SLOW COOKER RECIPES

COOKBOOK

THE

500

MOST HEALTHY
AND DELICIOUS
SLOW COOKER RECIPES

SLOW COOKER RECIPES COOKBOOK

The 500 Most Healthy And Delicious Slow Cooker Recipes

© H.B.F. Editorial, 2014
© Arthur H. Graham
   Master Resell Rights

ISBN-13: 978-1502594051
ISBN-10: 1502594056

EDITORIAL

SLOW COOKER

RECIPES

COOKBOOK

THE

500

MOST HEALTHY
AND DELICIOUS
SLOW COOKER RECIPES

1- Mushroom Lentil Barley Stew

2 quarts vegetable broth
2 cups sliced fresh button mushrooms
1 ounce dried shiitake mushrooms, torn
into pieces
3/4 cup uncooked pearl barley
3/4 cup dry lentils
1/4 cup dried onion flakes

2 teaspoons minced garlic
2 teaspoons dried summer savory
3 bay leaves
1 teaspoon dried basil
2 teaspoons ground black pepper salt to
taste

In a slow cooker, mix the broth, button mushrooms, shiitake mushrooms, barley, lentils, onion flakes, garlic, savory, bay leaves, basil, pepper, and salt. Cover, and cook 4 to 6 hours on High or 10 to 12 hours on Low. Remove bay leaves before serving.

2- Hearty Pork N Beans

1 pound ground beef
1 medium green pepper, chopped
1 small onion, chopped
1 (1 pound) package smoked sausage,
halved lengthwise and thinly sliced
1 (16 ounce) can pork and beans,
undrained
1 (15 ounce) can lima beans, rinsed and
drained

1 (15 ounce) can pinto beans, rinsed and
drained
1 cup ketchup
1/2 cup packed brown sugar
1 teaspoon salt
1/2 teaspoon garlic powder
1/4 teaspoon pepper

In a skillet, cook beef, green pepper and onion over medium heat until meat is no longer pink; drain. In a slow cooker, combine the remaining ingredients. Stir in beef mixture. Cover and cook on high for 4-5 hours or until heated through.

3- Slow Cooker Mediterranean Stew

1 butternut squash - peeled, seeded, and
cubed
2 cups cubed eggplant, with peel
2 cups cubed zucchini
1 (10 ounce) package frozen okra,
thawed
1 (8 ounce) can tomato sauce
1 cup chopped onion
1 ripe tomato, chopped

1 carrot, sliced thin
1/2 cup vegetable broth
1/3 cup raisins
1 clove garlic, chopped
1/2 teaspoon ground cumin
1/2 teaspoon ground turmeric
1/4 teaspoon crushed red pepper
1/4 teaspoon ground cinnamon
1/4 teaspoon paprika

In a slow cooker, combine butternut squash, eggplant, zucchini, okra, tomato sauce, onion, tomato, carrot, broth, raisins, and garlic. Season with cumin, turmeric, red pepper, cinnamon, and paprika. Cover, and cook on Low for 8 to 10 hours, or until vegetables are tender.

4- Mushroom Slow Cooker Roast Beef

1 pound sliced fresh mushrooms
1 (4 pound) standing beef rib roast
1 (1.25 ounce) envelope onion soup mix

1 (12 fluid ounce) bottle beer
ground black pepper

Place the mushrooms in the bottom of a slow cooker; set the roast atop the mushrooms; sprinkle the onion soup mix over the beef and pour the beer over everything; season with black pepper. Set slow cooker to LOW; cook 9 to 10 hours until the meat is easily pulled apart with a fork.

5- Slow Cooker Adobo Chicken

1 small sweet onion, sliced
8 cloves garlic, crushed
3/4 cup low sodium soy sauce

1/2 cup vinegar
1 (3 pound) whole chicken, cut into pieces

Place chicken in a slow cooker. In a small bowl mix the onion, garlic, soy sauce, and vinegar, and pour over the chicken. Cook on Low for 6 to 8 hours.

6- Texas Black Bean Soup

2 (15 ounce) cans black beans, rinsed and drained
1 (14.5 ounce) can stewed tomatoes
1 (14.5 ounce) can diced tomatoes, or diced tomatoes with green chilies
1 (14.5 ounce) can chicken broth

1 (11 ounce) can Mexicorn, drained
2 (4 ounce) cans chopped green chilies
4 green onions, thinly sliced
2 tablespoons chili powder
1 teaspoon ground cumin
1/2 teaspoon dried minced garlic

In a slow cooker, combine all ingredients. Cover and cook on high for 4-5 hours or until heated through.

7- Angel Chicken

4 Ounces Philadelphia Cream Cheese, Softened
1 (10.75 Ounce) Can Reduced- Sodium Condensed Cream Of Mushroom Soup
1/4 Cup Kraft Tuscan House Italian Dressing And Marinade

1/4 Cup Dry White Wine
1 1/2 Pounds Boneless Skinless Chicken Thighs, Cut Into Bite-Size Pieces
1/2 Pound Angel Hair Pasta, Uncooked
2 Tablespoons Chopped Fresh Parsley

Beat cream cheese, soup, dressing and wine with whisk until blended; pour over chicken in slow cooker. Cook on LOW 4 to 5 hours (or on HIGH 2 to 3 hours). Cook pasta as directed on package about 15 min. before chicken is done; drain. Serve topped with chicken mixture and parsley.

8- Slow Cooker Beef Stew II

2 pounds stew meat, trimmed and cubed
3 (10.75 ounce) cans condensed cream of
chicken soup

1 (16 ounce) package egg noodles

Spray the inside of a slow cooker with the vegetable cooking spray. Add the meat and the soups to the slow cooker. Cook on low setting for 8 to 10 hours. Prepare noodles according to package directions. When stew is ready, pour over the noodles and serve hot.

9- Slow-Cooked Broccoli

2 (10 ounce) packages frozen chopped
broccoli, partially thawed
1 (10.75 ounce) can condensed cream of
celery soup, undiluted
1 1/2 cups shredded sharp
Cheddar cheese, divided

1/4 cup chopped onion
1/2 teaspoon Worcestershire sauce
1/4 teaspoon pepper
1 cup crushed butter-flavored crackers
2 tablespoons butter

In a large bowl, combine broccoli, soup, 1 cup cheese, onion, Worcestershire sauce and pepper. Pour into a 3-qt. greased slow cooker. Sprinkle crackers on top; dot with butter. Cover and cook on high for 2-1/2 to 3 hours. Sprinkle with remaining cheese. Cook 10 minutes longer or until the cheese is melted.

10- Slow Cooker Tomato Chicken

5 (6 ounce) skinless, boneless chicken
breast halves
1 (16 ounce) can diced tomatoes with
basil

2 tablespoons minced garlic
2 tablespoons soy sauce
1 tablespoon dry mustard
1/2 (10 ounce) package frozen peas

Place the chicken breasts in a slow cooker. Stir together the tomatoes, garlic, soy sauce, and dry mustard; pour over the chicken breasts. Cook on Low 7 hours; stir in peas and cook 1 hour more.

11- Bacon Wrapped Smokies

1 pound sliced bacon, cut into thirds
1 (14 ounce) package beef cocktail
wieners

3/4 cup brown sugar, or to taste
Preheat the oven to 325 degrees F (165
degrees C).

Refrigerate 2/3 of the bacon until needed. It is easier to wrap the wieners with cold bacon. Wrap each cocktail wiener with a piece of bacon and secure with a toothpick. Place on a large baking sheet. Sprinkle brown sugar generously over all. Bake for 40 minutes in the preheated oven, until the sugar is bubbly. To serve, place the wieners in a slow cooker and keep on the low setting.

12- Quick and Easy Clam Chowder

1 (10.75 ounce) can condensed cream of celery soup
1 (10.75 ounce) can condensed cream of potato soup

1 (10.75 ounce) can New England clam chowder
2 (6.5 ounce) cans minced clams
1 quart half-and-half cream
1 pint heavy whipping cream

Mix cream of celery soup, cream of potato soup, clam chowder, 1 can undrained clams, 1 can drained clams, half-and-half cream, and whipping cream into a slow cooker. Cover, and cook on low for 6 to 8 hours.

13- Slow-Cooked Autumn Brisket

1 (3 pound) boneless beef brisket
1 small head cabbage, cut into wedges
1 large sweet potato, peeled and cut into 1-inch pieces
1 large onion, cut into wedges
1 medium Granny Smith apple, cored and cut into wedges

2 (10.75 ounce) cans Campbell's®
Condensed Cream of Celery Soup
(Regular or 98% Fat Free)
1 cup water
2 teaspoons caraway seeds (optional)

Place the brisket in a 6-quart slow cooker. Top with the cabbage, sweet potato, onion and apple. Stir the soup, water and caraway seed, if desired, in a small bowl. Pour the soup mixture over the brisket and vegetable mixture. Cover and cook on LOW for 8 to 9 hours* or until the brisket is fork- tender. Season as desired.

14- Tender Pork Roast

1 (3 pound) boneless pork roast
1 (8 ounce) can tomato sauce
3/4 cup soy sauce

1/2 cup sugar
2 teaspoons ground mustard

Cut roast in half; place in a 5-qt. slow cooker. Combine remaining ingredients; pour over roast. Cover and cook on low for 8-9 hours or until a meat thermometer reads 160 degrees F-170 degrees F. Remove roast to a serving platter and keep warm. If desired, skim fat from pan juices and thicken for gravy.

15- Krista's Queso

1 (16 ounce) package bulk pork breakfast sausage
1 (16 ounce) package processed cheese food, cubed

1 (4 ounce) jar mushrooms, drained
1 (14 ounce) can diced tomatoes with green chile peppers, drained

Cook the sausage in a large skillet over medium heat until completely browned; drain.

Combine the cooked sausage, cheese, mushrooms, and diced tomatoes with green chile peppers in a slow cooker. Set slow cooker to Low. Cook until the cheese melts completely, stirring occasionally, 30 to 40 minutes.

16- Chili Cheese Dip I

60 ounces chili with beans
2 (8 ounce) packages cream cheese, softened

2 cups shredded Cheddar cheese

In a slow cooker, combine chili, cream cheese, and Cheddar cheese. Set the slow cooker to a low temperature, and let the dip cook until all of the cheeses have melted. Serve warm.

17- Colonial Hot Buttered Rum

2 cups brown sugar
1/2 cup butter
1 pinch salt
2 quarts hot water
3 cinnamon sticks

6 whole cloves
2 cups rum
1 cup sweetened whipped cream ground nutmeg to taste.

Combine the brown sugar, butter, salt and hot water in 5 quart slow cooker. Add cinnamon sticks and cloves. Cover and cook on Low for 5 hours. Stir in rum. Ladle from the slow cooker into mugs, and top with whipped cream and a dusting of nutmeg.

18- Red Beans and Rice

2 cups dried red beans
1/2 teaspoon dried minced garlic
1 tablespoon dried minced onion
2 teaspoons salt
1 bay leaf
1 teaspoon white sugar

1/4 teaspoon ground cayenne pepper
1 teaspoon celery seed
1 teaspoon ground cumin
1/4 teaspoon crushed red pepper flakes
1 ham hock
1 pound smoked sausage, sliced

Pick over the dried beans, and soak them in water overnight. The next day, drain off the soaking water, and place the beans in a large pot or slow cooker. Cover with water, and stir in the dried garlic and onion, salt, bay leaf, sugar, cayenne pepper, celery seed, cumin, and crushed red pepper flakes. Push the ham hock down into the beans. Bring to a boil, reduce the heat, and simmer over low heat for 3 to 4 hours. Stir in the smoked sausage, simmer for 20 more minutes, and serve.

19- Turkey with Mushroom Sauce

1 (3 pound) boneless turkey breast, halved
2 tablespoons butter or margarine, melted

2 tablespoons dried parsley flakes
1/2 teaspoon dried tarragon
1/2 teaspoon salt (optional)
1/8 teaspoon pepper

1 (4.5 ounce) jar sliced mushrooms, drained
1/2 cup white wine or chicken broth

2 tablespoons cornstarch
1/4 cup cold water

Place the turkey, skin side up, in a slow cooker. Brush with butter. Sprinkle with parsley, tarragon, salt if desired and pepper. Top with mushrooms. Pour wine or broth over all. Cover and cook on low for 7-8 hours. Remove turkey and keep warm. Skim fat from cooking juices. In a saucepan, combine cornstarch and water until smooth. Gradually add cooking juices. Bring to a boil; cook and stir for 2 minutes or until thickened. Serve with the turkey.

20- Fisherman's Catch Chowder

1 1/2 pounds cod fillets, cubed
1 (16 ounce) can whole peeled tomatoes, mashed
1 (8 ounce) jar clam juice
1/2 cup chopped onion
1/2 cup chopped celery
1/2 cup chopped carrots

1/2 cup dry white wine
1/4 cup chopped fresh parsley
1/4 teaspoon dried rosemary
1 teaspoon salt
3 tablespoons all-purpose flour
3 tablespoons butter, melted
1/3 cup light cream

In a slow cooker, stir together the cod, tomatoes, clam juice, onion, celery, carrots, wine, parsley, rosemary, and salt. Cover, and cook on Low 7 to 8 hours or on High 3 to 4 hours. One hour prior to serving, mix flour, butter, and light cream in a small bowl. Stir into the slow cooker until the fish mixture is thickened.

21- Slow Cooker Roast Beef

3 pounds beef chuck roast
1/3 cup soy sauce

1 (1 ounce) package dry onion soup mix
2 teaspoons freshly ground black pepper

Pour the soy sauce and dry onion soup mix into the slow cooker. Mix well. Place chuck roast into slow cooker. Add water until the top 1/2 inch of the roast is not covered. Add the fresh ground pepper over the top. Cover and cook on low for 22 hours.

22- Sweet-And-Sour Smokies

2 (16 ounce) packages miniature smoked sausages
2 (21 ounce) cans cherry pie filling

1 (20 ounce) can pineapple chunks, drained
3 tablespoons brown sugar

Place sausages in a slow cooker. In a bowl, combine the pie filling, pineapple and brown sugar; pour over sausages. Cover and cook on low for 4 hours.

23- Sleeper Heater Lentil Soup

3 cups brown lentils
1/4 cup chopped fresh parsley

1/4 cup curry paste
1 tablespoon grated fresh ginger root

2 tablespoons chopped fresh oregano
2 cloves garlic, chopped

1 tablespoon all-purpose flour
1 teaspoon paprika

Place the lentils, parsley, curry paste, ginger, oregano, garlic, flour and paprika into a 2.5 quart (5 liter) slow cooker. Mix until blended. Fill with water to within 1/2 inch of the top. Cover, and cook on high for 4 hours, or longer if you can.

24- Smokey Black Beans

1 pound dry black beans, soaked overnight
4 teaspoons bacon drippings
1 onion, chopped

2 teaspoons hickory-flavored liquid smoke
2 tablespoons dark molasses
1/2 cup packed brown sugar
4 slices pickled jalapeno peppers

Drain the black beans from their soaking water and place in a slow cooker. Fill with enough fresh water to cover them. Cover and set to High. Heat bacon drippings in a skillet over medium heat. Add onions; cook and stir until tender. Stir this into the beans along with the brown sugar, liquid smoke, molasses and jalapeno slices. Stir to blend, then cover and cook on High for 5 to 6 hours, or until beans are tender.

25- Slow Cooker Cranberry Roast

1 (1 ounce) envelope dry onion soup mix
1 (3 pound) beef chuck roast
1 (16 ounce) can jellied cranberry sauce

2 tablespoons butter
2 tablespoons all-purpose flour

Place onion soup mix in the bottom of a slow cooker. Place roast in the slow cooker, and top with cranberry sauce. Cover, and cook 8 hours on Low. Remove roast, and set aside. Set slow cooker to High. Whisk together butter and flour, and slowly mix into the liquid remaining in the slow cooker to create a thick gravy. Serve with the roast.

26- Rogan Josh, Lamb Shanks

2/3 cup sour cream
1 tablespoon all-purpose flour
1/2 teaspoon chili powder
1 teaspoon ground coriander
1/2 teaspoon ground ginger
2 cubes chicken bouillon
4 whole cardamom pods, broken
1 (14.5 ounce) can diced tomatoes
1 cup water
ground nutmeg to taste

salt and ground black pepper to taste
2 tablespoons cornstarch
1/4 cup water
1 large onion, cut into wedges
3 lamb shanks
1 (15 ounce) can carrots, drained
1 (15 ounce) can whole new potatoes, drained
1/2 pound button mushrooms, quartered (optional)

Stir the sour cream and all-purpose flour together in a small bowl until smooth and set aside. In a separate small bowl, mix together the cornstarch and water to make a paste. Combine the chili powder, coriander, ginger, bouillon cubes, cardamom, tomatoes, water, nutmeg, salt and pepper in a medium saucepan; bring to a boil over high heat. Slowly add the cornstarch paste to the tomato mixture, stirring constantly; simmer for 2 minutes. Remove the saucepan from the heat and slowly stir in the sour cream and flour mixture. Arrange the onions across the bottom of a slow cooker, lay the shanks on top of the onions and pour the prepared tomato mixture over the meat. Place the carrots, potatoes and mushrooms on top of the sauce. Cover and cook in the slow cooker on High for 8 hours.

27- Kielbasa Made Easy

2 (16 ounce) packages kielbasa sausage, cut into 1 inch pieces

2 (16 ounce) cans whole cranberry sauce
1 (18 ounce) bottle barbecue sauce

Brown the kielbasa in a large skillet over medium high heat. Place the browned kielbasa, cranberry sauce and barbeque sauce in a slow cooker set on low. Allow the mixture to simmer at least 1 hour before serving warm.

28- Black Bean Chili

1 1/2 pounds boneless pork, cut into 1/2-inch cubes
2 (15.5 ounce) cans black beans, drained
1 cup chopped onion
1 cup chopped yellow bell pepper
1 cup thick and chunky salsa
1 (15 ounce) can canned diced tomatoes

2 cloves garlic, minced
1 teaspoon chili powder
1/2 teaspoon cumin
1/4 teaspoon crushed red pepper
Garnish: sour cream, shredded Cheddar cheese (optional)

Combine all ingredients except garnishes in 3 1/2-quart slow cooker. Cover and cook on low heat setting 7 to 8 hours. Top individual bowls with sour cream and Cheddar cheese.

29- Sauerkraut and Smokies

8 apples - peeled, cored and sliced
1 (32 ounce) package sauerkraut with juice
4 (16 ounce) packages cocktail- size smoked link sausages

1 (12 fluid ounce) can cola- flavored carbonated beverage
1 1/2 cups apple juice
1/2 cup brown sugar, or to taste

Place the apples, sauerkraut with juice, and smoked sausages into a slow cooker.
In a bowl, stir together the cola, apple juice, and brown sugar until the sugar dissolves. Pour the cola mixture into the slow cooker. Stir to combine, cook on High for 2 hours, then on Low for 6 to 8 hours.

30- Beer-Baked Irish Beef

6 slices bacon, diced
1/3 cup all-purpose flour

1 teaspoon salt
1/2 teaspoon ground black pepper

1 teaspoon ground allspice
2 1/2 pounds cubed beef stew meat
4 carrots, peeled and cut diagonally into
1-inch pieces
4 large onions, cut into eighths
2 cloves garlic, chopped

1/4 cup minced fresh parsley
1 teaspoon dried rosemary, crushed
1 teaspoon dried marjoram
1 bay leaf
1 (12 fluid ounce) can or bottle Irish stout beer

Place the bacon in a large nonstick skillet, and cook over medium heat until crisp and brown. Remove the bacon pieces and set aside, leaving the drippings in the skillet. Place the flour, salt, black pepper, and allspice in a large plastic zipper bag, and shake a few times to combine. Place the beef stew meat into the bag, and shake to coat the meat with flour mixture. Place the meat pieces in the skillet with the bacon drippings, and cook the meat until brown on all sides. Remove the browned meat to a slow cooker, and add the carrots, onions, garlic, parsley, rosemary, marjoram, and bay leaf to the cooker. Pour the beer into the skillet, and bring to a boil over medium-low heat, scraping all the browned bits of flavor from the bottom of the skillet. Pour the beer into the slow cooker, over the meat and vegetables. Cover, and cook on Medium setting until the meat is very tender, 4 to 5 hours. Before serving, remove the bay leaf, and sprinkle the stew with the reserved bacon pieces.

31- Peking Pork Chops

6 thick cut pork chops (1 inch)
1/4 cup brown sugar
1 teaspoon ground ginger
1/2 cup soy sauce

1/4 cup ketchup
1 clove garlic, crushed salt and pepper to taste

Trim excess fat from pork chops and place in slow cooker. Mix brown sugar, ginger, soy sauce, ketchup, garlic, salt and pepper in small bowl and pour over meat. Cover, turn to low and cook 4 to 6 hours, or until tender. Season with salt and pepper, if needed.

32- Amazing Pork Tenderloin in the Slow Cooker

1 (2 pound) pork tenderloin
1 (1 ounce) envelope dry onion soup mix
1 cup water
3/4 cup red wine

3 tablespoons minced garlic
3 tablespoons soy sauce freshly ground black pepper to taste

Place pork tenderloin in a slow cooker with the contents of the soup packet. Pour water, wine, and soy sauce over the top, turning the pork to coat. Carefully spread garlic over the pork, leaving as much on top of the roast during cooking as possible. Sprinkle with pepper, cover, and cook on low setting for 4 hours. Serve with cooking liquid on the side as au jus.

33- Bean and Sausage Soup

12 ounces dry mixed beans
1 1/2 pounds Italian turkey sausage links
1 (29 ounce) can diced tomatoes

2 (14 ounce) cans chicken broth
1 cup white wine
1 red bell pepper, chopped

1 onion, chopped

2 stalks celery, chopped

2 large carrots, chopped

2 cups frozen green peas, thawed

Pick through and rinse beans. Place in a 4 quart pot, and cover with at least 2 inches of water. Bring to a boil for 2 to 3 minutes. Cover, and let stand in the refrigerator overnight. Drain and rinse beans. Place beans in slow cooker with canned tomatoes, broth, white wine, and vegetables. Cover, and cook on low for 7 to 8 hours. In a skillet, cook the sausage over medium heat until done. Slice links into 1/2 inch pieces. Add meat to slow cooker, and cook soup another 30 to 60 minutes.

34- Beer Chops I

1 onion, sliced

2 pork chops butterfly cut

1 (12 fluid ounce) can or bottle beer

2 cubes chicken bouillon

Arrange onion slices on bottom of slow-cooker. Cut butterfly chops in half and place on top of onions. Pour in beer and add chicken bouillon cubes. Cover and cook and low 6 to 8 hours.

35 - Swiss Steak Stew

1/4 cup all-purpose flour

1/2 teaspoon salt

1 1/2 pounds boneless round steak, cut into bite size pieces

1 (14.5 ounce) can Italian-style diced tomatoes

3/4 cup water

3 cups peeled and quartered new red potatoes

1 onion, diced

1 cup sweet corn

In medium bowl combine flour and salt mix well. Add beef and coat well. Coat a nonstick skillet with cooking spray and heat over medium heat. Add beef and cook until browned. In a slow cooker layer potatoes, beef and onion. Stir tomatoes with juice, water and any remaining flour mixture together. Pour over top. Cover and cook on low setting for 7 to 8 hours or until beef is tender. Add corn, cover and cook an additional 25 minutes.

36- Pork Roast with Sauerkraut and Kielbasa

1 (2 pound) boneless pork loin roast

2 tablespoons olive oil

2 sprigs fresh thyme leaves salt and pepper to taste

4 pounds sauerkraut

1 pound kielbasa, cut into 3-inch pieces

Preheat the oven broiler. Place the roast in a roasting pan, brush with olive oil, sprinkle with thyme leaves, and season with salt and pepper. Place under the broiler for 10 minutes, until lightly browned in several places. Place 2 pounds sauerkraut in a slow cooker. Arrange kielbasa pieces around the edges of the slow cooker pot, and place the roast in the center. Cover with remaining sauerkraut. Cover slow cooker, and cook roast 6 hours on High.

37- Red Zone Chili

1 (12 ounce) package Hebrew
NationalB® Beef Franks, sliced
1/2 pound ground sirloin beef, uncooked
1 (28 ounce) can Hunt'sB® Petite
Diced Tomatoes, undrained
1 (15 ounce) can Ranch StyleB® Black
Beans
1 (15 ounce) can Ranch StyleB® Pinto
Beans
1 (8 ounce) can Hunt'sB® Tomato
Sauce-No Salt Added

1 cup finely chopped onion
1 cup finely chopped poblano chile with
seeds
2 tablespoons finely chopped jalapeno
chile with seeds
2 tablespoons GebhardtB® Chili
Powder
1 tablespoon ancho chile powder
1 tablespoon brown sugar
1 tablespoon minced garlic
2 teaspoons ground cumin

Place all ingredients in 4-quart slow cooker; stir to combine thoroughly. Cook on LOW setting 6-1/2 hours or until vegetables are tender.

38- Chicken and Corn Chili

4 skinless, boneless chicken breast halves
1 (16 ounce) jar salsa
2 teaspoons garlic powder
1 teaspoon ground cumin

1 teaspoon chili powder salt to taste
ground black pepper to taste
1 (11 ounce) can Mexican-style corn
1 (15 ounce) can pinto beans

Place chicken and salsa in the slow cooker the night before you want to eat this chili. Season with garlic powder, cumin, chili powder, salt, and pepper. Cook 6 to 8 hours on Low setting. About 3 to 4 hours before you want to eat, shred the chicken with 2 forks. Return the meat to the pot, and continue cooking. Stir the corn and the pinto beans into the slow cooker. Simmer until ready to serve.

39- Yankee Beans

1 pound dried great Northern beans,
soaked overnight
1 teaspoon canola oil
1 large onion, chopped
1/2 pound bacon, diced
3 cloves garlic, minced
1 teaspoon dried thyme
1 pinch red pepper flakes
1/4 cup pure maple syrup

1/4 cup tomato puree
2 tablespoons Worcestershire sauce
1 tablespoon mustard powder
1 ham bone with some meat
3 cups boiling water, or as needed
1 bay leaf
1 1/2 tablespoons apple cider vinegar
1 dash hot pepper sauce, or to taste
salt and pepper to taste

Heat oil in a large skillet over medium-high heat. Add onions and bacon, and cook until onions are tender and golden, about 5 minutes. Add garlic, thyme and red pepper flakes to the skillet, and cook for a minute to blend flavors. Place the soaked beans in a 3 1/2 quart or larger slow cooker. Stir in the onion and bacon mixture, maple syrup, tomato puree, Worcestershire sauce, and mustard powder. Bury the ham bone in the beans, and fill the slow cooker with enough hot water to cover the beans. Add bay leaves to the top. Cover and cook for 5 hours on High, or 10 to 11 hours on Low. Remove bay leaves, and season with vinegar, hot sauce, salt and pepper before serving.

4- Slow Cooker Ham and Bean Stew

1 (15 ounce) can black-eyed peas, undrained
1 (15 ounce) can black beans, undrained
1 (15 ounce) can garbanzo beans, drained
1 (16 ounce) can chili beans in sauce

1 large onion, chopped
1 pound cooked ham, cubed
1 clove garlic, minced, or to taste
1 tablespoon sour cream

Stir the black-eyed peas, black beans, garbanzo beans, chili beans, onion, ham, and garlic together in a slow cooker. Cook on Low for 5 hours. Top with sour cream to serve.

41- Slow Cooker Spicy Black-Eyed Peas

6 cups water
1 cube chicken bouillon
1 pound dried black-eyed peas, sorted and rinsed
1 onion, diced
2 cloves garlic, diced
1 red bell pepper, stemmed, seeded, and diced

1 jalapeno chile, seeded and minced
8 ounces diced ham
4 slices bacon, chopped
1/2 teaspoon cayenne pepper
1 1/2 teaspoons cumin salt, to taste
1 teaspoon ground black pepper

Pour the water into a slow cooker, add the bouillon cube, and stir to dissolve. Combine the black-eyed peas, onion, garlic, bell pepper, jalapeno pepper, ham, bacon, cayenne pepper, cumin, salt, and pepper; stir to blend. Cover the slow cooker and cook on Low for 6 to 8 hours until the beans are tender.

42- Quick Chick!

3 boneless, skinless chicken breast halves
1 (12 ounce) jar turkey gravy
1/2 teaspoon paprika

1/2 teaspoon salt-free herb seasoning blend
1 teaspoon soy sauce

Place chicken and gravy into a slow cooker. Season with paprika, seasoning blend and soy sauce. Cook on high for 4 hours or for 6 to 8 hours on medium. Tear chicken into pieces. Serve over rice, noodles or potatoes.

43- Slow Cooker Tipsy Chicken

1 tablespoon butter
8 chicken thighs
salt and pepper to taste

1 (10.75 ounce) can condensed cream of celery soup
1 (10.75 ounce) can condensed cream of mushroom soup

1 (5 ounce) jar pimento-stuffed green
olives
1 (8 ounce) package sliced fresh
mushrooms

1 1/4 cups Chablis wine
1 tablespoon all-purpose flour

Melt the butter in a large skillet over medium-high heat. Season the chicken with salt and
pepper, and brown for 2 to 3 minutes each side. Place in a slow cooker. In a saucepan over
medium heat, blend the cream of mushroom soup and cream of celery soup. Pour over the
chicken in the slow cooker, then add olives, mushrooms, wine, and flour.
Cover, and cook on Low for 8 hours.

44- Campbell's® Slow Cooker Hearty Beef and Bean

1 1/2 pounds ground beef
1 large onion, chopped
2 cloves garlic, minced
1 (10.75 ounce) can Campbell's®
Condensed Tomato Soup (Regular or
25% Less Sodium)

1 (14.5 ounce) can diced tomatoes
1/2 cup water
2 (15 ounce) cans kidney beans, rinsed
and drained
1/4 cup chili powder
2 teaspoons ground cumin

Cook the beef in a 12-inch skillet over medium-high heat until it's well browned, stirring
often. Pour off any fat. Stir the beef, onion, garlic, soup, tomatoes, water, beans, chili powder
and cumin in a 3 1/2-quart slow cooker. Cover and cook on LOW for 8 to 9 hours.*

45- Slow Cooker Spaghetti Sauce I

5 (29 ounce) cans tomato sauce
3 (6 ounce) cans tomato paste
3 cloves garlic, minced
1 onion, chopped
3 tablespoons dried rosemary

3 tablespoons dried oregano
3 tablespoons dried thyme
3 tablespoons dried parsley
1 bay leaf
1 pinch crushed red pepper flakes

In a large slow cooker combine tomato sauce, tomato paste, garlic, onion, rosemary, oregano,
thyme, parsley, bay leaf and red pepper. Cook on high for 3 to 4 hours, stir frequently.

46- Jambalaya I

2 cups diced ham
2 onion, chopped
2 stalks celery, diced
1 green bell pepper, chopped
2 (14.5 ounce) cans stewed tomatoes
1/4 cup tomato paste
3 cloves garlic, minced

1 tablespoon minced fresh parsley
1/2 teaspoon dried thyme
2 whole cloves
2 tablespoons vegetable oil
1 cup converted long-grain white rice
1 pound medium shrimp – peeled and
deveined

In a slow cooker combine and thoroughly mix the ham, onions, celery, bell pepper, tomatoes,
tomato paste, garlic, parsley, thyme leaves, cloves, salad oil and rice. Cover and cook on low

for 8 to 10 hours. One hour before serving, turn slow cooker to high. Stir in the uncooked shrimp. Cover and cook until the shrimp are pink and tender.

47- Grandma Maul's Italian Beef

1 (4 pound) boneless beef chuck roast
1/2 cup all-purpose flour
salt and ground black pepper to taste
2 tablespoons olive oil
2 cloves garlic, minced
1 cup water

1 tablespoon anise seed
1 tablespoon sesame seed
1 large green bell pepper, julienned
Rinse and pat dry the roast. Coat the
roast evenly with the flour;
season with salt and pepper.

Heat the olive oil in a skillet over medium-high heat. Add the garlic to the hot oil; sear the beef in the oil until all sides are slightly browned. Transfer the roast to a slow cooker. Pour the water over the roast. Cook on Low for 5 hours. Add the anise seed and sesame seed to the slow cooker and cook another 4 hours. Add the green bell pepper and continue cooking until the meat is tender and easily pulled apart, about 1 hour more.

48- Chicken Soup with Drop-In Noodles

2 skinless, boneless chicken breasts
2 1/2 tablespoons mixed vegetable flakes
1 bay leaf
1 teaspoon dried parsley
1/4 teaspoon dried tarragon
3/4 teaspoon celery salt
1 onion, chopped
1/2 cup frozen diced carrots

2 (14.5 ounce) cans chicken broth
2 teaspoons chicken bouillon powder
salt to taste
2 cups all-purpose flour
1 tablespoon shredded Cheddar cheese
2 eggs
1 tablespoon milk

Place chicken breasts in a large slow cooker and cover with cold water, 3/4 of the way full. Add vegetable flakes, bay leaf, parsley, tarragon, celery salt and onion. Cook on high at least 6 hours or on low for 8 hours. 1 hour prior to serving add carrots, chicken bouillon, chicken broth and start making drop-in noodles. In a large stock pot bring 4 to 6 quarts of salted water to a boil. In a mixing bowl combine flour and cheese. In the center of flour mixture make a well and drop in eggs and milk. Mix with a fork until dough crumbles and looks like peas (if too dry add milk; if too moist add flour). Drop pea size dough pieces into boiling water and cook for twenty minutes. Drain and rinse the noodles with cold water. Once noodles are finished and vegetables in soup are tender ladle soup into serving bowls, drop in noodles and serve.

49- Slow-Cooked Oriental Chicken

1 (3 1/2) pound broiler-fryer chicken, cut
up
2 tablespoons vegetable oil
1/3 cup soy sauce
2 tablespoons brown sugar

2 tablespoons water
1 garlic clove, minced
1 teaspoon ground ginger
1/4 cup slivered almonds

In a large skillet over medium heat, brown the chicken in oil on both sides. Transfer to a slow cooker. Combine the soy sauce, brown sugar, water, garlic and ginger; pour over chicken. Cover and cook on high for 1 hour. Reduce heat to low; cook 4-5 hours longer or until the meat juices run clear. Remove chicken to a serving platter sprinkle with almonds. Spoon juices over chicken or thicken if desired.

50- Easy Cheesy Chicken I

6 skinless, boneless chicken breast halves
salt and pepper to taste
1 teaspoon garlic powder
1 (10.75 ounce) can condensed cream of
chicken soup

1 (10.75 ounce) can condensed cream of
mushroom soup
1 (11 ounce) can condensed cream of
Cheddar cheese soup
1 (8 ounce) container sour cream

Rinse chicken, and pat dry. Sprinkle with salt, pepper and garlic powder. Place in slow cooker. In a medium bowl, mix together cream of chicken soup, cream of mushroom soup and cream of Cheddar cheese soup. Cook on Low for 6 to 8 hours. Stir in sour cream just before serving.

51- Slow Cooker Guisado Verde

2 tablespoons vegetable oil
2 pounds boneless pork shoulder
1 large onion, coarsely chopped
3 cloves garlic, chopped
2 (12 ounce) cans tomatillos, drained and
chopped
1 (7 ounce) can diced green chile peppers
2 fresh jalapeno peppers, sliced

1/2 cup fresh chopped cilantro
1 teaspoon dried oregano salt and
pepper to taste
1 quart water
1 cup shredded Monterey Jack cheese
1/4 cup sour cream
4 sprigs fresh cilantro, for garnish

Heat the oil in a large skillet over medium heat, and brown the pork on all sides. Reserving the juices in the skillet, transfer the pork to a slow cooker. In the skillet with the pork juices over medium heat, saute the onion and garlic about 1 minute. Transfer to the slow cooker, along with skillet juices. Mix the tomatillos, green chile peppers, jalapeno peppers, and cilantro into the slow cooker. Season with oregano, salt, and pepper. Pour in 1 quart water, or enough to cover all ingredients. Cover, and cook on High for 6 to 7 hours. Shred the cooked pork with a fork. Spoon the slow cooker mixture into bowls, and top with Monterey Jack cheese, sour cream, and fresh cilantro sprigs to serve.

52- Creamy Chicken and Wild Rice

2 (10.75 ounce) cans Campbell's®
Condensed Cream of Chicken Soup
(Regular or 98% Fat Free)
1 1/2 cups water
4 large carrots, thickly sliced

1 (6 ounce) package uncooked seasoned
long-grain and wild rice mix
8 skinless, boneless chicken
breast halves

Stir the soup, water, carrots, rice and seasoning packet in a 3 1/2- quart slow cooker. Add the chicken and turn to coat. Cover and cook on LOW for 7 to 8 hours* or until the chicken is cooked through.

53- Duck Cassoulet

1 pound pork sausage links, sliced
1 tablespoon whole cloves
1 whole onion, peeled
3 sprigs fresh parsley
1 sprig fresh thyme
1/2 pound bacon
1 sprig fresh rosemary

1 pound dry navy beans, soaked overnight
1 bay leaf
3 carrots, peeled and sliced
3 cloves garlic, minced
1 pound skinned, boned duck breast halves, sliced into thin strips.
1 fresh tomato, chopped

In a large skillet, brown the sliced sausage over medium heat. Insert whole cloves into onion. Roll bacon up, and tie with a string. Tie together parsley, thyme, and rosemary. In a large slow cooker, place soaked beans, sausage, bacon, onion studded with cloves, fresh herbs, bay leaf, carrots, minced garlic, and duck. Add enough water to cover the other ingredients. Cook for 1 hour on HIGH. Reduce heat to LOW, and continue cooking for 6 to 8 hours. Remove onion, bacon, and herbs. Stir in chopped tomatoes. Continue cooking for 1/2 hour. Serve.

54- Slow Cooker Oatmeal

1 cup oats
3 cups water
1 pinch salt

1 cup half-and-half cream
1/4 cup brown sugar, or to taste

Just before going to bed, combine the oats and water in a slow cooker. Set on Low, cover, and let cook overnight. In the morning, stir in the salt and half-and-half. Scoop into bowls, and sprinkle brown sugar over the top.

55- Vegetable-Stuffed Peppers

2 (14.5 ounce) cans diced tomatoes, undrained
1 (16 ounce) can kidney beans, rinsed and drained
1 1/2 cups cooked rice
2 cups shredded Cheddar cheese, divided

1 (10 ounce) package frozen corn, thawed
1/4 cup chopped onion
1 teaspoon Worcestershire sauce
3/4 teaspoon chili powder
1/2 teaspoon pepper
1/4 teaspoon salt
6 medium green bell peppers

In a large bowl, combine the tomatoes, beans, rice, 1-1/2 cups cheese, corn, onion, Worcestershire sauce, chili powder, pepper and salt; mix well. Remove and discard tops and seeds of green peppers. Fill each pepper with about 1 cup of the vegetable mixture. Place in a

5-qt. slow cooker. Cover and cook on low for 8 hours. Sprinkle with remaining cheese. Cover and cook 15 minutes longer or until peppers are tender and cheese is melted.

56- Garlic Pork Roast

1 tablespoon vegetable oil
1 (2 pound) boneless pork roast salt and
pepper to taste
4 sweet potatoes, quartered

1 onion, quartered
6 cloves garlic
1 (14.5 ounce) can chicken broth

Heat oil in large heavy skillet. Season meat with salt and pepper, and brown in oil. In a slow cooker, layer sweet potatoes, onion and garlic. Place browned roast on top of vegetables, and pour in chicken broth. Cover, and cook on low setting for 6 hours.

57- Easy Slow Cooker French Dip

4 pounds rump roast
1 (10.5 ounce) can beef broth
1 (10.5 ounce) can condensed
French onion soup

1 (12 fluid ounce) can or bottle beer
6 French rolls
2 tablespoons butter

Trim excess fat from the rump roast, and place in a slow cooker. Add the beef broth, onion soup and beer. Cook on Low setting for 7 hours. Preheat oven to 350 degrees F (175 degrees C). Split French rolls, and spread with butter. Bake 10 minutes, or until heated through. Slice the meat on the diagonal, and place on the rolls. Serve the sauce for dipping.

58- Tender N Tangy Ribs

3/4 cup vinegar
1/2 cup ketchup
2 tablespoons sugar
2 tablespoons Worcestershire sauce
1 garlic clove, minced
1 teaspoon ground mustard

1 teaspoon paprika
1/2 teaspoon salt
1/8 teaspoon pepper
2 pounds pork spareribs
1 tablespoon vegetable oil

Combine the first nine ingredients in a slow cooker. Cut ribs into serving-size pieces; brown in a skillet in oil. Transfer to slow cooker. Cover and cook on low for 4-6 hours or until tender.

59- Easy Cheesy Crawfish Dip

2 pounds processed cheese food
(such as VelveetaB®), cubed
1 teaspoon condensed cream of
mushroom soup
1/2 cup butter, divided
2 onions, chopped
1 green bell pepper, chopped

1 tablespoon minced garlic
3 pounds peeled crawfish tails
1 teaspoon cayenne pepper, or to taste
salt and ground black pepper to taste
1 (10 ounce) can diced tomatoes with
green chile peppers (such as RO*TELB®)

Place the processed cheese and 1 teaspoon of cream of mushroom soup into a slow cooker. Turn the slow cooker to High and set aside. Melt half of the butter in a large skillet over medium heat. Stir in the onion and green pepper; cook and stir until the onion has softened and turned translucent, about 10 minutes. Scrape the onion mixture into a bowl and set aside. Melt the remaining butter in the skillet along with the garlic. Once the garlic begins to sizzle and is aromatic, add the crawfish tails, and season with cayenne pepper, salt and pepper. Cook and stir until the crawfish is hot, then stir into the onion and pepper mixture. Place the crawfish mixture into a food processor, and process until the mixture is finely ground, or to your desired consistency. Stir the crawfish mixture into the slow cooker along with the can of diced tomatoes. Cover, and continue to cook 45 minutes, stirring occasionally. Once hot, set the slow cooker to Low until ready to serve.

60- Baked Slow Cooker Chicken

1 (2 to 3 pound) whole chicken salt and   1 teaspoon paprika
pepper to taste

Wad three pieces of aluminum foil into 3 to 4 inch balls, and place them in the bottom of the slow cooker. Rinse the chicken, inside and out, under cold running water. Pat dry with paper towels. Season the chicken with the salt, pepper and paprika, and place in the slow cooker on top of the crumbled aluminum foil. Set the slow cooker to High for 1 hour, then turn down to Low for about 8 to 10 hours, or until the chicken is no longer pink and the juices run clear.

61- Marmalade-Glazed Carrots

2 pounds baby carrots   1/2 teaspoon ground cinnamon
1/2 cup orange marmalade   1/4 teaspoon salt
3 tablespoons cold water, divided   1/4 teaspoon ground nutmeg
2 tablespoons brown sugar   1/8 teaspoon pepper
1 tablespoon butter, melted   1 tablespoon cornstarch

In a 3-qt. slow cooker, combine the carrots, marmalade, 1 tablespoon water, brown sugar, butter and seasonings. Cover and cook on low for 5-6 hours or until carrots are tender. Combine cornstarch and remaining water until smooth; stir into carrot mixture. Cover and cook on high for 30 minutes or until thickened. Serve with a slotted spoon.

62- Slow Cooker Pumpkin Soup

1 tablespoon olive oil   1 sprig fresh thyme
1 medium sugar pumpkin, seeded and   1 sprig fresh sage
cubed   2 small cinnamon sticks
1 medium onion, chopped   2 bay leaves
3 cups chicken stock, or as needed   1/2 cup heavy cream
1 sprig fresh rosemary

Heat the olive oil in a large skillet over medium-high heat. Add pumpkin and onion; cook and stir until lightly browned. Transfer to a slow cooker. Pour in enough chicken broth to cover the pumpkin. Tie the rosemary, thyme, sage, cinnamon, and bay leaves into a piece of cheesecloth, and place in the slow cooker. Cover and cook on Low for 4 hours. After 4 hours, remove the herb sachet. Stir in the cream, and puree the soup with a hand blender until smooth. Serve.

63- Cheesy Italian Tortellini

1/2 pound ground beef
1/2 pound Italian sausage, casings removed
1 (16 ounce) jar marinara sauce
1 (4.5 ounce) can sliced mushrooms

1 (14.5 ounce) can Italian-style diced tomatoes, undrained
1 (9 ounce) package refrigerated or fresh cheese tortellini
1 cup shredded mozzarella cheese
1/2 cup shredded Cheddar cheese

Crumble the ground beef and Italian sausage into a large skillet. Cook over medium-high heat until browned. Drain. Combine the ground meats, marinara sauce, mushrooms, and tomatoes in a slow cooker. Cover, and cook on LOW heat for 7 to 8 hours. Stir in the tortellini, and sprinkle the mozzarella and cheddar cheese over the top. Cover and cook for 15 more minutes on LOW, or until the tortellini is tender.

64- Slow-Cooked Short Ribs

2/3 cup all-purpose flour
2 teaspoons salt
1/2 teaspoon pepper
4 pounds boneless beef short ribs
1/4 cup butter
1 large onion, chopped
1 1/2 cups beef broth

3/4 cup red wine vinegar
3/4 cup packed brown sugar
1/2 cup chili sauce
1/3 cup ketchup
1/3 cup Worcestershire sauce
5 cloves garlic, minced
1 1/2 teaspoons chili powder

In a large resealable plastic bag, combine the flour, salt and pepper. Add ribs in batches and shake to coat. In a large skillet, brown ribs in butter. Transfer to a 6-qt. slow cooker. In the same skillet, combine the remaining ingredients. Cook and stir until mixture comes to a boil; pour over ribs. Cover and cook on low for 9-10 hours or until meat is tender.

65- Warm Mexican Corn Dip

2 (8 ounce) packages cream cheese, softened
1 cup butter, softened

2 (15.25 ounce) cans white corn, drained
2 (14 ounce) cans diced tomatoes with green chile peppers

Combine the cream cheese, butter, corn, and tomatoes with green chile peppers in a slow cooker. Set the slow cooker to Low. Cook until the cream cheese and butter melt completely, about 1 hour.

66- Shredded Barbecue Beef

1 teaspoon celery salt
1 teaspoon garlic powder
1 teaspoon onion powder
1 (3 pound) fresh beef brisket*, halved
3 tablespoons liquid smoke

(optional)
1 tablespoon hot pepper sauce
1 (18 ounce) bottle barbecue sauce
12 sandwich rolls, split

Combine the celery salt, garlic powder and onion powder; rub over brisket. Place in a 5-qt. slow cooker. Combine liquid smoke if desired and hot pepper sauce; pour over brisket. Cover and cook on low for 6-8 hours or until the meat is tender. Remove roast and cool slightly. Strain cooking juices, reserving 1/2 cup. Shred met with two forks; place in a large saucepan. Add the barbecue sauce and reserved cooking juices; heat through. Serve about 1/3 cup meat mixture on each roll.

67- Texas Black Bean Soup

2 (15 ounce) cans black beans, rinsed and
drained
1 (14.5 ounce) can stewed tomatoes, or
Mexican stewed tomatoes, cut up
1 (14.5 ounce) can diced tomatoes, or
diced tomatoes with green chilies
1 (14.5 ounce) can chicken broth

1 (11 ounce) can Mexicorn, drained
2 (4 ounce) cans chopped green chilies
4 green onions, thinly sliced
3 tablespoons chili powder
1 teaspoon ground cumin
1/2 teaspoon dried minced garlic

In a slow cooker, combine all ingredients. Cover and cook on high for 4-5 hours or until heated through.

68- Shredded Beef

1 pound rump roast
1 cup water
1/4 cup barbeque sauce
2 tablespoons honey

1 tablespoon steak seasoning
1 teaspoon cumin
1/2 teaspoon onion powder
1/2 teaspoon garlic powder

Place the rump roast and water in a slow cooker. Cover, and cook 5 hours on High. Remove the roast from slow cooker, and shred using two forks. Discard fat. In the slow cooker, mix the barbeque sauce, honey, steak seasoning, cumin, onion powder, and garlic powder. Stir in the shredded beef. Cook 1 hour on Low. Allow to sit for 10 minutes before serving.

69- Slow Cooker Posole with Pork and Chicken

1 canned chipotle pepper in adobo sauce
1/4 cup water
1/2 pound boneless pork loin roast

1/2 pound skinless, boneless chicken
breast halves
1 (15.5 ounce) can white hominy, drained
1 (4 ounce) can chopped green chilies

1 medium onion, chopped
1 clove garlic, minced
2 (14.5 ounce) cans chicken broth
1 teaspoon dried oregano

1 teaspoon ground cumin
1/4 teaspoon ground black pepper to taste
1 bay leaf

Place the chipotle chile and water into a blender, and puree until smooth. Pour into a slow cooker, and add the pork, chicken, hominy, green chilies, onion, garlic, and chicken broth. Season with oregano, cumin, pepper, and the bay leaf. Cover, and cook on Low 6 to 7 hours until the meats are tender. Remove the bay leaf before serving.

70- Fruity Pork Chops

4 bone-in pork loin chops, 1 inch thick
1/2 teaspoon salt
1/4 teaspoon pepper
1/8 teaspoon dried rosemary, crushed
1/8 teaspoon dill weed
1/8 teaspoon ground ginger
2 tablespoons vegetable oil

1 (15.25 ounce) can fruit cocktail
2 tablespoons red wine vinegar or cider vinegar
1 tablespoon prepared mustard
1/4 teaspoon grated orange peel
2 tablespoons cornstarch
2 tablespoons cold water

Sprinkle pork chops with salt, pepper, rosemary, dill and ginger. In a skillet, brown chips on both sides in oil; transfer to a slow cooker. Drain fruit cocktail. In a bowl, combine the vinegar, mustard, orange peel and reserved fruit juice. Pour over pork. Cover and cook on low for 7-8 hours or until meat is tender. Remove chops and keep warm. Strain the cooking liquid into a small saucepan. Combine the cornstarch and water until smooth; stir into the cooking liquid. bring to a boil; cook and stir for 2 minutes or until thickened and bubbly. Add fruit cocktail; heat through. Serve over pork chops.

71- Candied Kielbasa

1 cup packed brown sugar
1/2 cup ketchup

1/4 cup prepared horseradish
2 pounds kielbasa sausage, sliced thin

In a slow cooker combine the sugar, ketchup and horseradish. Add the sausage, and mix well. Cook on High until it starts to boil. Reduce heat to Low, and cook until sauce thickens, about 45 minutes to 1 hour.

72- Craig's Mystic Wings

1 (18 ounce) bottle honey teriyaki barbeque sauce
1/2 cup Worcestershire sauce
1/4 cup honey
3 dashes liquid smoke flavoring
1 1/2 tablespoons grated fresh ginger
6 cloves crushed garlic

8 habanero peppers, seeded and minced
4 green chile peppers, chopped
3 tablespoons finely grated raw horseradish
18 chicken wings, separated at joints, tips discarded

In a medium saucepan mix together barbeque sauce, Worcestershire sauce, honey, liquid smoke, ginger, garlic, habanero peppers, green chile peppers, and horseradish. Simmer 1 hour over low heat, stirring occasionally. Place chicken wings in a large bowl, and coat with 3/4 of the sauce. Cover, and refrigerate for at least 6 hours. Preheat grill for low heat. Lightly oil grate. Discard marinade, and place chicken on the grill. Cook over low heat for 45 minutes to 1 hour, turning occasionally, until juices run clear. Transfer chicken to a slow cooker for serving, and stir in the remaining sauce. Set to the Low setting to keep chicken warm while serving.

73- Chicken Broth in a Slow Cooker

2 1/2 pounds bone-in chicken pieces
6 cups water
2 stalks celery, chopped

2 carrots, chopped
1 onion, quartered
1 tablespoon dried basil

Place the chicken pieces, water, celery, carrots, onion, and basil in a slow cooker. Cook on Low setting for 8 to 10 hours. Strain before using, and discard vegetables. Chicken may be removed from the bones, and used in soup.

74- Slow Cooker Blackberry Pork Tenderloin

1 (2 pound) pork tenderloin
1 teaspoon salt
1 teaspoon ground black pepper
1 tablespoon dried rubbed sage
1 tablespoon crushed dried rosemary, or to taste
1 (16 ounce) jar seedless blackberry jam

1/4 cup honey
2 tablespoons dry red wine (such as Cabernet Sauvignon, Merlot, or a blend)
1/2 cup dry red wine (such as Cabernet Sauvignon, Merlot, or a blend)
2 tablespoons honey
1 cup fresh blackberries

Season the pork tenderloin on all sides with salt, pepper, sage, and rosemary. Place the tenderloin into a slow cooker, and spoon the blackberry jam, 1/4 cup honey, and 2 tablespoons of red wine over the pork. Set the cooker to Low, and cook until very tender, 4 to 5 hours. About 15 minutes before serving time, pour 1/2 cup red wine, 2 tablespoons of honey, and the fresh blackberries into a saucepan. Bring to a boil over medium-low heat, and simmer until the sauce thickens slightly and some of the berries burst, about 15 minutes. To serve, slice the tenderloin and spoon blackberry-wine sauce over slices.

75- Slow Cooker Venison Stroganoff Meal

3 tablespoons olive oil
1 pound venison stew meat
1 teaspoon salt
1 teaspoon ground black pepper
1 teaspoon garlic powder
1 teaspoon onion powder

1 tablespoon all-purpose flour
1 cup water
1 (10.75 ounce) can condensed cream of mushroom soup
1 (16 ounce) package uncooked egg noodles

Heat the olive oil in a large skillet over medium-high heat. Toss the cubed venison with salt, pepper, garlic powder, and onion powder. Cook the venison in the hot oil until browned on all sides, about 8 minutes. Once browned, remove from the skillet and place into a slow cooker, leaving the remaining oil in the skillet. Reduce the heat to medium-low, and stir the flour into the remaining olive oil. Cook and stir until the flour has turned golden brown, about 5 minutes. Stir in the water and bring to a simmer, then pour into the slow cooker along with the cream of mushroom soup. Cover, and cook on Low for 4 hours, or until the venison is tender. Bring a large pot of lightly salted water to a boil. Add the egg noodles, and cook until al dente, 8 to 10 minutes; drain. Spoon the Stroganoff over the egg noodles to serve.

76- Original Homemade Italian Beef

3 pounds beef chuck roast
3 (1 ounce) packages dry Italian salad dressing mix

1 cup water
1 (16 ounce) jar pepperoncini peppers
8 hamburger buns, split

Place the roast into a slow cooker, and season with Italian dressing mix. Pour in the water. Cover, and cook on High for 6 to 7 hours. During the last hour, shred the meat with two forks - if it does not shred easily, cook longer. Add the peppers, and as much of the juice as you like for additional flavor. Serve on buns.

77- Slow-Cooked White Chili

3/4 pound skinless, boneless chicken breast halves - cubed
1 medium onion, chopped
1 garlic clove, minced
1 tablespoon vegetable oil
1 1/2 cups water
1 (15 ounce) can white kidney or cannelini beans, rinsed and drained

1 (15 ounce) can garbanzo beans, rinsed and drained
1 (11 ounce) can whole kernel corn, drained
1 (4 ounce) can chopped green chilies
1 teaspoon chicken bouillon granules
1 teaspoon ground cumin

In a large skillet, saute chicken, onion and garlic in oil until onion is tender. Transfer to a slow cooker. Stir in the remaining ingredients. Cover and cook on low for 7-8 hours or until chicken juices run clear and flavors are blended.

78- Authentic Cochinita Pibil (Spicy Mexican Pulled

1 red onion, sliced thin
3 habanero peppers, sliced
10 limes, juiced salt to taste
B
3 ounces dried guajillo chile peppers, seeded and deveined
1 tablespoon vegetable oil salt and pepper to taste

3 pounds boneless pork shoulder, cut into 1-inch cubes
3 cups fresh orange juice
1 cup white vinegar
1 bulb garlic, peeled
7 1/2 ounces achiote paste

Combine the onion, habanero peppers, lime juice, and salt in a bowl; cover and refrigerate while preparing and cooking the pork. Use rubber gloves when preparing the habanero peppers and avoid touching your eyes, nose, or skin while slicing peppers. Place the guajillo peppers in a bowl; pour enough hot water over the peppers to cover. Allow to soak until the peppers are softened, about 10 minutes. Heat the oil in a large skillet at medium-high heat. Season pork with salt and pepper; cook in the hot oil until completely browned, 15 to 20 minutes. Transfer the pork to a slow cooker. Combine the guajillo peppers, orange juice, vinegar, garlic, and achiote paste in a blender; blend until smooth. Pour the sauce over the pork cubes in the slow cooker. Cook on High until the pork easily falls apart, 6 to 8 hours. Remove the pork to a serving dish and shred with 2 forks. Pour the achiote sauce over the shredded pork. To serve, top with the onion- habanero salsa.

79- Italian Turkey Sandwiches

1 (5 1/2 pound) bone-in turkey breast, skin removed
1/2 cup chopped green pepper
1 medium onion, chopped
1/4 cup chili sauce

3 tablespoons white vinegar
2 tablespoons dried oregano or Italian seasoning
4 teaspoons beef bouillon granules
11 kaiser or hard rolls, split

Cut turkey breast in half along the bone. Place the turkey breast, green pepper and onion in a 5-qt. slow cooker coated with nonstick cooking spray. Combine the chili sauce, vinegar, oregano and bouillon; pour over turkey and vegetables. Cover and cook on low for 5-6 hours or until meat juices run clear and vegetables are tender. Remove turkey, reserving cooking liquid. Shred the turkey with two forks; return to cooking juices. Spoon 1/2 cup onto each roll.

80- Slow Cooker Chicken Cacciatore

6 skinless, boneless chicken breast halves
1 (28 ounce) jar spaghetti sauce
2 green bell pepper, seeded and cubed

8 ounces fresh mushrooms, sliced
1 onion, finely diced
2 tablespoons minced garlic

Put the chicken in the slow cooker. Top with the spaghetti sauce, green bell peppers, mushrooms, onion, and garlic. Cover, and cook on Low for 7 to 9 hours.

81- Hearty Pasta Tomato Soup

1 pound bulk Italian sausage
6 cups beef broth
1 (28 ounce) can stewed tomatoes
1 (15 ounce) can tomato sauce
2 cups sliced zucchini
1 large onion, chopped
1 cup sliced carrots
1 cup sliced fresh mushrooms

1 medium green pepper, chopped
1/4 cup minced fresh parsley
2 teaspoons sugar
1 teaspoon dried oregano
1 teaspoon dried basil
1 garlic clove, minced
2 cups frozen cheese tortellini grated Parmesan cheese

In a skillet, cook the sausage over medium heat until no longer pink; drain. Transfer to a 5-qt. slow cooker; add the next 13 ingredients. Cover and cook on high for 3-4 hours or until the vegetables are tender. Cook tortellini according to package directions; drain. Stir into slow cooker; cover and cook 30 minutes longer. Serve with Parmesan cheese if desired.

82- Barbecue Pork On Buns

1 (2 pound) boneless pork loin
1 onion, chopped
3/4 cup cola carbonated beverage

3/4 cup barbecue sauce
8 sandwich buns

Combine all ingredients except buns in a 4-quart slow-cooker; cook, covered, on high for 5-6 hours, until very tender. Drain and slice or shred pork; serve on buns with additional barbecue sauce, if desired.

83- Hamburger Soup II

1 1/2 pounds lean ground beef
2 large potatoes, sliced
2 stalks celery, sliced salt and pepper to taste
2 onions, thinly sliced

1 (15 ounce) can peas
3 small carrots, sliced
1 (10.75 ounce) can condensed tomato soup
1 1/4 cups water

Place ground beef in a large, deep skillet. Cook over medium-high heat until evenly brown. Drain, crumble, and set aside. Place a the potatoes in a layer to cover the bottom of the slow cooker. Sprinkle the celery over the potatoes, and cover with a layer of ground beef. Season each layer with salt and pepper. Throw in the carrots, onions and peas. Mix together the tomato soup and water, and pour over the top. Cover, and set to low for 6 to 8 hours.

84- Slow Cooker Tamale Pie

1 pound ground beef
1 (15 ounce) can kidney beans, drained and rinsed
1 (10 ounce) can enchilada sauce
1 1/2 teaspoons garlic powder

1 (8.5 ounce) package corn bread/muffin mix
1/3 cup milk
1 egg
2 tablespoons melted butter
1/2 cup shredded Cheddar cheese

Place the ground beef in a skillet over medium heat, and cook and stir the beef until it is browned, about 10 minutes, breaking up the meat as it cooks. Drain the beef, and place it into the slow cooker. Stir in the kidney beans, enchilada sauce, and garlic powder. In a bowl, combine the corn bread mix with milk, egg, and butter, and stir until just mixed. Stir in the Cheddar cheese. Spoon the corn bread mixture over the beef mixture in the slow cooker. Set the cooker to Low, cover, and cook until the corn bread topping is cooked through and set, about 5 hours.

85- Wassail Punch

2 quarts apple cider
2 cups orange juice
1/2 cup lemon juice
12 whole cloves

4 cinnamon sticks
1 pinch ground ginger
1 pinch ground nutmeg

In a slow-cooker or a large pot over low heat, combine apple cider, orange juice and lemon juice. Season with cloves, ginger and nutmeg. Bring to a simmer. If using a slow cooker, allow to simmer all day. Serve hot.

86- Chops With Fruit Stuffing

6 (1/2 inch thick) pork loin chops
1 tablespoon vegetable oil
1 (6 ounce) package herb stuffing mix
2 celery ribs, chopped
1 medium tart apple, peeled and
chopped

1 cup dried cherries or cranberries
1/2 cup chopped onion
2/3 cup chicken broth
1/4 cup butter, melted

In a large skillet, brown pork chops in oil on both sides. In a large bowl, combine the remaining ingredients. Place half of the stuffing mixture in a 3-qt. slow cooker. Top with pork and remaining stuffing mixture. Cover and cook on low for 3 hours or until a meat thermometer reads 160 degrees F.

87- Kevin's Sausage Dip

1 pound fresh, ground pork sausage
1/2 pound fresh, ground spicy pork
sausage

1 (8 ounce) package cream cheese
1 (14.5 ounce) can diced tomatoes
with green chile peppers

In a large skillet, brown sausage. Drain excess fat. Cut cream cheese blocks into small cubes. Place the cream cheese, tomatoes and sausage into a slow cooker. Heat over a medium heat. Stir continually. Serve as soon as cream cheese melts completely.

88- Cheesy Taco Dip

1 pound lean ground beef
3/4 cup water
1 (1.25 ounce) package taco seasoning
mix

1 (16 ounce) can crushed tomatoes
1 (1 pound) loaf processed
cheese, shredded

In a large skillet, brown ground beef. Drain fat. Stir in seasoning packet and water. Bring to a boil, reduce heat to simmer. Let cook for 5 minutes, stir occasionally. Place ground beef mixture into a slow cooker. Add tomatoes and cheese to the slow cooker.
Cook on low for 1 hour.

89- October Dinner Fondue

1 (10.75 ounce) can
Campbell'sB® Condensed Cream of
Chicken Soup (Regular or 98% Fat Free)
3/4 cup milk
1/2 teaspoon chili powder

1/2 teaspoon ground cumin
1 cup shredded Cheddar cheese
2 tablespoons chopped fresh cilantro
leaves

Suggested Dippers: chicken nuggets, tortellini, mini ravioli, steamed broccoli and/or
Cauliflower Heat the soup and milk in a 2-quart saucepan over medium heat until the mixture
is hot and bubbling, stirring occasionally. Stir in the chili powder, cumin and cheese. Cook
and stir until the cheese is melted. Stir in the cilantro. Pour the soup mixture into a fondue pot
or slow cooker. Serve warm with the Suggested Dippers.

90- Slowly Deviled Beef

2 pounds chuck roast
1 onion, chopped
1 (6 ounce) can tomato paste
3/4 cup water

1 (1.3 ounce) envelope sloppy joe
seasoning
2 tablespoons cider vinegar

Place the beef, onion, tomato paste, water, sloppy Joe seasoning mix and vinegar in a slow
cooker. Cook on low setting for 10 hours OR on high setting for 5 hours.

91- Simple Slow Cooker Meatloaf

1 pound Bob Evans® Original
Recipe Sausage Roll
1 pound ground beef
1 cup ketchup, divided

1 (1.25 ounce) envelope dry onion soup
mix
1/2 cup dry bread crumbs
2 eggs

In large bowl, combine sausage, beef, 1/2 cup ketchup, soup mix, bread crumbs and eggs.
When well combined, shape into loaf to fit your slow cooker (round or oval). Place into slow
cooker. Cover and cook on low heat 4-6 hours. Spread remaining 1/2 cup ketchup on top of
meatloaf 30 minutes before serving. Cover and continue cooking on low heat for 30 minutes.

92- BBQ Pork for Sandwiches

1 (14 ounce) can beef broth
3 pounds boneless pork ribs

1 (18 ounce) bottle barbeque sauce

Pour can of beef broth into slow cooker, and add boneless pork ribs. Cook on High heat for 4
hours, or until meat shreds easily. Remove meat, and shred with two forks. It will seem that
it's not working right away, but it will. Preheat oven to 350 degrees F (175 degrees C). Transfer
the shredded pork to a Dutch oven or iron skillet, and stir in barbeque sauce. Bake in the
preheated oven for 30 minutes, or until heated through.

93- Sweet Barbeque Beans

6 slices bacon, chopped
1 pound ground beef
2 (16 ounce) cans baked beans with pork
1 (15.5 ounce) can navy beans, rinsed
and drained
1 (15 ounce) can kidney beans, rinsed
and drained
3/4 cup ketchup

3/4 cup packed brown sugar
3 tablespoons distilled white vinegar
2 tablespoons honey garlic sauce
2 tablespoons sweet and sour sauce
1 teaspoon onion powder
1 teaspoon garlic salt
1 teaspoon ground mustard
1 teaspoon Worcestershire sauce

Fry the bacon pieces in a large skillet until browned and crisp, remove from the pan and set aside. Crumble the ground beef into the pan; cook and stir until no longer pink, then drain off grease. Transfer the ground beef and bacon to a slow cooker. Pour the baked beans, navy beans, kidney beans, ketchup, brown sugar and vinegar into the slow cooker. Season with honey garlic sauce, sweet and sour sauce, onion powder, garlic salt, mustard powder and Worcestershire sauce. Stir until everything is distributed evenly. Cover, and cook on High heat for 1 hour before serving.

94- Cantonese Dinner

2 pounds pork steak, cut into strips
2 tablespoons vegetable oil
1 onion, thinly sliced
1 (4.5 ounce) can mushrooms, drained
1 (8 ounce) can tomato sauce

3 tablespoons brown sugar
1 1/2 teaspoons distilled white vinegar
1 1/2 teaspoons salt
2 tablespoons Worcestershire sauce

In a large heavy skillet, heat oil over medium-high heat. Brown pork in oil. Drain off excess fat. Place pork, onion, mushrooms, tomato sauce, brown sugar, vinegar, salt and Worcestershire sauce in a slow cooker. Cook on High for 4 hours, or on Low for 6 to 8 hours.

95- Salmon with Spinach Sauce

1 (10 ounce) package frozen chopped
spinach, thawed and squeezed dry
3/4 cup mayonnaise
1 tablespoon Dijon mustard
2 teaspoons lemon juice

1/4 teaspoon garlic salt
1 1/2 cups water
2 (6 ounce) salmon fillets
1/2 teaspoon lemon-pepper seasoning
4 slices lemon

In a small bowl, combine the spinach, mayonnaise, mustard, lemon juice and garlic salt; cover and refrigerate until serving. Pour water into a pressure cooker. Place salmon on rack; sprinkle with lemon-pepper and top with lemon slices. Close cover securely; place pressure regulator on vent pipe. Bring cooker to full pressure over high heat. Reduce heat to medium-high and cook for 2 minutes. (Pressure regulator should maintain a slow steady rocking motion; adjust heat if needed.) Remove from the heat. Immediately cool according to manufacturers directions until pressure is completely reduced. Discard lemon slices. Serve salmon with spinach sauce.

96- Slow Cooker Chile Verde

3 tablespoons olive oil
1/2 cup onion, chopped
2 cloves garlic, minced
3 pounds boneless pork shoulder, cubed

5 (7 ounce) cans green salsa
1 (4 ounce) can diced jalapeno peppers
1 (14.5 ounce) can diced tomatoes

Heat the oil in a large skillet or Dutch oven over medium heat. Add the onion and garlic; cook and stir until fragrant. Add the cubed pork, and cook until browned on the outside. Transfer the pork, onions, and garlic to a slow cooker, and stir in the green salsa, jalapeno peppers, and tomatoes. Cover, and cook on High for 3 hours. Reduce the setting to Low, and cook for 4 to 5 more hours.

97- Ten Bean Soup II

1 (16 ounce) package dry mixed beans
1 (15 ounce) can tomato sauce
1 (14.5 ounce) can diced tomatoes with green chile peppers
3 stalks celery, diced
4 carrots, diced
16 ounces smoked turkey sausage, diced

salt to taste
ground black pepper to taste
1/4 teaspoon poultry seasoning
1/2 teaspoon onion powder
2 1/2 teaspoons minced garlic
Soak bean mix in water overnight.

Place drained soaked beans, tomato sauce, tomatoes and chilies, celery, carrots and sausage in slow cooker. Add enough water to cover all ingredients and season soup to taste with salt, pepper, chicken seasoning, onion powder, and garlic. Simmer on low for 8 to 10 hours until beans are tender.

98- Apple Butter I

8 apples - peeled, cored and chopped
4 cups white sugar
4 teaspoons ground cinnamon

1/4 teaspoon ground cloves
1/4 teaspoon salt

Fill a slow cooker with diced apples, sugar, cinnamon, cloves and salt. Cover, and cook on high for 1 hour. Reduce heat. Simmer, stirring occasionally, for 12 hours, or until thick and dark golden in color. Pack into small, freezer-safe containers leaving 3/4 inch space at the top. Store in the freezer.

99- Chicken Delicious

10 skinless, boneless chicken breast halves
1 teaspoon fresh lemon juice salt and pepper to taste
1/8 teaspoon celery salt
1 teaspoon paprika

1 (10.75 ounce) can condensed cream of mushroom soup
1 (10.75 ounce) can condensed cream of celery soup
1/3 cup dry sherry
1/4 cup grated Parmesan cheese

Rinse the chicken breasts and pat dry. Season with the lemon juice, salt, pepper, celery salt and paprika to taste. Place in a slow cooker. In a medium size bowl mix the mushroom and celery soups with the sherry/wine. Pour mixture over the chicken breasts and sprinkle with grated Parmesan cheese. Cook on LOW setting for 8 to 10 hours, OR on HIGH setting for 4 to 5 hours.

100- Slow Cooker Squirrel and Liver

1 tablespoon olive oil
2 squirrels - skinned, gutted, and cut into pieces
2 pounds beef liver, sliced into thin strips
2 large sweet onions, chopped
4 carrots, sliced
1 green bell pepper, seeded and sliced into strips

6 cloves garlic, minced
2 cups tomato juice
1 teaspoon salt
1 teaspoon ground black pepper
1 teaspoon dried oregano
1 teaspoon crushed dried thyme
1 bay leaf

Heat the olive oil in a large skillet over medium heat. Sear the squirrel and liver until browned on the outside. Transfer to a slow cooker. Add the onions, carrots, bell pepper and garlic. Stir in the tomato juice. Season with salt, pepper, oregano, thyme and bay leaf. Cover, and cook on High for 6 hours.

101- Daria's Slow Cooker Beef Stroganoff

1 1/2 pounds top round steak, cut into strips
salt and pepper to taste
1/2 onion, chopped
1 (10.75 ounce) can condensed cream of mushroom soup
1 (8 ounce) can canned mushrooms
1/4 cup water

1 tablespoon dried chives
1 clove garlic, minced
1 teaspoon Worcestershire sauce
1 cube beef bouillon
1/4 cup white wine
1 tablespoon all-purpose flour
1 (16 ounce) container sour cream
1/2 cup chopped fresh parsley

Place the beef in the bottom of a slow cooker, and season with salt and pepper to taste. Place onion on top of beef, and then add mushroom soup, mushrooms, and water. Season with chives, garlic, Worcestershire sauce, and bouillon. In a small bowl, mix together the wine with the flour. Pour over the beef. Cover, and cook on Low for 6 to 7 hours. Stir in the sour cream and parsley, and continue cooking for 1 hour.

102- Sauerkraut-Stuffed Slow-Cooked Pork Roast

1 (3 pound) boneless pork roast

1 (14.5 ounce) can sauerkraut, drained

Place pork roast on a cutting board. With a sharp knife, cut a 5-inch slit into the top of the roast, being careful not to cut clear through to the bottom of the roast. Spoon the sauerkraut into the pork roast, pressing it into the slit with the bottom of the spoon. Place the roast in the slow cooker, and cook on Low for 8 to 9 hours.

103- Creamy Slow Cooker Marsala Pork

1 cup flour
1 tablespoon minced fresh rosemary
1 teaspoon dry mustard powder
1 teaspoon salt
1 teaspoon garlic powder
1/2 teaspoon ground black pepper
6 (4 ounce) pork chops

2 tablespoons vegetable oil
1 onion, sliced
1 (4 ounce) package sliced mushrooms
1 clove garlic, minced
1 (10.75 ounce) can condensed cream of mushroom soup
1/2 cup Marsala wine

Stir together the flour, rosemary, mustard, salt, garlic powder, and pepper in a bowl. Dredge the pork chops in the seasoned flour, shake off excess, and set aside. Heat the vegetable oil in a large skillet over medium-high heat. Add the pork chops and cook until golden brown on both sides, about 4 minutes per side. Place the onion, mushrooms, and garlic into a slow cooker. Add the seared pork chops, then pour in the cream of mushroom soup and Marsala wine. Cover, and cook on Low until the chops are tender, 6 to 8 hours.

104- Barbecue Chicken Wings

3 pounds whole chicken wings
2 cups ketchup
1/2 cup honey
2 tablespoons lemon juice
2 tablespoons vegetable oil
2 tablespoons soy sauce

2 tablespoons Worcestershire sauce
1 tablespoon paprika
4 garlic cloves, minced
1 1/2 teaspoons curry powder
1/2 teaspoon pepper
1/8 teaspoon hot pepper sauce

Cut chicken wings into three sections; discard wing tips. Place wings in a greased 15-in. x 10-in. x 1-in. baking pan. Bake at 350 degrees F for 35-40 minutes or until juices run clear. In a bowl, combine the remaining ingredients. Pour 1/2 cup into a 3- qt. slow cooker. Drain chicken wings; add to slow cooker. Drizzle with remaining sauce. Cover and cook on low for 1 hour, basting occasionally.

105- Slow Cooker Chicken Curry with Quinoa

1 1/2 pounds diced chicken breast meat
3/4 cup chopped onion
1 1/4 cups chopped celery
1 3/4 cups chopped Granny Smith apples
1 cup chicken broth

1/4 cup nonfat milk
1 tablespoon curry powder
1/4 teaspoon paprika
1/3 cup quinoa

Place the chicken, onion, celery, apple, chicken broth, milk, curry powder, and paprika into a slow cooker; stir until mixed. Cover, and cook on Low for 4 to 5 hours. Stir in the quinoa during the final 35 minutes of cooking. Serve when quinoa is tender.

106- Citrus Pork Roast

1 (3 pound) boneless pork loin roast
1/2 teaspoon garlic powder
1/2 teaspoon dried thyme
1/2 teaspoon ground ginger
1/4 teaspoon pepper
1 tablespoon vegetable oil
1 cup chicken broth

2 tablespoons sugar
2 tablespoons lemon juice
2 tablespoons soy sauce
1 1/2 teaspoons grated orange peel
3 tablespoons cornstarch
1/2 cup orange juice

Cut roast in half. In a small bowl, combine the garlic powder, thyme, ginger and pepper; rub over roast. In a large skillet over medium heat, brown roast on all sides in oil. Place roast in a 5-qt. slow cooker. In a small bowl, combine the broth, sugar, lemon juice, soy sauce and orange peel; pour over roast. Cover and cook on low for 4 hours or until a meat thermometer reads 160 degrees F. Remove roast and keep warm. In a saucepan, combine the cornstarch and orange juice until smooth; stir in cooking juices. Bring to a boil; cook and stir for 2 minutes or until thickened. Serve with the roast.

107- Hot Crab Spread

1 1/2 cups chopped green onions
6 garlic cloves, minced
1 tablespoon butter
1 tablespoon mayonnaise

8 cups shredded Monterey Jack cheese
4 (6 ounce) cans crabmeat - drained,
flaked and cartilage removed
Assorted crackers

In a skillet, saute onions and garlic in butter until tender. Transfer to a 3-qt. slow cooker; add mayonnaise. Stir in cheese. Cover and cook on low for 30 minutes or until cheese is melted, stirring occasionally. Stir in crab; cover and cook 1 hour longer or until heated through. Serve spread warm with crackers.

108- Slow Cooker Lime Chicken with Rice

1 1/4 pounds skinless, boneless chicken
breast halves
1/3 cup lime juice
2 cups chicken broth
1 clove garlic, minced

1/2 teaspoon dried thyme leaves
1/4 teaspoon ground black pepper
2 tablespoons butter
2 cups uncooked instant rice

Place the chicken breasts into a slow cooker; pour in the lime juice and chicken stock. Add the garlic, thyme, pepper, and butter. Cover, and cook on Low until the chicken is very tender, 8 to 10. Stir in the rice during the last 15 minutes of cooking time.

109- Colorado Buffalo Chili

1 pound ground buffalo
1 1/2 teaspoons ground cumin
1/2 teaspoon ground cumin

1 (10 ounce) can diced tomatoes with
green chiles
1 (10.75 ounce) can tomato soup

1 (14.5 ounce) can kidney beans, drained
1 (14.5 ounce) can black beans, drained
1/2 medium onion, chopped
1/2 teaspoon minced garlic
1 Anaheim chile pepper, chopped

1 poblano chile pepper, chopped
2 tablespoons chili powder
1 teaspoon red pepper flakes salt and
pepper to taste

Brown the buffalo in a skillet over medium heat; season with 1/2 teaspoon cayenne pepper and 1/2 teaspoon cumin; drain. Combine the buffalo, tomatoes with green chiles, tomato soup, kidney beans, black beans, onion, garlic, Anaheim chile pepper, poblano chile pepper, chili powder, red pepper flakes, black pepper, and salt in a slow cooker. Cover and cook on Low overnight or 8 hours.

110- Our Favorite Olive Beef

2 pounds boneless chuck roast
2 (14.5 ounce) cans stewed tomatoes,
chopped

1 (8 ounce) jar pitted green olives,
chopped, 1/3 of liquid reserved
8 kaiser rolls

Place chuck roast, stewed tomatoes, and green olives with the reserved liquid into a slow cooker. Cook 6 hours on Low, until the roast falls apart easily. Serve over kaiser rolls.

111- Slow Cooker Sausage with Sauce

8 (4 ounce) links fresh Italian sausage
1 (26 ounce) jar spaghetti sauce

1 green bell pepper, seeded and sliced
into strips
1 onion, sliced

Place the Italian sausage links, spaghetti sauce, green pepper and onion into a slow cooker. Stir to coat everything in sauce. Cover, and cook on Low for 6 hours. Serve on hoagie rolls, or over rice.

112- Keon's Slow Cooker Curry Chicken

1 tablespoon butter
1 onion, chopped
1 (10.75 ounce) can condensed cream of
mushroom soup
1 (10.75 ounce) can condensed cream of
chicken soup
1 (14 ounce) can coconut milk
1 packet dry onion soup mix (such as
Knorr® French Onion Soup
Mix)

3 tablespoons curry powder, or to taste
1/2 teaspoon salt
1/2 teaspoon ground black pepper
2 teaspoons ground cayenne pepper, or
to taste
3 large skinless, boneless chicken breast
halves -- trimmed and cut into 1-inch
pieces
1 cup green peas
2 cups sliced fresh mushrooms

Set the slow cooker to the High setting. Heat the butter in a skillet over medium heat, and cook and stir the onion until browned, 5 to 10 minutes. Set the onion aside. In a large bowl, stir together cream of mushroom soup, cream of chicken soup, coconut milk, dry soup mix, curry powder, salt, pepper, and cayenne pepper until the mixture is thoroughly combined. Place the chicken into the bottom of the slow cooker, and pour the mixture over the chicken. Stir in onion, peas and mushrooms. Cook on High setting for 1 1/2 hours, then reduce heat to Low and cook an additional 1 1/2 to 2 hours.

113- Easy Slow Cooker Ham

1 (6 pound) bone-in country ham
30 whole cloves
3 cups apple cider, or as needed
1 cup brown sugar
1 cup maple syrup
2 tablespoons ground cinnamon

1 tablespoon ground nutmeg
2 teaspoons ground ginger
2 tablespoons ground cloves
1 tablespoon vanilla extract
(optional)
1 orange's peel

Press whole cloves into the ham so they are evenly distributed. You may score the ham for easier insertion if you wish. Place the ham in a slow cooker. Pour in apple cider until only about 2 inches of ham is above the surface. Pack the brown sugar on top of the ham, pressing into the cloves. This will get washed away in the next step but any that stays on is a bonus. Pour the maple syrup over the ham. Season the apple cider with cinnamon, nutmeg, ginger, ground cloves and vanilla. Add the orange peel to the pot. Fill the slow cooker as full as you can with apple cider without going over the fill line. Cover and set to Low. Cook for 8 to 10 hours.

114- Pork Chops a la Slow Cooker

1/2 cup all-purpose flour
1 teaspoon dry mustard
1 teaspoon seasoning salt
4 thick cut pork chops

2 tablespoons olive oil
1 (10.5 ounce) can condensed chicken with rice soup

In a pie plate or shallow dish, mix flour, dry mustard, and seasoned salt. Trim fat from pork chops. Heat oil in a skillet over medium heat. Dredge chops in flour mixture, then place them in the skillet, and brown both sides. Place in chops into a slow cooker, and pour the chicken and rice soup over them. Cover, and cook on Low about 8 hours.

115- Pork Chalupas

1 (4 pound) pork shoulder roast
1 pound dried pinto beans
3 (4 ounce) cans diced green chile peppers
2 tablespoons chili powder

2 tablespoons ground cumin
2 tablespoons salt
2 tablespoons dried oregano
2 tablespoons garlic powder
12 flour tortillas

Place the roast inside a slow cooker coated with cooking spray. In a separate bowl, stir together the beans, 2 cans of the chile peppers, chili powder, cumin, salt, oregano, and garlic powder. Pour the whole mixture over the roast, and add enough water so that the roast is mostly covered. Jiggle the roast a little to get some of the liquid underneath. Cover, and cook on Low for 8 to 9 hours. Check after about 5 hours to make sure the beans have not absorbed all of the liquid. Add more water if necessary 1 cup at a time. Use just enough to keep the beans from drying out. When the roast is fork-tender, remove it from the slow cooker, and place on a cutting board. Remove any bone and fat, then shred with forks. Return to the slow cooker, and stir in the remaining can of green chilies. Heat through, and serve with flour tortillas and your favorite toppings.

116- Slow Cooker Venison Stroganoff

1 tablespoon canola oil
1 1/2 pounds venison stew meat, cut into
1 inch cubes
1 bay leaf
1 small onion, thinly sliced
1 (8 ounce) jar sliced mushrooms,
drained

2 (14 ounce) cans low-sodium beef broth
Salt and pepper to taste
1/2 (16 ounce) package whole wheat
noodles
1 (8 ounce) container sour cream

Heat canola oil in a large skillet over medium-high heat. Add the venison cubes and fry on all sides until well browned, then place into a slow cooker. Add the bay leaf, onion, and mushroom to the slow cooker. Pour in the beef broth, and season to taste with salt and pepper. Set slow cooker on Low, and cook for 8 to 10 hours. Add the noodles, and water or additional beef broth if needed. Cover and cook for 30 minutes. Once the noodles are done, stir in the sour cream and serve.

117- Melt-In-Your-Mouth Meat Loaf

2 eggs
3/4 cup milk
2/3 cup seasoned bread crumbs
2 teaspoons dried minced onion
1 teaspoon salt
1/2 teaspoon rubbed sage

1 1/2 pounds ground beef
1/4 cup ketchup
2 tablespoons brown sugar
1 teaspoon ground mustard
1/2 teaspoon Worcestershire sauce

In a large bowl, combine the first six ingredients. Crumble beef over mixture and mix well (mixture will be moist.) Shape into a round loaf; place in a 5-qt. slow cooker. Cover and cook on low for 5-6 hours or until a meat thermometer reads 160 degrees F. In a small bowl, whisk the ketchup, brown sugar, mustard and Worcestershire sauce. Spoon over the meat loaf. Cook 15 minutes longer or until heated through. Let stand for 10-15 minutes before cutting.

118- Hungarian Noodle Side Dish

1 (16 ounce) package wide egg noodles
3 cubes chicken bouillon
1/4 cup water
1 (10.75 ounce) can condensed cream of
mushroom soup
1/2 cup chopped onion

2 tablespoons Worcestershire sauce
1 tablespoon poppy seeds
1/4 teaspoon garlic powder
1/4 teaspoon hot pepper sauce
2 cups cottage cheese
2 cups sour cream

1/4 cup grated Parmesan cheese   1 pinch paprika

Cook egg noodles in a large pot with boiling salted water. Drain well. In a large bowl dissolve chicken bouillon cube in boiling water. Mix in the cream of mushroom soup, chopped onion, Worcestershire sauce, poppy seeds, garlic powder, and hot pepper sauce. Stir in cottage cheese, sour cream, and cooked egg noodles. Transfer to lightly greased slow cooker and sprinkle the top with parmesan cheese and paprika. Cover and cook on high for 3 to 4 hours. Serve immediately.

119- Italian Beef Hoagies

1 (4 pound) boneless sirloin tip roast,   2 cups water
halved   1 (16 ounce) jar mild pepper rings,
2 (.7 ounce) packages Italian salad   undrained
dressing mix   18 hoagie buns, split

Place roast in a 5-qt. slow cooker. Combine the salad dressing mix and water; pour over roast. Cover and cook on low for 8 hours or until meat is tender. Remove meat; shred with a fork and return to slow cooker. Add pepper rings; heat through. Spoon 1/2 cup meat mixture onto each bun.

120- Slow Cooker Macaroni and Cheese II

2 cups evaporated milk   2 tablespoons butter
1/2 teaspoon paprika   3 1/2 cups cubed Cheddar cheese
1 teaspoon salt   1 (8 ounce) package macaroni
1 egg, beaten

Combine in slow cooker: evaporated milk, paprika, salt, egg, butter and cheese; stir. Cook on high for 1 hour. Bring a large pot of lightly salted water to a boil. Add macaroni and cook for 8 to 10 minutes or until al dente; drain. Stir cooked macaroni into cheese sauce, reduce temperature to low and cook for 3 to 5 hours.

121- Slow Cooker Mussaman Curry

2 potatoes, cut into large chunks   1/4 cup peanut butter
1 small onion, coarsely chopped   3 tablespoons curry powder
2 tablespoons butter   3 tablespoons Thai fish sauce
1 1/4 pounds beef chuck, cut into   3 tablespoons brown sugar
1-inch cubes   2 cups beef broth
3 cloves garlic, minced   1/2 cup unsalted, dry-roasted peanuts
1 (14 ounce) can coconut milk

Place the potatoes and onion in a slow cooker. Melt the butter in a skillet over medium-high heat. Cook the beef and garlic together in the melted butter until the beef is browned on all sides. Transfer the beef and garlic to the slow cooker while keeping the beef drippings in the skillet. Return the skillet to the medium-high heat. Stir the coconut milk, peanut butter, and curry powder into the reserved beef drippings; cook and stir until the peanut butter melts. Pour the coconut milk mixture into the slow cooker. Turn the slow cooker on to Low; stir the fish sauce, brown sugar, and beef broth into the slow cooker. Cook on Low until the beef is fork-tender, 4 to 6 hours. Stir the peanuts into the curry about 30 minutes before serving.

122- Spicy Beef Curry Stew for the Slow Cooker

1 tablespoon olive oil
1 pound beef stew meat salt and pepper to taste
2 cloves garlic, minced
1 teaspoon chopped fresh ginger
1 fresh jalapeno peppers, diced

1 tablespoon curry powder
1 (14.5 ounce) can diced tomatoes with juice
1 onion, sliced and quartered
1 cup beef broth

Heat the olive oil in a skillet over medium heat, and brown the beef on all sides. Remove from skillet, reserving juices, and season with salt and pepper. Cook and stir the garlic, ginger, and jalapeno in the skillet for 2 minutes, until tender, and season with curry powder. Mix in the diced tomatoes and juice. Place the onion in the bottom of a slow cooker, and layer with the browned beef. Scoop the skillet mixture into the slow cooker, and mix in the beef broth. Cover, and cook 6 to 8 hours on Low.

123- Deer Chop Hurry

2 pounds deer chops (venison)
1 cup ketchup
1/2 cup water

1 medium onion, chopped
1/2 cup packed brown sugar
1 (1 ounce) envelope dry onion soup mix

Thinly slice the deer chops and brown them in a heavy skillet over medium-high heat. Transfer the meat to a slow cooker. Mix in the ketchup, water, onion, brown sugar, and dry onion soup mix. Cook on LOW for 6 hours or until tender. If you want to cook it in a roaster, bake at 350 degrees F, for 1 hour.

124- Slow Cooker Spaghetti Sauce II

1 pound ground beef
1 onion, finely chopped
2 cloves garlic, chopped
2 (28 ounce) cans tomato puree

2 (6 ounce) cans tomato paste
1 teaspoon white sugar
2 teaspoons Italian seasoning salt to taste

Place ground beef in a large, deep skillet. Cook over medium high heat until evenly brown. Stir in onion and garlic; cook 1 to 2 minutes. In a slow cooker combine ground beef mixture, tomato puree, tomato paste, sugar, Italian seasoning and salt. Cook on low for 4 hours.

125- Vegetable Cheese Soup II

1 (16 ounce) package frozen mixed vegetables

2 (10.75 ounce) cans condensed cream of chicken soup

2 1/2 cups water
1 tablespoon minced onion
1/4 tablespoon garlic powder salt to taste

ground black pepper to taste
32 ounces processed cheese food, cubed

In a large microwave bowl, cook vegetables in microwave for 10 minutes on high. Stir and rotate midway. On a large slow cooker, mix soup and water. Add onions, vegetables, and garlic, salt, and pepper to taste, and mix. Add cheese and mix. Simmer approximately 2 hours or until soup is creamy and cheese is melted.

126- Moist Poultry Dressing

2 (4.5 ounce) jars sliced mushrooms, drained
4 celery ribs, chopped
2 medium onions, chopped
1/4 cup minced fresh parsley
3/4 cup butter, cubed
1 1/2 pounds day old bread, crusts removed and cubed

1 1/2 teaspoons salt
1 1/2 teaspoons rubbed sage
1 teaspoon poultry seasoning
1 teaspoon dried thyme
1/2 teaspoon pepper
2 eggs
1 (14.5 ounce) can chicken broth

In a large skillet, saute the mushrooms, celery, onions and parsley in butter until the vegetables are tender. In a large bowl, toss the bread cubes with salt, sage, poultry seasoning, thyme and pepper. Add the mushroom mixture. Combine eggs and broth; add to the bread mixture and toss. Transfer to 5-qt. slow cooker. Cover and cook on low for 4-5 hours or until a meat thermometer reads 160 degrees F.

127- Old-Fashioned Peach Butter

14 cups coarsely chopped peeled fresh or frozen peaches
2 1/2 cups sugar
4 1/2 teaspoons lemon juice

1 1/2 teaspoons ground cinnamon
3/4 teaspoon ground cloves
1/2 cup quick-cooking tapioca

In a large bowl, combine the peaches, sugar, lemon juice, cinnamon and cloves; mix well. Transfer to a 5-qt. slow cooker. Cover and cook on low for 8-10 hours or until peaches are very soft, stirring occasionally. Stir in tapioca. Cook, uncovered, on high for 1 hour or until thickened. Pour into jars or freezer containers; cool to room temperature, about 1 hour. Refrigerate or freeze.

128- Corned Beef and Cabbage

1 medium onion, cut into wedges
4 medium potatoes, peeled and quartered
1 pound baby carrots
3 cups water
3 garlic cloves, minced

1 bay leaf
2 tablespoons sugar
2 tablespoons cider vinegar
1/2 teaspoon pepper
2 1/2 pounds corned beef brisket with spice packet, cut in half

1 small head cabbage, cut into wedges

Place the onion, potatoes and carrots in a 5-qt. slow cooker. Combine water, garlic, bay leaf, sugar, vinegar, pepper and contents of spice packet; pour over the vegetables. Top with brisket and cabbage. Cover and cook on low for 8-9 hours or until the meat and vegetables are tender. Remove bay leaf before serving.

129- Hot Chili Cheese Dip

1 medium onion, finely chopped
2 garlic cloves, minced
2 teaspoons vegetable oil
2 (15 ounce) cans chili without beans
2 cups salsa
2 (3 ounce) packages cream cheese, cubed
2 (2.25 ounce) cans sliced ripe olives, drained
Tortilla chips

In a skillet, saute onion and garlic in oil until tender. Transfer to a slow cooker. Stir in the chili, salsa, cream cheese and olives. Cover and cook on low for 4 hours or until heated through, stirring occasionally. Stir before serving with tortilla chips.

130- Grandma B's Bean Soup

1 pound dry navy beans
3 carrots, peeled and shredded
2 medium potatoes, peeled and diced
3 stalks celery, sliced
1 medium onion, diced
2 cups cubed cooked ham

Place the beans in a slow cooker with enough water to cover, and soak 6 to 8 hours, or overnight. Drain the beans, and return to the slow cooker. Cover with water, and mix in the carrots, potatoes, celery, onion, and ham. Cover slow cooker, and cook soup on High for 3 1/2 hours. Switch to Low, and continue cooking at least 6 1/2 hours. The longer it cooks the more flavorful it becomes.

131- Pareve Cholent

1 cup dry kidney beans
1/2 cup dry white beans
1/2 cup barley
2 large potatoes, peeled and cubed
1 large sweet potato, peeled and cubed
1 large onion, cut into chunks
2 cloves garlic, minced
2/3 cup ketchup
1/4 cup barbeque sauce
1/4 cup soy sauce
1/4 cup brown sugar
2 teaspoons garlic powder
2 teaspoons onion powder
2 teaspoons paprika
2 teaspoons ground black pepper
1 tablespoon salt
4 cups water, or more as needed to cover

Place kidney beans, white beans, barley, potatoes, sweet potato, onion, garlic, ketchup, barbeque sauce, soy sauce, brown sugar, garlic powder, onion powder, paprika, pepper, salt, and water in a slow cooker. Mix well. Cook on High for 3 hours, then reduce heat to Low and continue cooking overnight until the beans are tender.

132- Minestrone Stew

1 pound ground beef
1 small onion, chopped
1 (19 ounce) can minestrone soup
1 (15 ounce) can pinto beans, rinsed and
drained
1 (14.5 ounce) can stewed tomatoes

1 (11 ounce) can whole kernel corn,
drained
1 (4 ounce) can chopped green chilies
1 teaspoon salt
1/2 teaspoon garlic powder
1/2 teaspoon onion powder

In a skillet, cook beef and onion over medium heat until meat is no longer pink; drain.
Transfer to a slow cooker. Add the remaining ingredients; mix well. Cover and cook on low
for 4-6 hours or until heated through.

133- Swiss-Style Veal and Mushrooms

1 3/4 cups Swanson® Chicken
Stock
1 (10.75 ounce) can Campbell's®
Condensed Cream of Potato Soup
1 teaspoon dried thyme leaves, crushed
1 1/2 pounds veal for stew
1 (8 ounce) package sliced mushrooms

8 green onions, sliced
2 tablespoons all-purpose flour
1/4 cup water
1 cup shredded Swiss cheese Hot cooked
egg noodles Freshly ground black
pepper

Stir the stock, soup, thyme, veal, mushrooms and green onions in a 3 1/2-quart slow cooker.
Cover and cook on LOW for 7 to 8 hours or until the veal is fork-tender. Stir the flour and
water in a small bowl until the mixture is smooth. Stir the flour mixture in the cooker. Turn
the heat to HIGH. Cover and cook for 5 minutes or until the mixture boils and thickens.
Stir in the cheese. Serve over the noodles. Season with the black pepper.

134- Spaghetti Pork Chops

3 (8 ounce) cans tomato sauce
1 (10.75 ounce) can condensed tomato
soup, undiluted
1 small onion, finely chopped
1 bay leaf

1 teaspoon celery seed
1/2 teaspoon Italian seasoning
6 (1 inch thick) bone-in pork chops
2 tablespoons olive or vegetable oil
Hot cooked spaghetti

In a 5-qt. slow cooker, combine the tomato sauce, soup, onion, bay leaf, celery seed and Italian
seasoning. In a large skillet, brown pork chops in oil. Add to the slow cooker. Cover and cook
on low for 6-8 hours or until meat is tender. Discard bay leaf. Serve chops and sauce over
spaghetti.

135- Slow Cooker Cider Pork Roast

1 large onion, roughly chopped
1 apple, peeled and roughly chopped

3 cloves garlic
2 cups apple cider

1 1/2 cups water
salt and pepper to taste
1/2 teaspoon ground ginger
1/4 cup all-purpose flour

1 (3 pound) pork loin roast
2 teaspoons vegetable oil
1 stalk celery, roughly chopped
4 large carrots, roughly chopped

Combine 1/4 of the onion, 1/2 of the apple, and the garlic in the bowl of a food processor. Process until smooth. Transfer to slow cooker along with the apple cider and water. Combine the salt, pepper, ginger and flour in a shallow container. Gently press the roast onto the flour mixture to coat all sides. Brush off any excess flour. Heat the oil in a large, heavy skillet. Brown the pork in the hot oil, turning until golden on all sides. Place the browned roast in the slow cooker and scatter the celery and the remaining onion and apple on top. Cook on low for 4 hours, then add carrots. Cook for an additional 3 hours. Remove the cooked roast to a heated platter, arrange carrots around roast and serve with the strained juices from the slow cooker.

136- Slow Cooker Vegetable Soup

1 pound boneless round steak, cut into
1/2 inch cubes
1 (14.5 ounce) can diced tomatoes,
undrained
3 cups water
2 medium potatoes, peeled and cubed
2 medium onions, diced
3 celery ribs, sliced

2 carrots, sliced
3 beef bouillon cubes
1/2 teaspoon dried basil
1/2 teaspoon dried oregano
1/2 teaspoon salt
1/4 teaspoon pepper
1 1/2 cups frozen mixed vegetables

In a slow cooker, combine the first 12 ingredients. Cover and cook on high for 6 hours. Add vegetables; cover and cook on high 2 hours longer or until the meat and vegetables are tender.

137- Home-Style Ribs

4 pounds boneless pork spareribs, cut
into pieces
1 medium onion, thinly sliced
1 cup ketchup
1/2 cup water
1/4 cup packed brown sugar

1/4 cup cider vinegar
2 tablespoons Worcestershire sauce
2 teaspoons ground mustard
1 1/2 teaspoons salt
1 teaspoon paprika

Place half of the ribs in a slow cooker; top with half of the onion. Repeat layers. Combine the remaining ingredients; pour over all. Cover and cook on low for 8-9 hours or until ribs are tender.

138- Slow Cooker Chops

1 (10.75 ounce) can condensed cream of
mushroom soup
1/4 cup water

1 1/2 pounds boneless pork chops
1 teaspoon ground black pepper
1 (14.5 ounce) can green beans

4 potatoes, peeled and cubed

Pour soup into slow cooker. Stir in water to thin soup slightly. Season each pork chop with a dash of pepper, and place chops in slow cooker. Cover, and cook on Low for 7 to 8 hours. Add green beans and potatoes, and cook on High for 2 to 2 1/2 hours. Stir, remove from heat, and serve.

139- Easy Beer and Ketchup Meatballs

1 (28 ounce) bottle ketchup
24 fluid ounces beer
1 1/2 pounds ground beef

2 teaspoons garlic powder
1 onion, chopped

Preheat oven to 400 degrees F (200 degrees C).Place the beer and ketchup in a slow cooker on high setting and allow to simmer. Meanwhile, in a large bowl, combine the ground beef, garlic powder and onion, mixing well. Form mixture into meatballs about 3/4 inch in diameter. Place meatballs in a 9x13 inch baking dish. Bake at 400 degrees F (200 degrees C) for 20 minutes. Transfer meatballs to the slow cooker with the beer and ketchup and simmer for 3 hours; sauce will thicken.

140- Slow-Cooked Sweet 'n' Sour Pork

2 1/2 tablespoons paprika
2 1/2 pounds boneless pork loin roast, cut into 1-inch strips
1 tablespoon canola oil
1 (20 ounce) can unsweetened pineapple chunks
1 medium onion, chopped
1 medium green pepper, chopped

1/4 cup cider vinegar
3 tablespoons brown sugar
3 tablespoons reduced-sodium soy sauce
1 tablespoon Worcestershire sauce
1/2 teaspoon salt
2 tablespoons cornstarch
1/4 cup cold water
Hot cooked rice

Place paprika in a large resealable plastic bag. Add pork, a few pieces at a time, and shake to coat. In a nonstick skillet, brown pork in oil in batches over medium-high heat. Transfer to a 3-qt. slow cooker. Drain pineapple, reserving juice; refrigerate the pineapple. Add the pineapple juice, onion, green pepper, vinegar, brown sugar, soy sauce, Worcestershire sauce and salt to slow cooker; mix well. Cover and cook on low for 6-8 hours or until meat is tender. Combine cornstarch and water until smooth; stir into pork mixture. Add pineapple. Cover and cook 30 minutes longer or until sauce is thickened. Serve over rice if desired.

141- Cranberry Apple Cider

4 cups water
4 cups apple juice
1 (12 ounce) can frozen apple juice concentrate, thawed

1 medium apple - peeled, cored and diced
1 cup fresh or frozen cranberries
1 medium orange, peeled and sectioned
1 cinnamon stick

In a 5-qt. slow cooker, combine all ingredients. Cover and cook on low for 2 hours or until cider reaches desired temperature. Discard cinnamon stick. If desired, remove fruit with a slotted spoon before serving.

142- Slow Cooker Thai Pork with Peppers

1 cup chicken broth
1/3 cup soy sauce
1/3 cup creamy peanut butter
3 tablespoons honey
6 cloves garlic, minced

2 tablespoons minced fresh ginger root
1 teaspoon crushed red pepper flakes
2 red bell peppers, thinly sliced and cut into bite-size lengths
1 pound boneless pork chops

Place the chicken broth, soy sauce, peanut butter, honey, garlic, ginger, crushed red pepper flakes, red bell peppers, and pork chops into a slow cooker, stir together, and set the cooker on Low. Cook for 5 to 6 hours until the pork is tender, and remove the pork from the sauce. Shred the pork, return to the sauce, let cook until hot, and serve.

143- Corn Spoon Bread

1 (8 ounce) package cream cheese, softened
1/3 cup sugar
1 cup milk
1/2 cup egg substitute
2 tablespoons butter, melted
1 teaspoon salt

1/4 teaspoon ground nutmeg
Dash pepper
2 1/3 cups frozen corn, thawed
1 (14.75 ounce) can cream-style corn
1 (8.5 ounce) package corn bread/muffin mix

In a large mixing bowl, beat cream cheese and sugar until smooth. Gradually beat in milk. Beat in the egg substitute, butter, salt, nutmeg and pepper until blended. Stir in corn and cream-style corn. Stir in corn bread mix just until moistened. Pour into a greased 3-qt. slow cooker. Cover and cook on high for 3-4 hours or until center is almost set.

144- Slow-Cooked Flank Steak

1 (1 1/2-pound) flank steak, cut in half
1 tablespoon vegetable oil
1 large onion, sliced
1/3 cup water
1 (4 ounce) can chopped green chilies
2 tablespoons vinegar

1 1/4 teaspoons chili powder
1 teaspoon garlic powder
1/2 teaspoon sugar
1/2 teaspoon salt
1/8 teaspoon pepper

In a skillet, brown steak in oil; transfer to a slow cooker. In the same skillet, saute onion for 1 minute. Gradually add water, stirring to loosen browned bits from pan. Add remaining ingredients; bring to a boil. Pour over the flank steak. Cover and cook on low for 7-8 hours or until the meat is tender. Slice the meat; serve with onion and pan juices.

145- Mexican Beef and Bean Stew

1 1/2 pounds beef for stew, cut in
1 inch pieces
2 tablespoons all-purpose flour
1 tablespoon vegetable oil
1 (10.5 ounce) can Campbell's®
Condensed Beef Consomme
1 cup Pace® Thick & Chunky
Salsa

1 large onion, coarsely chopped
1 (15 ounce) can pinto beans, rinsed and
drained
1 (16 ounce) can whole kernel corn,
drained
2 tablespoons chili powder
1 teaspoon ground cumin
1/4 teaspoon garlic powder

Coat the beef with flour. Heat the oil in a 12-inch skillet over medium-high heat. Add the beef and cook in 2 batches until it's well browned, stirring often. Stir the beef, consomme, salsa, onion, beans, corn, chili powder, cumin and garlic powder in a 3 1/2-quart slow cooker. Cover and cook on LOW for 8 to 9 hours* or until the beef is fork- tender.

146- Slow Cooker Country-Style Spareribs

4 pounds pork spareribs salt and pepper
to taste
1 onion, chopped
1 green bell pepper, chopped
2 stalks celery, chopped

2 (8 ounce) cans tomato sauce
3 tablespoons brown sugar
2 tablespoons white wine vinegar
1/4 cup lemon juice
2 tablespoons Worcestershire sauce

Season ribs with salt and pepper to taste. In a large skillet, over medium-high heat, brown ribs on all sides. Place half of the onion, green pepper, and celery in the bottom of a slow cooker. Place half of the ribs on top the vegetables, then repeat layering with the remaining vegetables and ribs. In a medium bowl, stir together the tomato sauce, brown sugar, vinegar, lemon juice, and Worcestershire sauce. Pour mixture over the top of the ribs. Cover, and cook on High for 1 hour. Reduce to Low, and cook for another 8 to 9 hours.

147- Dee's Special Chicken

4 skinless, boneless chicken breast halves
salt and pepper to taste
1 teaspoon dried rosemary
1 teaspoon dried sage

1 teaspoon dried thyme
6 cloves garlic
1 (12 fluid ounce) can or bottle beer
2 sprigs fresh parsley, for garnish

Salt and pepper the chicken breasts and broil them until golden brown. Place the chicken in a slow cooker with the rosemary, sage, thyme, garlic and beer. Cook on high for 3 to 4 hours. Remove the chicken breasts, garnish with parsley and serve.

148- Slow Cooker Mock-Roast

1 pound beef sirloin roast
1 pinch seasoned salt, or to taste

1 pinch ground black pepper, or to taste
1 teaspoon vegetable oil

3/4 cup chopped onion
1/4 cup chopped carrot
1/4 cup chopped celery
4 large potatoes, cubed
6 carrots, cut into bite-size pieces
2 teaspoons dried Italian herb seasoning
2 teaspoons dried parsley

1/4 teaspoon celery salt
1 (12 fluid ounce) can or bottle
caffeinated citrus-flavored soda (such as
Mountain Dew®)
4 1/2 teaspoons steak sauce
(such as A1 Steak Sauce®)

Sprinkle the beef with seasoned salt and black pepper to taste. Heat the vegetable oil in a skillet over medium heat, and brown the roast on all sides, about 3 minutes per side. Place the browned roast into a slow cooker, and sprinkle the onion, chopped carrot, and celery over the meat. Scatter the potatoes and carrot pieces over the other ingredients, sprinkle on the Italian seasoning, parsley, and celery salt, and pour the can of soda over everything. Sprinkle the steak sauce on top. Cover, and cook on Low setting for 8 hours.

149- Wildfire Pulled Pork Sandwiches

3 1/2 pounds pork roast
1/4 cup water
1 cup Bob Evans® Wildfire BBQ Sauce

1 small red pepper, thinly sliced
1 teaspoon chili powder
12 sandwich buns

Place pork roast into slow cooker. Add 1/4 cup water. Combine Wildfire sauce, red pepper and chili powder. Pour over pork. Cover and heat on low for 6 to 8 hours. Remove pork from slow cooker and shred with 2 forks. Combine with sauce in slow cooker. Serve on buns.

150- Slow Cooker Butter Chicken

2 tablespoons butter
2 tablespoons vegetable oil
4 large skinless, boneless chicken thighs,
cut into bite-sized pieces
1 onion, diced
3 cloves garlic, minced
2 teaspoons curry powder

1 tablespoon curry paste
2 teaspoons tandoori masala
1 teaspoon garam masala
1 (6 ounce) can tomato paste
15 green cardamom pods
1 (14 ounce) can coconut milk
1 cup plain yogurt salt to taste

Melt the butter and vegetable oil in a large skillet over medium heat. Stir in the chicken, onion, and garlic. Cook and stir until the onion has softened and turned translucent, about 10 minutes. Stir in the curry powder, curry paste, tandoori masala, garam masala, and tomato paste until no lumps of tomato paste remain. Pour into a slow cooker, and stir in the cardamom pods, coconut milk, and yogurt. Season to taste with salt. Cook on High 4 to 6 hours, or on Low 6 to 8 hours until the chicken is tender and the sauce has reduced to your desired consistency. Remove and discard the cardamom pods before serving.

151- Old Virginia Wassail Cider

2 quarts apple cider
2 cups orange juice

1 (46 fluid ounce) can pineapple juice
2 (3 inch) cinnamon sticks

1 tablespoon whole cloves

1/2 cup honey

In a large stock pot over medium heat, combine the apple cider, orange juice, pineapple juice, cinnamon sticks, cloves and honey. Bring to a boil, then simmer over low heat, or transfer to a slow cooker to keep warm while serving. Strain out cinnamon sticks and cloves before serving if desired.

152- Slow Cooker Salisbury Steak

2 pounds lean ground beef

1 (1 ounce) envelope dry onion soup mix

1/2 cup Italian seasoned bread crumbs

1/4 cup milk

1/4 cup all-purpose flour

2 tablespoons vegetable oil

2 (10.75 ounce) cans condensed cream of chicken soup

1 (1 ounce) packet dry au jus mix

3/4 cup water

In a large bowl, mix together the ground beef, onion soup mix, bread crumbs, and milk using your hands. Shape into 8 patties. Heat the oil in a large skillet over medium-high heat. Dredge the patties in flour just to coat, and quickly brown on both sides in the hot skillet. Place browned patties into the slow cooker stacking alternately like a pyramid. In a medium bowl, mix together the cream of chicken soup, au jus mix, and water. Pour over the meat. Cook on the Low setting for 4 or 5 hours, until ground beef is well done.

153- Slow Cooker Chicken Dinner

6 medium red potatoes, cut into chunks

4 medium carrots, cut into 1/2 inch pieces

4 boneless, skinless chicken breast halves

1 (10.75 ounce) can condensed cream of chicken soup, undiluted

1 (10.75 ounce) can condensed cream of mushroom soup, undiluted

1/8 teaspoon garlic salt

2 tablespoons mashed potato flakes (optional)

Place potatoes and carrots in a slow cooker. Top with chicken. Combine the soups and garlic salt; pour over chicken. Cover an cook on low for 8 hours. To thicken if desired, stir potato flakes into the gravy and cook 30 minutes longer.

154- BBQ Meatballs

1 (16 ounce) package frozen meatballs

1 (18 ounce) bottle barbecue sauce

1/4 cup ketchup

Place prepared meatballs, barbeque sauce, and ketchup in a slow cooker. Let cook on a low heat for 4 hours, stirring occasionally.

155- All-Day Meatballs

1 cup milk

3/4 cup quick-cooking oats

3 tablespoons finely chopped onion

1 1/2 teaspoons salt

1 1/2 pounds ground beef
1 cup ketchup
1/2 cup water

3 tablespoons vinegar
2 tablespoons sugar

In a bowl, combine the first four ingredients. Crumble beef over the mixture and mix well. Shape into 1-in. balls. Place in a slow cooker. In a bowl, combine the ketchup, water, vinegar and sugar; mix well. Pour over meatballs. Cover and cook on low for 6-8 hours or until the meat is no longer pink.

156- Italian Style Beef Sandwiches

2 1/2 cups water
1 packet dry onion soup mix
2 tablespoons Worcestershire sauce
1 teaspoon garlic powder
1 teaspoon dried marjoram

1 teaspoon dried thyme
1 teaspoon dried oregano
4 pounds chuck roast
1 (10 ounce) package frozen bell pepper stir-fry mix

In a slow cooker combine the water, soup mix, Worcestershire sauce, garlic powder, marjoram, thyme and oregano. Add the meat and the stir-fry mix. Cook for half a day on high setting or all day on low setting, or until the meat falls apart. Pull the meat apart and stir all together.

157- Vegetarian Southwest One-Pot Dinner

1 1/2 cups dried black-eyed peas, soaked overnight
1 green bell pepper, diced
1 onion, chopped
garlic cloves, chopped
1 (10 ounce) can sweet corn, drained

1 (28 ounce) can diced tomatoes
1/4 cup chili powder
2 teaspoons ground cumin
2 cups cooked rice
1/2 cup shredded Cheddar cheese

Drain and rinse black-eyed peas thoroughly. Place peas, green pepper, onion, garlic, corn, and tomatoes, in slow cooker. Season with chili powder, and cumin; stir until well blended. Cover and cook on high for 2 hours. Stir in rice, and cheese. Continue to cook for a further 30 minutes.

158- Slow Cooker Taco Soup

1 pound ground beef
1 onion, chopped
1 (16 ounce) can chili beans, with liquid
1 (15 ounce) can kidney beans with liquid
1 (15 ounce) can whole kernel corn, with liquid

1 (8 ounce) can tomato sauce
2 cups water
2 (14.5 ounce) cans peeled and diced tomatoes
1 (4 ounce) can diced green chile peppers
1 (1.25 ounce) package taco seasoning mix

In a medium skillet, cook the ground beef until browned over medium heat. Drain, and set aside. Place the ground beef, onion, chili beans, kidney beans, corn, tomato sauce, water, diced tomatoes, green chile peppers and taco seasoning mix in a slow cooker. Mix to blend, and cook on Low setting for 8 hours.

159- Slow Cooker Apple-Scented Venison Roast

1 tablespoon olive oil
3 pounds boneless venison roast
1 large apple, cored and quartered
2 small onions, sliced

4 cloves crushed garlic
1 cup boiling water
1 cube beef bouillon

Spread the olive oil on the inside of a slow cooker. Place the venison roast inside, and cover with apple, onions, and garlic. Turn to Low, and cook until the roast is tender, about 6 to 8 hours. When the roast has cooked, remove it from the slow cooker, and place onto a serving platter. Discard the apple. Stir the water and bouillon into the slow cooker until the bouillon has dissolved. Serve this as a sauce with the roast.

160- Gone-All-Day Casserole

1 cup uncooked wild rice, rinsed and drained
1 cup chopped celery
1 cup chopped carrots
2 (4 ounce) cans mushroom stems and pieces, drained
1 large onion, chopped

1 garlic clove, minced
1/2 cup slivered almonds
3 beef bouillon cubes
2 1/2 teaspoons seasoned salt
2 pounds boneless round steak, cut into 1-inch cubes
3 cups water

Place ingredients in order listed in a slow cooker (do not stir). Cover and cook on low for 6-8 hours or until rice is tender. Stir before serving.

161- Cousin David's Slow Cooker Brisket

1 (3 pound) beef brisket
2 (12 ounce) bottles chili sauce

1 (1 ounce) envelope dry onion soup mix
2 teaspoons garlic powder

Place the beef brisket into a slow cooker. In a medium bowl, mix together the chili sauce, onion soup mix, and garlic powder. Pour over the brisket. Cover, and cook on the Low setting for 8 to 10 hours. Slice the brisket against the grain, and pour the gravy over the slices.

162- Savory Slow Cooker Squash and Apple Dish

1 (3 pound) butternut squash - peeled, seeded, and cubed
4 apples - peeled, cored and chopped
3/4 cup dried cranberries

1/2 white onion, diced (optional)
1 tablespoon ground cinnamon
1 1/2 teaspoons ground nutmeg

Combine the squash, apples, cranberries, onion, cinnamon, and nutmeg in a slow cooker. Cook on HIGH for 4 hours or until the squash is tender and cooked through. Stir occasionally while cooking.

163- Slow Cooker Pork Chops

4 pork chops   16 ounces sauerkraut with juice

Place the chops in the bottom the slow cooker and pour the sauerkraut over the top. Cook on low for 8 to 9 hours or on high for 4 to 5 hours.

164- Chicken in Mushroom Sauce

4 boneless, skinless chicken breast halves   1 cup sour cream
1 (10.75 ounce) can condensed cream of   4 bacon strips, cooked and crumbled
mushroom soup, undiluted

Place chicken in a slow cooker. Combine soup and sour cream; pour over chicken. Cover and cook on low for 4-5 hours or until chicken is tender. Sprinkle with bacon.

165- Beef 'N' Bean Starter

2 1/2 pounds beef stew meat, cut into 1   1 (15.5 ounce) can great northern beans,
inch cubes   rinsed and drained
2 (14.5 ounce) cans diced tomatoes with   1 teaspoon salt
oil, garlic and onions, undrained   1/2 teaspoon pepper
1 (16 ounce) can kidney beans, rinsed
and drained

In a slow cooker, combine all ingredients; mix well. Cover and cook on low for 8-9 hours or until beef is tender. Cool. Transfer to two freezer bags or containers, 4 cups in each. May be frozen for up to 3 months.

166- Slow Cooker Bean Casserole AKA Sweet Chili

1/2 cup ketchup   1/2 teaspoon ground black pepper
1/4 cup molasses   4 slices bacon
1 teaspoon dry mustard   1 large green bell pepper, chopped
1 (16 ounce) can baked beans with pork   1 1/2 pounds ground beef
1 teaspoon salt

In a slow cooker, mix together ketchup, molasses, mustard, pork and beans, salt, and pepper. Cook bacon and bell pepper in a large skillet over medium heat for about 5 to 7 minutes, then add to the slow cooker. In same skillet, brown beef, and stir into the slow cooker. Cover, and cook on High setting for 1 hour.

167- Amazing Hawaiian Chicken Chili

2 pounds skinless, boneless chicken breast halves
1 cup barbeque sauce
2 tablespoons butter, divided
1 large onion, diced
2 cloves garlic, minced
1 large roasted red pepper, chopped
1 (6 ounce) can tomato paste
3 tablespoons chili powder
1 tablespoon ancho chile powder
1 tablespoon ground cumin

1 teaspoon ground ginger
1 tablespoon vanilla extract
1/2 teaspoon white sugar
1 (20 ounce) can pineapple chunks
1 (15 ounce) can kidney beans, drained
1 (15 ounce) can black beans, drained
1 (28 ounce) can chopped tomatoes, drained
1 (24 ounce) jar chipotle salsa
salt and pepper to taste

Place the chicken breasts and barbecue sauce in a gallon-sized zip top bag and allow to marinate for 30 minutes in the refrigerator. Melt 1 tablespoon of butter in a large skillet placed over high heat, and add the chicken. Cook the chicken until it is browned and almost cooked through, about 5 minutes per side. Remove chicken from skillet, chop into 1 inch pieces, and place in the crock of a slow cooker. Heat the remaining 1 tablespoon of butter in the skillet over medium-high heat, add the diced onion, garlic, and roasted red pepper, and cook and stir until the onion is softened, about 5 minutes. Stir in the tomato paste, chili powder, ancho chile powder, ground cumin, ground ginger, vanilla, and sugar. Cook, stirring, until blended, about 2 minutes. Transfer the mixture to the slow cooker. Drain the canned pineapple and reserve the fruit. Stir the pineapple juice, kidney beans, black beans, tomatoes, and chipotle salsa into the ingredients in the slow cooker and set the heat to High. Allow the chili to cook on High until it begins to bubble, about 20 minutes. Turn the slow cooker to Low and cook for 1 additional hour. Stir the reserved pineapple into the chili and continue to cook until the pineapple is warm, about 15 minutes. Salt and pepper the chili to taste and serve piping hot.

168- Hot Cranberry Citrus Punch

2 quarts cranberry juice cocktail
3 cups orange juice
1/4 cup white sugar
1/4 cup brown sugar

2 tablespoons fresh lemon juice
1 pinch salt
2 (3 inch) cinnamon sticks

In a 4 quart or larger slow cooker, combine the cranberry juice, orange juice, white sugar, brown sugar, lemon juice, salt and cinnamon sticks. Stir to dissolve sugar. Cook on High for 4 to 6 hours. Turn heat to Low and keep warm for serving.

169- Cocktail Meatballs

1 pound lean ground beef
1 egg
2 tablespoons water
1/2 cup bread crumbs
3 tablespoons minced onion

1 (8 ounce) can jellied cranberry sauce
3/4 cup chili sauce
1 tablespoon brown sugar
1 1/2 teaspoons lemon juice

Preheat oven to 350 degrees F (175 degrees C). In a large bowl, mix together the ground beef, egg, water, bread crumbs, and minced onion. Roll into small meatballs. Bake in preheated oven for 20 to 25 minutes, turning once. In a slow cooker or large saucepan over low heat, blend the cranberry sauce, chili sauce, brown sugar, and lemon juice. Add meatballs, and simmer for 1 hour before serving.

170- Hearty Split Pea Soup

16 ounces dried split peas
2 cups diced fully cooked lean ham
1 cup diced carrots
1 medium onion, chopped
2 garlic cloves, minced

2 bay leaves
1/2 teaspoon salt
1/2 teaspoon pepper
5 cups boiling water
1 cup hot milk

In a slow cooker, layer the first nine ingredients in order listed (do not stir). Cover and cook on high for 4-5 hours or until vegetables are tender. Stir in milk. Discard bay leaves before serving.

171- Slow Cooker Italian Moose Roast Sandwiches

1 (4 pound) moose roast
10 cloves garlic
10 cubes beef bouillon
1 (16 ounce) jar sliced pepperoncini peppers, with liquid

2 tablespoons Worcestershire sauce
1 (.7 ounce) package dry Italian salad dressing mix
12 (6 inch) hard-crusted French rolls

Cut 20 small, deep slits all over the roast; stuff the slits with garlic and bouillon cubes, and place into a slow cooker. Drain half of the liquid from the peppers, then pour the remaining peppers and liquid over the roast. Season with Worcestershire sauce, and sprinkle the Italian dressing mix overtop. Cook on Low for 10 to 12 hours until the meat can easily be pulled apart. Shred the meat finely, and serve mounded on French rolls; dip into juices if desired.

172- Chicken Tagine

2 tablespoons olive oil
8 skinless, boneless chicken thighs, cut into 1-inch pieces
1 eggplant, cut into 1 inch cubes
2 large onions, thinly sliced
4 large carrots, thinly sliced
1/2 cup dried cranberries
1/2 cup chopped dried apricots
2 cups chicken broth
2 tablespoons tomato paste

2 tablespoons lemon juice
2 tablespoons all-purpose flour
2 teaspoons garlic salt
1 1/2 teaspoons ground cumin
1 1/2 teaspoons ground ginger
1 teaspoon cinnamon
3/4 teaspoon ground black pepper
1 cup water
1 cup couscous

Heat olive oil in a skillet over medium-high heat. Place the chicken pieces and eggplant in the heated oil; stir and cook until the chicken is browned on all sides but not cooked through.

Remove the skillet from the heat. Place the browned chicken and eggplant on the bottom of a slow cooker. Layer the onion, carrots, dried cranberries, and apricots over the chicken. Whisk together the chicken broth, tomato paste, lemon juice, flour, garlic salt, cumin, ginger, cinnamon, and ground black pepper in a bowl. Pour the broth mixture into the slow cooker with the chicken and vegetables. Cook on High setting for 5 hours, or on Low setting for 8 hours. Bring water to boil in a saucepan. Stir in couscous, and remove from heat. Cover, and let stand about 5 minutes, until liquid has been absorbed. Fluff with a fork.

173- Slow Cooker Ham

2 cups packed brown sugar   1 (8 pound) cured, bone-in picnic ham

Spread about 1 1/2 cups of brown sugar on the bottom of the slow cooker crock. Place the ham flat side down into the slow cooker - you might have to trim it a little to make it fit. Use your hands to rub the remaining brown sugar onto the ham. Cover, and cook on Low for 8 hours.

174- Ministerls Delight

1 (21 ounce) can cherry or apple pie   1/2 cup butter, melted
filling   1/3 cup chopped walnuts
1 (18.25 ounce) package yellow cake mix

Place pie filling in a 1-1/2 qt. slow cooker. Combine dry cake mix and butter (mixture will be crumbly); sprinkle over filling. Sprinkle with walnuts if desired. Cover and cook on low for 2-3 hours. Serve in bowls.

175- Southern Pulled Pork

1 tablespoon butter   4 cloves garlic, crushed
2 pounds boneless pork roast   4 cups water
1 tablespoon Cajun seasoning   1 tablespoon liquid smoke flavoring
1 medium onion, chopped

Cut the pork roast into large chunks. Sea son generously with the Cajun seasoning. Melt butter in a large skillet over medium-high heat. Add pork, and brown on all sides. Remove from the skillet, and transfer to a slow cooker. Add the onion and garlic to the skillet, and cook for a few minutes until tender. Stir in the water scraping the bottom to include all of the browned pork bits from the bottom of the pan, then pour the whole mixture into the slow cooker with the pork. Stir in liquid smoke flavoring. Cover, and cook on High for 6 hours, or until meat is falling apart when pierced with a fork. Remove pieces of pork from the slow cooker, and shred. Return to the slow cooker to keep warm while serving.

176- Christmas Morning Oatmeal

1/3 cup brown sugar   2 Granny Smith apples - peeled, cored,
2 teaspoons ground cinnamon   and sliced 1/4 inch thick
1 teaspoon ground nutmeg   3/4 cup dried cranberries

1/4 cup butter, cut into pieces
2 cups regular rolled oats
2 cups water
1 cup apple juice

1 cup cranberry juice
1/4 teaspoon salt
3/4 cup candied walnuts (optional)

Mix the brown sugar, cinnamon, and nutmeg together in a bowl. Add the apples and cranberries, tossing to coat evenly with the sugar mixture. Pour into a slow cooker. Top with butter pieces. Mix the oatmeal together with the water, apple juice, cranberry juice, and salt in a bowl, and pour over the apple mixture in the slow cooker. Do not stir. Cover, and cook on Low for 8 hours. Stir before serving. Spoon into bowls and top with candied walnuts, if desired.

177- Meat Loaf Burgers

1 large onion, sliced
1 celery rib, chopped
2 pounds lean ground beef
1 1/2 teaspoons salt, divided
1/4 teaspoon pepper
2 cups tomato juice

4 garlic cloves, minced
1 tablespoon ketchup
1 bay leaf
1 teaspoon Italian seasoning
6 hamburger buns, split

Place onion and celery in a slow cooker. Combine beef, 1 teaspoon salt and pepper; shape into six patties. Place over onion mixture. Combine tomato juice, garlic, ketchup, bay leaf, Italian seasoning and remaining salt. Pour over the patties. Cover and cook on low for 7-9 hours or until meat is tender. Discard bay leaf. Separate patties with a spatula if necessary; serve on buns.

178- Slow-Cooked Pulled Pork Shoulder

1 (3 pound) pork shoulder
4 cups water, or as needed
8 cups white vinegar, or as needed
1/4 cup kosher salt
1 large onion, cut into 8 wedges

1 tablespoon ground cumin
1 tablespoon ground mustard
1 tablespoon chili powder
1/2 cup brown sugar

Place the pork shoulder into the ceramic bowl of a slow cooker. Pour enough water and white vinegar into the slow cooker to assure the pork is completely covered, maintaining a 2-to-1 ratio of vinegar to water. Add the salt. Put the ceramic bowl in the refrigerator and allow the pork to marinate at least 12 hours and up to 24 hours. Drain enough of the liquid from the ceramic bowl until about 1/2- inch of pork is left exposed. Add the onion to the remaining liquid. Season the exposed surface of the pork with the cumin, mustard, chili powder, and brown sugar. Place the bowl into the base of the slow cooker and cook on High until the pork is tender and falls apart easily, 8 to 10 hours. Carefully remove the pork to a cutting board; shred the meat into strands using a pair of forks. Remove and discard any excess fat.

179- Hot Chicken Sandwiches I

12 eggs
1 (1 pound) loaf white bread, cubed

3 (2 to 3 pound) boiler chickens salt to taste
ground black pepper to taste

Boil the chickens until done, and let cool. When the chicken meat is completely cool to the touch, pick the chicken meat from the bones; set aside. Reserve a little of the broth for later. Cube the loaf of bread, and put it in a large bowl. Mix in the 12 eggs with the cubed bread. Add the chicken meat you picked from the bone and enough broth from the chicken to moisten. Add salt and pepper to your own taste. Mix well. Spread mixture into a lightly greased casserole dish, and bake in a preheated 350 degrees F (175 degrees C) oven for 30 minutes. Or spray a slow cooker with cooking spray to prevent sticking, and pour in the chicken mixture. Let cook on low for about 6 hours. Serve by scooping onto buns.

180- Meatballs and Sauce

5 pounds Italian meatballs
1 (10.75 ounce) can condensed cream of mushroom soup

3/4 cup water
2 cups sour cream

Combine meatballs, mushroom soup, water, and sour cream. Cover and refrigerate overnight so that the meatballs can absorb the flavors. Pour the mixture into a slow cooker and heat until the meatballs are heated through. Serve hot.

181- Asian Style Country Ribs

1/4 cup lightly packed brown sugar
1 cup soy sauce
1/4 cup sesame oil
2 tablespoons olive oil
2 tablespoons rice vinegar

2 tablespoons lime juice
2 tablespoons minced garlic
2 tablespoons minced fresh ginger
1 teaspoon Sriracha hot pepper sauce
12 boneless country-style pork ribs

Stir together the brown sugar, soy sauce, sesame oil, olive oil, rice vinegar, lime juice, garlic, ginger, and Sriracha in the crock of a slow cooker. Add the ribs; cover and refrigerate. Allow ribs to marinate in the refrigerator for 8 hours or overnight. Before cooking, drain marinade and discard. Cook on Low for 9 hours. Drain cooked meat and shred, using 2 forks.

182- Spicy Chicken Thai Noodle Soup

5 cups chicken broth
1 cup white wine
1 cup water
1 onion, chopped
3 green onions, chopped
3 cloves garlic, chopped
4 large carrots, cut into 1 inch pieces

4 large stalks celery, cut into 1 inch pieces
1/2 teaspoon salt
1 teaspoon ground black pepper
1 tablespoon curry powder
1/2 tablespoon dried sage
1/2 tablespoon poultry seasoning

1/2 tablespoon dried oregano
1 teaspoon ground cayenne pepper
2 tablespoons vegetable oil
3 skinless, boneless chicken breast halves
- cut into 1 inch cubes

1 fresh red chile pepper, seeded and
chopped
1/2 (12 ounce) package dried rice
noodles

In a slow cooker on low heat, combine chicken broth, wine, water, onion, green onion, garlic, carrots, celery, salt, black pepper, curry, sage, poultry seasoning, oregano and cayenne. In a skillet over medium heat, cook chicken in oil until brown. Stir into slow cooker. Cook soup 8 hours on low or 5 hours on high. About halfway through the cooking time, stir in the red pepper. 15 minutes prior to serving, stir in the noodles.

183- Italian Sausage Dip

1 pound ground Italian sausage
2 tomatoes, chopped
2 chopped green bell peppers
2 onions, chopped

2 (4 ounce) cans chopped green chile
peppers
1 (16 ounce) container sour cream
1 (8 ounce) package cream cheese

Place Italian sausage in a large, deep skillet. Cook over medium high heat until evenly brown. Drain and set aside. In a large bowl, mix together sausage, tomatoes, green bell peppers, onions, green chile peppers, sour cream and cream cheese. Transfer mixture to a slow cooker. Cook on high heat approximately 1 hour, or until vegetables are soft. Reduce heat and simmer until serving.

184- Slow Cooked Apple Peach Sauce

10 Macintosh apples, cored and chopped
4 fresh peaches, pitted and chopped

1 tablespoon ground cinnamon

Put fruit into a slow-cooker; sprinkle with cinnamon. Turn slow- cooker to high. Cover, and cook for 3 hours on high, then switch to low for 2 hours. Stir before serving.

185- Slow Cooker Northern White Bean Bacon

1 1/2 cups dried great Northern beans,
rinsed
2 cups water
6 slices bacon
1 carrot, chopped
1 stalk celery, chopped
1 onion, chopped

1 potato - peeled and cubed
1 teaspoon Italian-style seasoning
1/8 teaspoon ground black pepper
3 (14.5 ounce) cans low-sodium chicken
broth
1 cup milk

Place beans in a large bowl with the water, cover, and soak overnight. In a large skillet over medium to medium high heat, fry the bacon until crispy. Drain the bacon fat and crumble the bacon; set aside. In a slow cooker, combine the carrot, celery, onion, potato, Italian- style seasoning, ground black pepper, reserved beans and crumbled bacon. Pour the broth over all.

Cover and cook on low setting for 7 1/2 to 9 hours, or until beans are crisp to tender. Transfer 2 cups at a time to a blender or food processor and puree until smooth. Return all to slow cooker, add the milk, cover and heat on high for about 10 to 15 minutes, or until heated through.

186- Easy Slow Cooker Carne Guisada

3 pounds chuck roast, cut into 1
1/2-inch cubes
3 medium potatoes, unpeeled and diced
1 medium onion, chopped
2 red bell peppers, cut into strips
3 cloves garlic, crushed

1/4 cup all-purpose flour
1/4 cup chili powder
1 teaspoon cumin
1 teaspoon salt
3 cups beef broth

Combine beef, potatoes, onion, peppers, and garlic in a large bowl. In a small bowl, mix together the flour, chili powder, cumin, and salt. Toss the beef mixture with the flour mixture until evenly coated. Place the mixture into a slow cooker, and pour in enough beef broth to barely cover the meat. If you don't have quite enough, you can fill the rest of the way with water. Cook on Low until the beef is tender, 6 to 8 hours.

187- Easiest BBQ Pork Chops

1 (10.75 ounce) can condensed cream of
mushroom soup
1 cup ketchup

1 tablespoon Worcestershire sauce
1/2 cup chopped onion
6 pork chops

Combine soup, ketchup, Worcestershire sauce, and onions in slow cooker. Add pork chops. Cover, and cook on Low for 6 hours.

188- Smoked Beef Brisket

2 1/2 pounds beef brisket
1 tablespoon liquid smoke flavoring
1 teaspoon salt
1/2 teaspoon pepper

1/2 cup chopped onion
1/2 cup ketchup
2 teaspoons Dijon mustard
1/2 teaspoon celery seed

Cut the brisket in half; rub with Liquid Smoke, salt and pepper. Place in a 3-qt. slow cooker. Top with onion. Combine the ketchup, mustard and celery seed; spread over meat. Cover and cook on low for 8-9 hours. Remove brisket and keep warm. Transfer cooking juices to a blender; cover and process until smooth. Serve with brisket.

189- BBQ Cola Meatballs

1 1/2 pounds lean ground beef
1 1/4 cups dry bread crumbs
1 egg
3 tablespoons grated onion

1 (1 ounce) package dry Ranch- style
dressing mix
1 cup ketchup
2 tablespoons apple cider vinegar

3/4 cup cola-flavored carbonated beverage
1/2 cup chopped onion
1/2 cup chopped green bell pepper

1 teaspoon seasoning salt
1/2 teaspoon ground black pepper
1 tablespoon Worcestershire sauce

Preheat the oven to 375 degrees F (190 degrees C). In a large bowl, mix together the ground beef, bread crumbs, egg, grated onion and Ranch dressing mix until well blended. Shape into 1 inch meatballs, and place on a 10x15 inch jellyroll pan, or any baking sheet with sides to catch the grease. Bake for 30 minutes in the preheated oven, turning them over half way through. While the meatballs are roasting, mix together the ketchup, cider vinegar, cola, chopped onion and green pepper in a slow cooker. Season with seasoning salt, pepper, and Worcestershire sauce. Remove meatballs from the baking sheet, and place into the sauce in the slow cooker. Cover and cook on Low for 3 hours, then remove the lid and cook for an additional 15 minutes before serving.

190- Meat-Lover's Slow Cooker Spaghetti Sauce

2 tablespoons olive oil
2 small onions, chopped
1/4 pound bulk Italian sausage
1 pound ground beef
1 teaspoon dried Italian herb seasoning
1 teaspoon garlic powder
1/2 teaspoon dried marjoram
1 (29 ounce) can tomato sauce
1 (6 ounce) can tomato paste

1 (14.5 ounce) can Italian-style diced tomatoes
1 (14.5 ounce) can Italian-style stewed tomatoes
1/4 teaspoon dried thyme leaves
1/4 teaspoon dried basil
1/2 teaspoon dried oregano
2 teaspoons garlic powder
1 tablespoon white sugar

Heat olive oil in a skillet over medium heat; cook and stir onions and Italian sausage until the sausage is browned, about 10 minutes. Transfer the sausage and onions to a slow cooker. In the same skillet, cook and stir the ground beef, Italian seasoning, 1 teaspoon of garlic powder, and marjoram, breaking the meat up as it cooks, until the meat is browned, about 10 minutes. Transfer the ground beef into the slow cooker. Stir in the tomato sauce, tomato paste, diced tomatoes, stewed tomatoes, thyme, basil, oregano, and 2 teaspoons of garlic powder. Set the cooker on Low, and cook the sauce for 8 hours. About 15 minutes before serving, stir in the sugar. Serve hot.

191- Rachael's Superheated Cajun Boiled Peanuts

1 pound raw peanuts, in shells
1 (3 ounce) package dry crab boil (such as Zatarain'sB® Crab and Shrimp Boil)
1/2 cup chopped jalapeno peppers

1 tablespoon garlic powder
1/2 cup salt
2 tablespoons Cajun seasoning
1/2 cup red pepper flakes

Place peanuts, crab boil, jalapenos, garlic powder, salt, Cajun seasoning, and red pepper flakes into a slow cooker. Pour in water to cover the peanuts and stir to combine. Cover and cook on Low until peanuts are soft, at least 24 hours. Stir occasionally, and add water as needed to keep peanuts covered. Drain; serve hot or cold.

192- Sloppied Flank Steak Sandwiches

1 1/2 pounds beef flank steak
1 tablespoon steak seasoning (such as
Montreal Steak Seasoning®)
1 tablespoon olive oil
1/4 cup brown sugar
1 small onion, chopped

1 small red bell pepper, chopped
1 tablespoon apple cider vinegar
1 tablespoon Worcestershire sauce
2 cups tomato sauce
2 tablespoons tomato paste
6 hamburger buns, split and toasted

Sprinkle the beef flank steak with steak seasoning on both sides. Heat olive oil in a skillet over medium heat until the oil shimmers, and place the flank steak into the hot oil. Quickly brown the steak on both sides, about 5 minutes per side. Set the beef aside. Stir brown sugar, onion, red bell pepper, apple cider vinegar, Worcestershire sauce, tomato sauce, and tomato paste together in a slow cooker until the brown sugar dissolves. Place the flank steak into the slow cooker, immersing it in the sauce. Set the cooker on on High and cook 4 hours, or set on Low and cook 8 hours. To serve, shred the meat with 2 forks, or remove the meat, chop, and return to the sauce. Toast buns, and serve the sloppied steak on the toasted buns.

193- Slow Cooker Sweet and Sour Kielbasa

6 tablespoons butter
2 large onions, sliced
1 cup packed brown sugar
1/2 (28 ounce) bottle ketchup
3 tablespoons cider vinegar

1 1/2 teaspoons spicy brown mustard
1 tablespoon Worcestershire sauce
2 teaspoons hot pepper sauce
1 pound kielbasa sausage, cut into 1 inch
pieces

Melt butter in a large skillet over medium heat. Saute onions until tender. Stir in brown sugar, ketchup, vinegar, mustard, Worcestershire sauce and pepper sauce. Simmer, stirring occasionally, for 20 minutes. Place sausage in a slow cooker with the sauce and onions. Cook on low for 4 to 5 hours. The longer it simmers the better!

194- Manhattan Clam Chowder

3 celery ribs, sliced
1 large onion, chopped
1 (14.5 ounce) can sliced potatoes,
drained
1 (14.5 ounce) can sliced carrots, drained
2 (6.5 ounce) cans chopped clams
2 cups tomato juice

1 1/2 cups water
1/2 cup tomato puree
1 tablespoon dried parsley flakes
1 1/2 teaspoons dried thyme
1 teaspoon salt
1 bay leaf
2 whole black peppercorns

In a slow cooker, combine all ingredients; stir. Cover and cook on low for 8-10 hours or until the vegetables are tender. Remove bay leaf and peppercorns before serving.

195- Party Kielbasa

2 pounds kielbasa sausage
2 cups ketchup

2 cups grape jelly
Slice kielbasa into strips or circles.

Pour ketchup and jelly into a slow cooker. Turn the heat to a medium temperature, stir occasionally while the jelly and ketchup melt together. When the mixture forms into a thin glaze, add the kielbasa and cook until the kielbasa is hot.

196- Kona Chicken

2 (2 pound) broiler chickens, quartered
1/2 cup chopped green onion
1/2 cup soy sauce
1/4 cup dry white wine

1/2 cup water
1/2 cup honey
ground black pepper to taste

Place chicken quarters into a slow cooker. Stir together the green onion, soy sauce, white wine, water, honey and pepper in a cup or small bowl. Pour over the chicken. Cover, and cook on high for 4 hours.

197- Jennie's Heavenly Slow Cooker Chicken

2 tablespoons butter
1 (.7 ounce) package dry Italian- style salad dressing mix
1 (10.75 ounce) can condensed golden mushroom soup

1 (8 ounce) container chive and onion cream cheese
1/2 cup dry white wine
4 skinless, boneless chicken breast halves

Melt the butter in a saucepan over medium heat, and stir in the salad dressing mix, mushroom soup, cream cheese, and wine until the sauce mixture is hot, smooth and well combined. Place the chicken breasts into the bottom of a slow cooker, and pour the sauce mixture over the chicken. Cover and cook on Low setting until chicken is tender, about 4 hours.

198- Mushroom Potatoes

7 medium potatoes, peeled and thinly sliced
1 medium onion, sliced
4 garlic cloves, minced
2 green onions, chopped
1 (8 ounce) can mushroom stems and pieces, drained
1/4 cup all-purpose flour

2 teaspoons salt
1/2 teaspoon pepper
1/4 cup butter or margarine, cubed
1 (10.75 ounce) can condensed cream of mushroom soup, undiluted
1 cup shredded Colby-Monterey Jack cheese

In a slow cooker, layer half of the potatoes, onion, garlic, green onions, mushrooms, flour, salt, pepper and butter. Repeat layers. Pour soup over the top. Cover and cook on low for 6-8 hours or until potatoes are tender; sprinkle with cheese during the last 30 minutes of cooking time.

199- Slow Cooker Beef Barley Soup

1 1/2 pounds boneless lean beef, cubed
3 tablespoons vegetable oil
1 teaspoon salt
1 teaspoon ground black pepper
2 teaspoons garlic powder
3 (10.5 ounce) cans beef broth
6 cups water

4 stalks celery, chopped
6 carrots, chopped
6 green onions, chopped
1/2 cup chopped fresh parsley
1 cup barley
1 teaspoon dried thyme

In a skillet over medium heat, saute the beef in the oil for 5 minutes, or until browned. Stir in the salt, pepper and garlic powder and place seasoned meat in a slow cooker. Add a little water to the skillet and stir to pick up the browned bits. Add to the slow cooker. Add the broth, water, celery, carrots, green onions, parsley and barley. Cover and cook on low setting for 6 to 8 hours, or until the vegetables and barley are tender. Add the thyme just before serving.

200- Cajun Roast Beef

2 teaspoons garlic, minced
1/2 teaspoon prepared horseradish
1 teaspoon hot pepper sauce
1 teaspoon dried thyme
1/2 teaspoon salt

1/2 teaspoon ground black pepper
2 teaspoons Cajun seasoning
2 tablespoons olive oil
2 tablespoons malt vinegar
2 pounds beef eye of round roast

Stir the garlic, horseradish, hot pepper sauce, thyme, salt, pepper, Cajun seasoning, olive oil, and malt vinegar together in a bowl until thoroughly blended. Pierce the beef roast all over with a meat fork. Place the roast in a large, resealable plastic bag. Spoon in the marinade and turn the roast so it's well coated. Refrigerate overnight, turning occasionally if desired. When ready to cook, place the roast in a slow cooker along with any remaining marinade. Do not add water. Roast on Low for 8 to 10 hours, or until desired doneness. For medium-rare, a meat thermometer should read 135 degrees F (57 degrees C). Remove from the slow cooker to a serving plate, and allow to rest 15 minutes before slicing across the grain.

201- Honey Mustard Beer Brats

10 fresh bratwurst sausages
1 green bell pepper, sliced into long strips
1 red bell pepper, sliced into long strips
1 large sweet onion, sliced into rings and separated

2 cloves garlic, sliced
2 bay leaves
1 teaspoon liquid smoke flavoring
2 cups honey mustard barbecue sauce
1 (12 fluid ounce) can beer, or as needed
10 hoagie rolls, split lengthwise

Place half of the bratwurst in the bottom of a 5 quart slow cooker. Arrange half of the green pepper, red pepper, and onion over them. Layer the remaining bratwurst over the top, and top with the remaining red and green bell peppers and onion. Throw in the garlic and bay leaves. In a separate bowl, mix together HALF of the honey mustard sauce, liquid smoke and beer. Pour into the slow cooker. Add more beer if necessary to cover everything in the pot. Cover, and cook on Low for 4 to 5 hours. Preheat an outdoor grill for high heat, and lightly oil grate. Remove bratwurst from the slow cooker, but leave onions and peppers inside. Place bratwurst on the grill and baste with some of the remaining honey mustard sauce. Turn occasionally until slightly charred. Place bratwurst on rolls, and use tongs to pull out a few of the onions and peppers from the slow cooker and drape them over the sausage. The onions and peppers are very tasty so don't forget this part!

202- Slow-Cooker Pork and Apple Curry

2 pounds boneless pork loin roast, cut into 1-inch cubes
1 medium tart apple, peeled and chopped
1 small onion, chopped
1/2 cup orange juice
1 tablespoon curry powder
1 teaspoon chicken bouillon granules
1 garlic clove, minced

1/2 teaspoon salt
1/2 teaspoon ground ginger
1/4 teaspoon ground cinnamon
2 tablespoons cornstarch
2 tablespoons cold water
Hot cooked rice
1/4 cup raisins
1/4 cup flaked coconut, toasted

In a 3-qt. slow cooker, combine the first 10 ingredients. Cover and cook on low for 5-6 hours or until meat is tender. Increase heat to high. In a small bowl, combine cornstarch and water until smooth; stir into slow cooker. Cover and cook for 30 minutes or until thickened, stirring once. Serve over rice if desired. Sprinkle with raisins and coconut.

203- Moist N Tender Wings

25 whole chicken wings
1 (12 ounce) bottle chili sauce
1/4 cup lemon juice
1/4 cup molasses
2 tablespoons Worcestershire sauce

6 garlic cloves, minced
1 tablespoon chili powder
1 tablespoon salsa
1 teaspoon garlic salt
3 drops hot pepper sauce

Cut chicken wings into three sections; discard wing tips. Place the wings in a 5-qt. slow cooker. In a bowl, combine the remaining ingredients; pour over chicken. Stir to coat. Cover and cook on low for 8 hours or until chicken is tender.

204- Tangy Barbecue Sandwiches

3 cups chopped celery
1 cup chopped onion
1 cup ketchup
1 cup barbecue sauce

1 cup water
2 tablespoons vinegar
2 tablespoons Worcestershire sauce
2 tablespoons brown sugar

1 teaspoon chili powder
1 teaspoon salt
1/2 teaspoon pepper
1/2 teaspoon garlic powder

1 (3 pound) boneless chuck roast,
trimmed and cut in half
14 hamburger buns, split

In a slow cooker, combine the first 12 ingredients; mix well. Add roast. Cover and cook on high for 1 hour. Reduce heat to low and cook 7-8 hours longer or until meat is tender. Remove roast; cool. Shred meat and return to sauce; heat through. Use a slotted spoon to serve on buns.

205- Tangy Vegan Crockpot Corn Chowder

2 (12 ounce) cans whole kernel corn
3 cups vegetable broth
3 potatoes, diced
1 large onion, diced
1 clove garlic, minced
2 red chile peppers, minced
1 tablespoon chili powder

2 teaspoons salt
1 tablespoon parsley flakes black pepper
to taste
1 3/4 cups soy milk
1/4 cup margarine
1 lime, juiced

Place the corn, vegetable broth, potatoes, onion, garlic, red chile peppers, chili powder, salt, parsley, and black pepper in a slow cooker; cover. Cook on Low for 7 hours. Pour the vegetable mixture into a blender, filling the pitcher no more than halfway full. Hold the lid of the blender with a folded kitchen towel and carefully start the blender using a few quick pulses before leaving it on to puree. Puree in batches until smooth and pour into a clean pot. Alternately, you can use a stick blender and puree the mixture in the cooking pot. Once everything has been pureed, return it to the slow cooker. Stir the soy milk and margarine to the mixture; cook on Low for 1 hour more. Add the lime juice to serve.

206- Super Sunday Salsa Wings

2 pounds chicken wings
1 (16 ounce) jar Newman's Own
All-Natural Bandito Salsa, Medium

1/2 cup apple juice
1/4 cup prepared mustard
1/2 cup firmly packed brown sugar

Cut wings into 3 sections, discarding wing tips. Combine all ingredients in a 2-quart slow cooker. Cook on low for 4 to 6 hours.

207- Slow Cooker Fifteen Bean Soup

1 large, meaty ham hock
4 slices bacon, diced
3 onions, chopped
3 carrots, diced
1 small head cabbage, shredded
3 tablespoons chili powder

1 clove garlic, minced
1 (8 ounce) package 15 bean mixture,
soaked overnight
1 (28 ounce) can crushed tomatoes
1 teaspoon chopped fresh sage
salt and pepper to taste

Place the ham hock in a 5 to 6 quart slow cooker, and fill half way full with water. Set to High. Heat a large skillet over medium heat. Cook the bacon for a few minutes, then add onions, carrots, and cabbage. Cook, stirring frequently for about 5 minutes. Stir in chili powder and garlic; cook for 2 more minutes. Transfer the mixture to the slow cooker, and add beans, tomatoes, and sage. Cover, and cook 2 hours on High. Reduce heat to Low, and cook for 6 to 7 hours, or until beans are tender. Transfer ham hock to a cutting board, remove meat from bone, and return meat to slow cooker. Season with salt and fresh ground pepper to taste.

208- Elaine's Sweet and Tangy Loose Beef BBQ

7 pounds boneless chuck roast
1 cup water
3 tablespoons white vinegar
4 tablespoons brown sugar
2 teaspoons dry mustard
4 tablespoons Worcestershire sauce

3 cups ketchup
2 teaspoons salt
3/4 teaspoon ground black pepper
1/4 teaspoon cayenne pepper
6 cloves garlic, minced

Place the roast into a slow cooker along with the water. Cover, and cook on LOW for 2 to 4 hours, or until beef can be easily shredded with a fork. Shred the beef, removing fat as you go. Remove 1/2 cup of the broth from the slow cooker, and reserve for later. Add the vinegar, brown sugar, dry mustard, Worcestershire sauce and ketchup. Mix in the salt, pepper, cayenne, and garlic. Stir so that the meat is well coated. Cover, and continue to cook beef on LOW for an additional 4 to 6 hours. Add the reserved broth only if necessary to maintain moisture. Serve on toasted buns. The meat can be frozen for future use.

209- Slow-Cooker Posole

1 tablespoon canola oil
1 (2 pound) boneless pork loin roast, cut into 1-inch cubes
2 (14.5 ounce) cans enchilada sauce
2 (15.5 ounce) cans white hominy, drained
1 onion, sliced

1/2 cup green chilies, diced
4 cloves garlic, minced
1/2 teaspoon cayenne pepper, or to taste
2 teaspoons dried oregano
1/4 cup cilantro, chopped
1/2 teaspoon salt

Heat the canola oil in a skillet over high heat. Add the pork; cook and stir just until meat is browned on all sides, about 5 minutes. Place the meat in a 4 quart slow cooker. Pour the enchilada sauce over the meat. Top with the hominy, onion, chilies, garlic, cayenne pepper, and oregano. Pour in enough water to fill the slow cooker. Cover, and cook on High for 6 to 7 hours. Stir in the cilantro and salt. Cook on Low for 30 minutes more.

210- Teddy's Duck Gumbo

2 (3 to 3 1/2 pound) domestic whole ducklings, dressed
3 cups water

2 (8 ounce) cans diced tomatoes with green chilies, undrained
6 cloves garlic, minced
1 1/2 cups chopped onion

1 1/2 cups chopped celery
1 1/2 cups chopped green bell pepper
2 bay leaves
1 (4.5 ounce) package gumbo base, as in Zatarian's

2 pounds frozen sliced okra
1 (16 ounce) package frozen cooked shrimp (peeled and deveined)
1 pound smoked sausage, cut into 1/2 inch slices

Place the ducks in a slow cooker, fill with enough water to cover, and cook on Low until juices run clear, about 8 hours. Remove, reserving 3 cups of duck broth, and debone, discarding bones. Place the water and 3 cups of duck broth into a slow cooker. Add the tomatoes, garlic, onion, celery, bell pepper, bay leaves, and gumbo base mix. Cook on High until the mixture boils. Reduce heat, and stir in the duck meat, okra, shrimp, and sausage. Cook until thickened, about 30 minutes. Serve hot.

211- Sauerkraut Soup II

1 (10.75 ounce) can condensed cream of mushroom soup
1 (10.75 ounce) can condensed cream of chicken soup
2 1/2 cups water
4 cups chicken broth
1/2 pound sauerkraut
1 onion, finely diced

1 (15 ounce) can carrots, drained
1 (15 ounce) can sliced potatoes, drained
1 pound smoked sausage of your choice, sliced
1 teaspoon dried dill weed
1 teaspoon minced garlic (optional)
salt and pepper to taste

In a 4 to 6 quart slow cooker, blend the cream of mushroom soup, cream of chicken soup, water, and chicken broth. Stir in sauerkraut, onion, carrots, potatoes, and sausage. Season with dill and garlic. Cover, and cook on High for 4 hours, or Low for up to 8 hours. Taste, and season with salt and pepper to your liking.

212- Slow Cooker Stuffing

1 cup butter
2 cups chopped onion
2 cups chopped celery
1/4 cup fresh parsley
12 ounces fresh mushrooms, sliced
12 1/2 cups dry bread cubes
1 teaspoon poultry seasoning

1 1/2 teaspoons dried sage
1 teaspoon dried thyme
1/2 teaspoon dried marjoram
1 1/2 teaspoons salt
1/2 teaspoon ground black pepper
4 1/2 cups chicken broth
2 eggs, beaten

Melt butter or margarine in a skillet over medium heat. Cook onion, celery, mushroom, and parsley in butter, stirring frequently. Spoon cooked vegetables over bread cubes in a very large mixing bowl. Season with poultry seasoning, sage, thyme, marjoram, and salt and pepper. Pour in enough broth to moisten, and mix in eggs. Transfer mixture to slow cooker, and cover. Cook on High for 45 minutes, then reduce heat to Low, and cook for 4 to 8 hours.

213- Simple Hot Spiced Apple Cider

1 (64 fluid ounce) bottle apple cider
3 cinnamon sticks
1 teaspoon whole allspice

1 teaspoon whole cloves
3 tablespoons SPLENDA® Brown
Sugar Blend

In a slow cooker, combine apple cider and cinnamon sticks. Wrap allspice and cloves in a small piece of cheesecloth, and add to pot. Stir in SPLENDA® Brown Sugar Blend. Bring to a boil over high heat. Reduce heat, and keep warm.

214- Chicken Wild Rice Soup III

1 cup uncooked wild rice
3 cups diced, cooked chicken breast meat
2 tablespoons chicken bouillon granules
1 onion, chopped

5 cups water
4 potatoes, cubed
1 1/2 cups milk
2 tablespoons all-purpose flour

In a large saucepan over medium-high heat, bring rice, chicken, bouillon, onion and water to a boil. Remove from heat and pour into slow cooker. Stir in potatoes. Combine milk and flour and stir until smooth. Stir into soup mixture. Cook 6 to 8 hours, until rice and potatoes are tender and flavors are well blended.

215- Potato Sausage Supper

4 medium potatoes, peeled and sliced
1 pound fully cooked kielbasa or Polish
sausage, cut into 1/2-inch pieces
2 medium onions, sliced, separated into
rings

1 (10.75 ounce) can condensed cheddar
cheese soup, undiluted
1 (10.75 ounce) can condensed cream of
celery soup, undiluted
1 (10 ounce) package frozen peas,
thawed

In a greased 5-qt. slow cooker; layer a third of the potatoes, sausage, onions and cheese soup. Repeat layers twice. Pour cream of celery soup over the top. Cover and cook on low for 5-1/2 hours or until the potatoes are tender. Add the peas and cook 30 minutes longer.

216- SwansonB® Greek-Style Beef Stew

2 pounds boneless beef bottom round
roast or chuck pot roast, cut into 1-inch
pieces
1 (16 ounce) bag frozen whole small
white onions
1 (16 ounce) package fresh or frozen
whole baby carrots
2 tablespoons all-purpose flour

1 3/4 cups SwansonB® Beef Broth
(Regular, 50% Less Sodium or Certified
Organic)
1 (5.5 ounce) can Campbell'sB® V8B®
100% Vegetable Juice
1 tablespoon packed brown sugar
Bouquet Garni
Hot cooked egg noodles

Place the beef, onions and carrots into a 3 1/2- to 6-quart slow cooker. Sprinkle with the flour and toss to coat. Stir the broth, vegetable juice and brown sugar in a medium bowl. Pour the broth mixture over the beef and vegetables. Submerge the Bouquet Garni into the broth mixture. Cover and cook on LOW for 8 to 9 hours* or until the beef is fork- tender. Remove the Bouquet Garni. Serve the beef mixture over the noodles.

217- Slow Cooker Beef Roast

1 (2 pound) beef round roast
2 large carrots, chopped
1 large onion, thinly sliced
2 stalks celery, chopped

1 teaspoon garlic powder ground black
pepper to taste
1/2 cup Worcestershire sauce
1/2 cup barbeque sauce

Place beef round roast in slow cooker, then add carrots, onion, and celery. Season with garlic powder and black pepper. Pour Worcestershire and barbeque sauce over meat and vegetables. Cook on Low until the meat is tender, 6 to 8 hours.

218- Island Kielbasa in a Slow Cooker

2 pounds kielbasa sausage, sliced into 1/2
inch pieces
2 cups ketchup

2 cups brown sugar
1 (15 ounce) can pineapple chunks,
undrained

Place the sausage, ketchup, sugar and pineapple in the slow cooker and mix together. Cook on low setting for 5 to 6 hours, until sausage is cooked through.

219- Slow Cooker Pork Chops II

1/4 cup olive oil
1 cup chicken broth
2 cloves garlic, minced
1 tablespoon paprika
1 tablespoon garlic powder

1 tablespoon poultry seasoning
1 teaspoon dried oregano
1 teaspoon dried basil
4 thick cut boneless pork chops salt and
pepper to taste

In a large bowl, whisk together the olive oil, chicken broth, garlic, paprika, garlic powder, poultry seasoning and basil. Pour into the slow cooker. Cut small slits in each pork chop with the tip of a knife, and season lightly with salt and pepper. Place pork chops into the slow cooker, cover, and cook on High for 4 hours. Baste periodically with the sauce.

220- Spicy Slow Cooker Black Bean Soup

1 pound dry black beans, soaked
overnight
4 teaspoons diced jalapeno peppers
6 cups chicken broth
1/2 teaspoon garlic powder
1 tablespoon chili powder

1 teaspoon ground cumin
1 teaspoon cayenne pepper
3/4 teaspoon ground black pepper
1/2 teaspoon hot pepper sauce
Drain black beans, and rinse.

Combine beans, jalapenos, and chicken broth in a slow cooker. Season with garlic powder, chili powder, cumin, cayenne, pepper, and hot pepper sauce. Cook on High for 4 hours. Reduce heat to Low, and continue cooking for 2 hours, or until you are ready to eat.

221- Chocolate Pudding Cake IV

1 (18.25 ounce) package chocolate cake mix
1 (3.9 ounce) package instant chocolate pudding mix
2 cups sour cream
4 eggs

1 cup water
3/4 cup vegetable oil
1 cup semisweet chocolate chips
Preheat oven to 350 degrees F (175 degrees C). Grease and flour a 10 inch Bundt pan.

In a large bowl, stir together cake mix and pudding mix. Make a well in the center and pour in sour cream, eggs, water and oil. Beat on low speed until blended. Scrape bowl, and beat 4 minutes on medium speed. Stir in chocolate chips. Pour batter into prepared pan. Bake in the preheated oven for 45 to 50 minutes, or until a toothpick inserted into the center of the cake comes out clean. Let cool in pan for 10 minutes, then turn out onto a serving plate. Serve warm. Alternate cooking directions: Pour batter into a 5 quart slow cooker that has been coated with non stick cooking spray. Cover and cook on low for 6 hours. Spoon into individual dishes.

222- Slow Cooker Pheasant with Mushrooms

3/4 cup all-purpose flour salt
1/4 teaspoon ground black pepper
2 pheasants, rinsed, patted dry, and cut into pieces
2 tablespoons olive oil
1 onion, sliced into rings

1 cup sliced crimini mushrooms
1 tablespoon chopped garlic
1 cup white wine
1 cup chicken broth
1/2 cup sliced black olives

Place the flour, salt, and pepper into a resealable plastic bag; shake to mix. Place the pheasant pieces into the flour mixture, and shake until evenly coated. Heat the olive oil in a large skillet over medium-high heat. Shake any excess flour off of the pheasant pieces, and place them in the hot oil. Cook until the pheasant is brown on both sides, about 3 minutes per side. Place the pheasant into a slow cooker, reserving the oil in the skillet. Cook the onion in the remaining oil until they soften, about 3 minutes. Stir in the mushrooms and garlic, and continue cooking and stirring until the mushrooms have softened and the garlic has mellowed, about 5 minutes more. Pour the wine into the skillet and bring to a boil. Boil for 5 minutes, then pour in the chicken broth and return to a boil. Pour the mushroom mixture into the slow cooker, and sprinkle with sliced black olives. Cover, and cook on High for 4 hours, or Low for 7 hours.

223- Bill and Annette's One Pot Kraut Special

2 Granny Smith apples - peeled, cored and diced
1 large onion, diced

1 (3 pound) boneless pork loin
1/4 cup brown sugar
1 (32 ounce) jar sauerkraut, drained

1 (20 ounce) bottle peach-flavored   iced tea

Place apples and onion into a slow cooker. Set the pork loin on top, then add the sugar, sauerkraut, and iced tea. Cover and cook on High 6 to 8 hours until the pork is tender.

224- Slow Cooker Chicken Tetrazzini

6 skinless, boneless chicken breast halves
2 tablespoons melted butter
1 (.7 ounce) package dry Italian- style
salad dressing mix
2 tablespoons butter
1 small onion, sliced and separated into
rings

3 cloves garlic, minced
1 (10.75 ounce) can condensed cream of
chicken soup
1/2 cup chicken broth
1 (8 ounce) package cream cheese,
softened

Place chicken in the slow cooker crock. Top with 2 tablespoons melted butter; sprinkle with Italian dressing mix. Cover, and cook on High for 3 hours. Heat the remaining 2 tablespoons of butter in a large skillet over medium heat. Stir in onion and garlic; cook and stir until onion is soft, about 5 minutes. Mix in the cream of chicken soup, chicken broth, and cream cheese. Pour mixture over the cooked chicken in the slow cooker. Cover, and continue to cook on Low until chicken in fork tender and the sauce has thickened, about 1 additional hour.

225- Bourbon-Mango Pulled Pork

2 mangos
1 (4 pound) pork shoulder roast
2 tablespoons ground black pepper
1 teaspoon kosher salt
1 teaspoon chipotle chile powder
1/4 cup balsamic vinegar

2 cups water
1 teaspoon chipotle chile powder
2 teaspoons honey
1 (1.5 fluid ounce) jigger bourbon
whiskey
2 (12 ounce) bottles barbeque sauce

Peel the mangos and remove the pits. Place the pits into a slow cooker, then roughly chop the mango and set aside. Place the pork shoulder into the slow cooker, and season with the black pepper, kosher salt, and 1 teaspoon chipotle powder; pour in the balsamic vinegar and water. Cover, and cook on Low 5 to 8 hours until the meat is very tender. Once done, drain the pork, discarding the cooking liquid and mango pits, and shred with two forks. While the pork is cooking, puree the chopped mango in a blender until smooth, then pour into a saucepan along with the honey, 1 teaspoon chipotle powder, and whiskey. Bring to a simmer. Reduce heat to medium-low, and simmer, stirring frequently until the mango has reduced and darkened slightly, about 10 minutes. Stir in the barbeque sauce, and remove from the heat. Return the shredded pork to the slow cooker, and stir in the mango barbeque sauce. Cover, and cook on High 1 to 2 hours until the pork absorbs the barbeque sauce.

226- Easy Peasy Venison Stew

2 pounds venison, cut into cubes salt and
pepper to taste

1 kiwi, peeled and sliced
1 1/2 cups red wine

1/4 cup all-purpose flour extra-virgin
olive oil
2 cloves garlic, minced
1 onion, cut into chunks
1 sprig rosemary leaves, minced
1 sprig thyme leaves, minced balsamic
vinegar

1/2 cup beef stock
5 potatoes, peeled and cubed
1 carrots, cut into 1/2 inch pieces
1 parsnips, cut into 1/2 inch pieces
1 (8 ounce) package sliced fresh
mushrooms

Season the venison with salt and pepper, and place into a bowl. Stir in the kiwi slices and red wine until evenly mixed. Cover, and marinate in the refrigerator overnight. Drain the venison, reserving the red wine marinade. Pick out the pieces of kiwi from the venison, and place them with the red wine marinade. Squeeze as much marinade from the venison as you can. Heat the olive oil in a large skillet or saucepan over medium-high heat. Place the floured venison cubes in the hot oil, and cook until browned on all sides, 5 to 10 minutes. Remove the venison cubes to a slow cooker. Stir the garlic, onion, rosemary, and thyme into the skillet, and cook until the edges of the onion begins to soften, about 3 minutes. Pour in the balsamic vinegar and the reserved red wine marinade. Bring to a boil and cook for 5 minutes. Pour the onion mixture into the slow cooker, and stir in the beef stock, potatoes, carrots, parsnips, and mushrooms until evenly mixed. Add water if needed to just cover the vegetables. Cover the slow cooker, and set to LOW. Cook until the venison is easily pulled apart with a fork and the vegetables are tender, about 4 hours. Season to taste with salt and pepper before serving.

227- Texas Deer Chili

2 tablespoons vegetable oil
2 1/2 pounds venison, cut into cubes
1 large onion, chopped
1 clove garlic, minced
1 (4 ounce) can diced green chile peppers
2 (15 ounce) cans kidney beans, drained
and rinsed

2 (10.5 ounce) cans beef broth
2 teaspoons dried oregano
2 teaspoons ground cumin
1/2 teaspoon salt
1 1/2 teaspoons paprika

In a large skillet over medium heat, cook venison, onion and garlic in oil until meat is browned. Transfer to a slow cooker and stir together with chiles, beans, broth oregano, cumin, salt and paprika. Cook on medium 4 to 5 hours.

228- Slow Cooker Venison Stew

3 stalks celery, diced
1/2 cup chopped onion
2 cloves garlic, minced
1 tablespoon chopped fresh parsley
2 tablespoons vegetable oil

2 pounds venison stew meat salt and
pepper to taste
dried oregano to taste dried basil to taste
1 cup tomato sauce
1/2 cup dry red wine
1/2 cup water

Place the celery, onion, garlic, and parsley in the bottom of a slow cooker. Heat the oil in a large frying pan over medium-high heat. Brown the venison well in two batches, and add to the slow cooker. Season to taste with salt, pepper, oregano, and basil. Pour in the tomato sauce, red wine, and water. Cook on Low for 7 to 10 hours.

229- Slow Cooker Cheesy Chicken and Tortillas

4 skinless, boneless chicken breast halves
1 (1 ounce) package mild taco seasoning mix
5 1/4 cups Swanson® Chicken Stock
2 tablespoons butter

2 (10.75 ounce) cans Campbell's® Condensed Cream of Chicken Soup (Regular or 98% Fat Free)
10 fajita-size flour tortillas (10- inch), cut into 1-inch pieces
4 cups shredded Mexican cheese blend
Hot cooked regular long-grain white rice

Place the chicken into a 3 1/2-quart slow cooker. Top with all but 2 tablespoons of the taco seasoning. Pour 3 1/2 cups of the stock over the chicken. Cover and cook on LOW for 4 to 5 hours or until the chicken is cooked through. Remove the chicken to a cutting board. Using 2 forks, shred the chicken. Heat the oven to 350 degrees F. Heat the butter in a 3-quart saucepan over medium heat. Stir the remaining taco seasoning, stock and soup in the saucepan. Stir in the chicken. Layer half of the chicken mixture, tortillas, and cheese in a 3-quart shallow baking dish. Repeat the layer. Bake for 30 minutes or until the mixture is hot and bubbling. Serve over the rice.

230- Ham and Chickpea Slow Cooker Soup

1 pound dry garbanzo beans
1 meaty ham bone
10 new potatoes, halved

5 carrots, chopped
1/2 cup frozen corn
ground black pepper to taste

Place the garbanzo beans into a large container and cover with several inches of cool water; let stand 8 hours to overnight. The next day, rinse the soaked beans and place them into a slow cooker; place the ham bone in the cooker, and pour in enough water to cover the beans and ham bone by several inches. Set the cooker to Low, and cook for 8 hours. Skim any foam from the top of the soup, and remove the ham bone. Strip as much meat as possible from the ham bone, and return the meat to the slow cooker; discard the bone. Stir in potatoes, carrots, frozen corn, and black pepper to taste. Set the cooker on Low, and cook for 1 hour; then turn the heat up to High and cook 1 more hour (10 hours total cooking time).

231- Mexican Pintos With Cactus

2 cups dry pinto beans, rinsed
3 tablespoons salt, divided
3 slices bacon, chopped

2 large flat cactus leaves (nopales)
1 jalapeno pepper, seeded and chopped
2 slices onion

Place the pinto beans into a slow cooker, and fill to the top with hot water. Add the bacon, 2 tablespoons of salt, jalapeno and onion. Cover, and cook on High for 3 to 4 hours, adding water as needed, until beans are tender. Remove any thorns from the cactus leaves, and slice into small pieces. Place in a saucepan with 1 tablespoon of salt, and fill with enough water to cover. Bring to a boil, and cook for 15 minutes. Drain and rinse with cold water for 1 minute. Add to the beans when they are soft, and cook for 15 more minutes on High.

232- Portuguese Chourico and Peppers

2 pounds chorizo sausage, casings removed and crumbled
2 green bell peppers, seeded and chopped
2 sweet onion, peeled and chopped

1 (6 ounce) can tomato paste
1 cup red wine
1 cup water
2 tablespoons crushed garlic

In a slow cooker, combine the sausage, green pepper, onion, tomato paste, wine, water, and crushed garlic. Stir so that everything is evenly distributed. Cover, and set on Low. Cook for 8 hours. Uncover the pot, and cook an additional 2 hours to allow some of the liquid to evaporate. Serve over rice, or with Portuguese rolls.

233- Slow Cooker German-Style Pork Roast

6 white potatoes, peeled and quartered
1 tablespoon minced garlic salt and pepper to taste

1 (3 pound) boneless pork loin roast
1 (32 ounce) jar sauerkraut with liquid
2 teaspoons caraway seeds

Place the potatoes, garlic, salt, and pepper in a slow cooker; stir to coat. Season the pork roast with salt and pepper; lay atop the potatoes. Pour the sauerkraut over the roast; sprinkle with caraway seeds. Cook in slow cooker on Low 8 to 10 hours.

234- Spicy Kielbasa Soup

1/2 pound reduced-fat smoked turkey kielbasa, sliced
1 medium onion, chopped
1 medium green pepper, chopped
1 celery ribs with leaves, thinly sliced
4 garlic cloves, minced
2 (14.5 ounce) cans reduced sodium chicken broth

1 (15.5 ounce) can great northern beans, rinsed and drained
1 (14.5 ounce) can stewed tomatoes, cut up
1 small zucchini, sliced
1 medium carrot, shredded
1 tablespoon dried parsley flakes
1/4 teaspoon crushed red pepper flakes
1/4 teaspoon pepper

In a nonstick skillet, cook kielbasa over medium heat until lightly browned. Add the onion, green pepper, celery and garlic. Cook and stir for 5 minutes or until vegetable are tender. Transfer to a slow cooker. Stir in the remaining ingredients. Cover and cook on low for 8-9 hours.

235- A Nice Slow-Cooked Pork

1 (3 pound) pork shoulder roast
1 quart vegetable broth
1 cup sherry
3 cups peeled, chopped potatoes
2 cups pearl onions

2 cups sliced fresh mushrooms
1 tablespoon dried rosemary
1 teaspoon ground black pepper salt to taste

Place the pork roast in a slow cooker. Pour in the vegetable broth and sherry. Mix in the potatoes, onions, mushrooms, rosemary, and pepper. Cover, and cook on Low at least 8 hours, to an internal temperature of 160 degrees F (70 degrees C). Season with salt to taste.

236- Amelia's Slow Cooker Brunswick Stew

1 tablespoon vegetable oil
1 pound country style pork ribs
1 onion, chopped
1 roasted chicken, deboned and shredded
1 (28 ounce) can diced tomatoes
3/4 cup ketchup
1/2 (10 fluid ounce) bottle steak sauce
1/2 cup cider vinegar

2 tablespoons Worcestershire sauce
1 tablespoon hot sauce
1 lemon, juiced
2 cubes chicken bouillon
1/2 tablespoon ground black pepper
1 (15 ounce) can whole kernel corn, undrained
1 cup frozen lima beans, thawed

Heat the vegetable oil in a skillet over medium heat, and brown the ribs on all sides. Transfer to a slow cooker. Place onion in the skillet, cook until tender, and transfer to the slow cooker. Place the chicken in the slow cooker, and mix in tomatoes, ketchup, steak sauce, cider vinegar, Worcestershire sauce, hot sauce, lemon, chicken bouillon, and pepper. Cover, and cook 6 hours on High. Remove ribs, discard bones, and shred. Return meat to slow cooker. Mix in corn and lima beans, cover, and continue cooking 2 hours on High.

237- Slow Cooker Kielbasa Stew

2 pounds kielbasa sausage, cut into 1 inch pieces
1 1/2 pounds sauerkraut, drained and rinsed
2 Granny Smith apples - peeled, cored and sliced into rings

3/4 onion, sliced into rings
2 pounds red potatoes, quartered
1 1/2 cups chicken broth
1/2 teaspoon caraway seeds
1/2 cup shredded Swiss cheese

Place half the sausage in a slow cooker, and top with the sauerkraut. Cover with the remaining sausage, apples, and onion. Top with the potatoes. Pour chicken broth over all, and sprinkle with caraway seeds. Cover, and cook on High 4 hours, or until potatoes are tender. Top each serving with Swiss cheese.

238- Slow Cooker Moose Roast

2 tablespoons vegetable oil	2 cups apple juice
4 pounds moose roast	1 (1 ounce) envelope dry onion soup mix

Heat oil in a large skillet over medium-high heat. Brown the roast on all sides in the hot oil. Remove, and transfer to a slow cooker. Sprinkle onion soup mix over the roast, then pour in the apple juice. Cover and cook on MEDIUM for 6 to 8 hours, or until meat is very tender. Check occasionally to make sure there is sufficient liquid, and add more juice if necessary. Serve roast with juices, or thicken them for a tasty gravy.

239- Easy and Delicious Chicken

6 skinless, boneless chicken breast halves	1 cup chicken broth
1 (8 ounce) bottle Italian-style salad dressing	1 (8 ounce) package cream cheese
	1/2 teaspoon dried basil
1 (10.75 ounce) can condensed cream of chicken soup	1/2 teaspoon dried thyme salt and pepper to taste

In a slow cooker, combine the chicken breasts and Italian-style dressing. Cover, and cook on Low for 6 to 8 hours. Drain off the juices, and shred the chicken meat. In a medium bowl, mix the soup, broth, cream cheese, basil, thyme, salt, and pepper. Pour over the chicken in the slow cooker. Continue cooking on Low for 1 hour.

240- Slow Cooker Thanksgiving Turkey

5 slices bacon	1 (10.5 ounce) can turkey gravy
1 (5 1/2 pound) bone-in turkey breast, skin removed	2 tablespoons all-purpose flour
	1 tablespoon Worcestershire sauce
1/2 teaspoon garlic pepper	1 teaspoon dried sage

Place bacon in a skillet over medium-high heat, and cook until evenly brown. Drain and crumble. Spray a slow cooker with cooking spray. Place turkey in the slow cooker. Season with garlic pepper. In a bowl, mix the bacon, gravy, flour, Worcestershire sauce, and sage. Pour over turkey in the slow cooker. Cover slow cooker, and cook turkey 8 hours on Low.

241- Ham and Bean Stew

2 (16 ounce) cans baked beans	1 celery rib, chopped
2 medium potatoes, peeled and cubed	1/2 cup water
2 cups cubed fully cooked ham	

In a slow cooker, combine all ingredients; mix well. Cover and cook on low for 7 hours or until the potatoes are tender.

242- Chicken and Fresh Tomato Slow Cooker Stew

5 potatoes, peeled and cubed
1 1/2 cups chopped fresh tomato
1 cup sliced carrot
1 onion, chopped
2 bay leaves
3 large skinless boneless chicken breast
halves

2 (8 ounce) cans tomato sauce
1 (14.5 ounce) can chicken broth
1 1/2 teaspoons Italian seasoning
1/4 teaspoon red pepper flakes water, as
needed

Combine the potatoes, tomato, carrot, onion, and bay leaves in a slow cooker. Place the chicken breasts atop the vegetables. Stir the tomato sauce, chicken broth, and Italian seasoning in a bowl; pour over the chicken breasts. Add water as needed to assure the chicken is completely covered. Cook on Low for 6 hours. Remove the chicken breasts and cut into bite sized chunks and return to slow cooker. Continue cooking until the vegetables are tender, another 1 to 2 hours.

243- Lots-A-Veggies Stew

1 pound ground beef
1 medium onion, diced
2 garlic cloves, minced
1 (16 ounce) can baked beans, undrained
1 (16 ounce) can kidney beans, rinsed
and drained
1 (15 ounce) can butter beans, rinsed and
drained
1 (14.5 ounce) can beef broth
1 (11 ounce) can whole kernel corn,
undrained

1 (10.5 ounce) can condensed vegetable
soup, undiluted
1 (6 ounce) can tomato paste
1 medium green pepper, diced
1 cup sliced carrots
1 cup sliced celery
2 tablespoons chili powder
1 teaspoon dried oregano
1 teaspoon dried thyme
1 teaspoon salt
1/2 teaspoon dried marjoram
1/2 teaspoon pepper

In a skillet, cook beef, onion and garlic over medium heat until meat is no longer pink; drain. Transfer to a 5-qt. slow cooker. Add the remaining ingredients and mix well. Cover and cook on low for 5 hours or until vegetables are tender.

244- Zesty Slow-Cooker Italian Pot Roast

4 medium potatoes, cut into quarters
2 cups fresh or frozen whole baby carrots
1 stalk celery, cut into 1-inch pieces
1 medium Italian plum tomato, diced
2 1/2 pounds beef bottom round roasts or
beef chuck pot roast
1/2 teaspoon ground black pepper
1 (10.75 ounce) can Campbell's®
Condensed Tomato Soup

1/2 cup water
1 tablespoon chopped roasted garlic* or
chopped fresh garlic
1 teaspoon dried basil leaves, crushed
1 teaspoon dried oregano leaves, crushed
1 teaspoon dried parsley flakes, crushed
1 teaspoon vinegar

Place potatoes, carrots, celery and tomato in 3 1/2-quart slow cooker. Season roast with pepper and place on top. Mix soup, water, pepper, garlic, basil, oregano, parsley and vinegar. Pour over all. Cover and cook on LOW 10 to 12 hour or until done.**

245- The Spiced Cider Project

2 oranges
60 whole cloves
2 (6 ounce) cans frozen apple juice
concentrate, thawed

3 1/2 cups water
4 (2 inch) sticks cinnamon sticks

Cut each orange into 10 slices. Place 3 cloves into each slice. Combine apple juice concentrate and water in a slow cooker. Add oranges and cinnamon sticks. Cook on HIGH for 25 minutes, or until warm.

246- Shrimp Marinara

1 (14.5 ounce) can Italian diced tomatoes,
undrained
1 (6 ounce) can tomato paste
1/2 cup water
2 garlic cloves, minced
2 tablespoons minced fresh parsley
1 teaspoon salt (optional)

1 teaspoon dried oregano
1/2 teaspoon dried basil
1/4 teaspoon pepper
1 pound fresh or frozen shrimp, cooked,
peeled and deveined
1 pound spaghetti, cooked and drained
shredded Parmesan cheese (optional)

In a slow cooker, combine the first nine ingredients. Cover and cook on low for 3-4 hours. Stir in shrimp. Cover and cook 20 minutes longer or just until shrimp are heated through. Serve over spaghetti. Garnish with Parmesan cheese if desired.

247- Creamy Drunken Mushroom Pork Chops

4 thick cut bone-in pork chops
1 (10.75 ounce) can reduced-fat, reduced-
sodium cream of mushroom soup
1 (3 ounce) can chopped mushrooms,
drained

1/3 cup red wine
2 cloves garlic, minced ground black
pepper to taste

Place the pork chops in the bottom of a slow cooker. Stir the mushroom soup, mushrooms, red wine, garlic, and pepper together in a bowl; pour over the pork chops. Cover and cook on Low 6 to 8 hours.

248- White Bean with Fennel Soup

4 cups Swanson® Vegetable Broth
(Regular or Certified Organic)
1/8 teaspoon ground black pepper
1 small bulb fennel, trimmed and sliced

1 medium onion, chopped
2 cloves garlic, minced
1 (10 ounce) package frozen leaf spinach,
thawed

1 (14.5 ounce) can diced tomatoes, undrained

1 (16 ounce) can white kidney beans (cannellini), undrained

Stir the broth, black pepper, fennel, onion and garlic in a 5 1/2- to 6- quart slow cooker. Cover and cook on LOW for 6 to 7 hours. Add the spinach, tomatoes and beans. Turn the heat to HIGH. Cover and cook for 1 hour or until the vegetables are tender.

249- Chili Verde

3 tablespoons Worcestershire sauce
1 tablespoon garlic pepper
3 pounds pork picnic roast
1 large onion, diced
1 (14.5 ounce) can chicken broth

2 (4 ounce) cans diced green chilies, drained
3 (7 ounce) cans green salsa
2 (15.5 ounce) cans great Northern beans, drained (optional)

Pour half of the Worcestershire sauce into the pan of a slow cooker, and half of the garlic pepper. Place the roast in the pan, and sprinkle remaining Worcestershire sauce and garlic pepper over the top. Add the onions, and chilies, and pour in the chicken broth. Cover, and cook on Low for 8 to 10 hours. When the roast is tender enough to pull apart with a fork, add the green salsa, and the beans, if desired. Continue cooking until heated through. Serve as soup or over chimichangas.

250- Mulled Cranberry Cider

2 quarts cranberry juice
2 oranges, zested
14 whole cloves
1 1/2 cups dried cranberries

1 teaspoon vanilla extract
1 1/3 cups honey
2 cinnamon sticks

Pour cranberry juice into a slow cooker; set on high. To the juice add the zest from the oranges, cloves, cranberries, vanilla extract, honey and cinnamon sticks. Heat, stirring occasionally, until hot and steamy, about 20 minutes.

251- Zippy Slow-Cooked Chili

1 pound lean ground beef
1 (28 ounce) can diced tomatoes, undrained
1 medium onion, chopped
1 medium green pepper, chopped
1 (15 ounce) can fat-free vegetarian chili
1 (8 ounce) can tomato sauce
2 tablespoons chili powder
2 tablespoons minced fresh parsley

1 tablespoon dried basil
2 teaspoons ground cumin
4 garlic cloves, minced
1 teaspoon dried oregano
3/4 teaspoon pepper
1/8 teaspoon hot pepper sauce
6 tablespoons shredded reduced- fat Cheddar cheese
1 tablespoon minced chives

In a nonstick skillet, cook beef over medium heat until no longer pink; drain. Transfer to a 3-qt. slow cooker. Add the tomatoes, onion, green pepper, chili, tomato sauce, chili powder, parsley, basil, cumin, garlic, oregano, pepper and hot pepper sauce. Cover and cook on low for 6-8 hours. Sprinkle with cheese and chives before serving.

252- Slow Cooker Lemon Garlic Chicken I

6 skinless, boneless chicken breasts
3 cups white wine
1 1/2 cups lemon juice
1 medium head garlic, crushed

4 drops hot pepper sauce
2 teaspoons poultry seasoning
2 teaspoons salt

Combine the white wine, lemon juice, crushed garlic, pepper sauce, poultry seasoning and salt. Mix well. Place chicken in slow cooker. Pour lemon/garlic mixture over chicken. Cook on low for 8 to 10 hours.

253- Funky Cholent

2 teaspoons vegetable oil
1 large onion, chopped
2 cloves garlic, chopped
1 pound beef stew meat, cubed
5 large potatoes, cubed
1 sweet potato, cubed
1 (16 ounce) can baked beans

1 tablespoon ketchup
1 tablespoon barbecue sauce
1 tablespoon prepared yellow mustard
2 teaspoons dry onion soup mix
2 teaspoons seasoned salt
1 teaspoon steak seasoning
1/2 cup pearl barley

Heat the oil in a large soup pot over medium heat; cook and stir the onion and garlic until the onion is translucent, about 5 minutes. Add the beef stew meat, and quickly brown the pieces on all sides. Stir in the potatoes, sweet potato, baked beans, ketchup, barbecue sauce, mustard, onion soup mix, seasoned salt, and steak seasoning, and pour in enough water to cover. Bring the mixture to a boil, reduce to a simmer, and cook on low heat until the beef is tender, 1 1/2 to 2 hours, stirring occasionally. Stir in the pearl barley, and transfer the stew to a slow cooker set on Low until the barley is tender, about 12 hours.

254- Slow-Cooked Swiss Steak

1 tablespoon all-purpose flour
1/4 teaspoon salt
1/8 teaspoon pepper
3/4 pound boneless top round steak, cut in half

1/2 medium onion, cut into 1/4 inch slices
1/3 cup chopped celery
1 (8 ounce) can tomato sauce

In a large resealable plastic bag, combine the flour, salt and pepper. Add beef; seal bag and shake to coat. Place onion in a 3-qt. slow cooker coated with nonstick cooking spray. Layer with the beef, celery and tomato sauce. Cover and cook on low for 8 hours or until meat is tender.

255- Sweet Sausage InI Beans

1/2 cup thinly sliced carrots
1/2 cup chopped onion
2 cups frozen lima beans, thawed
2 cups frozen cut green beans
1 pound smoked sausage, cut into
1/4 inch slices

1 (16 ounce) can baked beans
1/2 cup ketchup
1/3 cup packed brown sugar
1 tablespoon cider vinegar
1 teaspoon prepared mustard

In a slow cooker, layer carrots, onion, lima beans, green beans, sausage and baked beans. Combine ketchup, brown sugar, vinegar and mustard; pour over beans. Cover and cook on high for 4 hours or until vegetables are tender. Stir before serving.

256- Slow Cooker Corn Chowder

5 potatoes, peeled and cubed
2 onions, chopped
2 cups diced ham
3 stalks celery, chopped
1 (15.25 ounce) can whole kernel corn, undrained

2 tablespoons margarine salt and pepper
to taste
2 cubes chicken bouillon
1 (12 fluid ounce) can evaporated milk

In a slow cooker, place the potatoes, onions, ham, celery, corn, butter or margarine and salt and pepper to taste. Add water to cover and two bouillon cubes. Cook on low setting for 8 to 9 hours and then stir in the evaporated milk. Cook for 30 more minutes.

257- Spiced Slow Cooker Applesauce

8 apples - peeled, cored, and thinly sliced
1/2 cup water

3/4 cup packed brown sugar
1/2 teaspoon pumpkin pie spice

Combine the apples and water in a slow cooker; cook on Low for 6 to 8 hours. Stir in the brown sugar and pumpkin pie spice; continue cooking another 30 minutes.

258- Beezie's Black Bean Soup

1 pound dry black beans
1 1/2 quarts water
1 carrot, chopped
1 stalk celery, chopped
1 large red onion, chopped
6 cloves garlic, crushed
2 green bell peppers, chopped
2 jalapeno pepper, seeded and minced
1/4 cup dry lentils

1 (28 ounce) can peeled and diced
tomatoes
2 tablespoons chili powder
2 teaspoons ground cumin
1/2 teaspoon dried oregano
1/2 teaspoon ground black pepper
3 tablespoons red wine vinegar
1 tablespoon salt
1/2 cup uncooked white rice

In a large pot over medium-high heat, place the beans in three times their volume of water. Bring to a boil, and let boil 10 minutes. Cover, remove from heat and let stand 1 hour. Drain, and rinse. In a slow cooker, combine soaked beans and 1 1/2 quarts fresh water. Cover, and cook for 3 hours on High. Stir in carrot, celery, onion, garlic, bell peppers, jalapeno pepper, lentils, and tomatoes. Season with chili powder, cumin, oregano, black pepper, red wine vinegar, and salt. Cook on Low for 2 to 3 hours. Stir the rice into the slow cooker in the last 20 minutes of cooking. Puree about half of the soup with a blender or food processor, then pour back into the pot before serving.

259- Pork Chile Rojo (Pulled Pork with Red Chile Sauce)

1 (4 pound) boneless pork shoulder
roast, trimmed
3 tablespoons chili powder
1 cup chopped onions

4 cups water
2 (16 ounce) jars salsa
2 (10 ounce) cans diced tomatoes with
green chilies, undrained

Place the pork roast into an oven roasting bag set inside a slow cooker. Sprinkle the chili powder over the roast and arrange onions on top of the roast. Loosely close the top of the bag with a nylon tie. Use scissors to cut 3 vents, 1-inch long in the top of the bag. Pour the water into the bottom of the slow cooker, around the bag, so that it is at least 1 inch deep. Cover and cook the pork on Low for 6 to 8 hours. Remove the pork and onions from the bag and place in a large Dutch oven; reserve 3/4 cup of liquid from the bag. Shred the pork by pulling it apart using two forks. Stir the salsa, tomatoes, and cooking liquid in with the shredded pork. Bring to a boil over high heat, then reduce the heat to low. Cover and simmer for 1 hour, stirring occasionally.

260- Simmered Smoked Links

2 (16 ounce) packages miniature smoked
sausage links
1 cup packed brown sugar

1/2 cup ketchup
1/4 cup prepared horseradish

Place sausages in a slow cooker. Combine brown sugar, ketchup and horseradish; pour over sausages. Cover and cook on low for 4 hours.

261- Corny Ham and Potato Scallop

5 potatoes, peeled and cubed
1 1/2 cups cubed cooked ham
1 (15 ounce) can whole kernel corn,
drained
1/4 cup chopped green bell pepper

2 teaspoons instant minced onion
1 (10.75 ounce) can condensed
Cheddar cheese soup
1/2 cup milk
3 tablespoons all-purpose flour

In a slow cooker, combine potatoes, ham, corn, green pepper, and onion. In a small bowl, stir together soup, milk, and flour until smooth. Pour soup mixture over ham and vegetables, and stir gently to coat. Cover, and cook on Low for about 8 hours, or until potatoes are tender.

262- Swink's Chili

2 pounds ground beef
1 onion, chopped
1 (1.25 ounce) package chili seasoning mix
2 cups water
1 (6 ounce) can tomato paste

1 (16 ounce) can chili beans, undrained
1 (16 ounce) can baked beans
1 (10.75 ounce) can condensed tomato soup
1 (10 ounce) can diced tomatoes with green chile peppers

In a large skillet over medium heat, cook beef and onion until beef is brown. Stir in chili seasoning and water. Pour beef mixture into a slow cooker and stir in tomato paste, chili beans, baked beans, tomato soup and diced tomatoes with green chiles. Cook on low 2 hours.

263- Awesome Slow Cooker Pot Roast

2 (10.75 ounce) cans condensed cream of mushroom soup
1 (1 ounce) package dry onion soup mix

1 1/4 cups water
5 1/2 pounds pot roast

In a slow cooker, mix cream of mushroom soup, dry onion soup mix and water. Place pot roast in slow cooker and coat with soup mixture. Cook on High setting for 3 to 4 hours, or on Low setting for 8 to 9 hours.

264- Creamy Blush Sauce with Turkey and Penne

4 turkey thighs, skin removed
1 (25.75 ounce) jar Prego® Chunky Garden Mushroom & Green Pepper Italian Sauce

1/2 teaspoon crushed red pepper
1/2 cup half-and-half
Hot cooked penne pasta
Grated Parmesan cheese

Place the turkey into a 3 1/2- to 5-quart slow cooker. Pour the sauce over the turkey and sprinkle with the red pepper. Cover and cook on LOW for 7 to 8 hours* or until the turkey is cooked through. Remove the turkey from the cooker to a cutting board. Let stand for 10 minutes. Remove the turkey meat from the bones. Stir the turkey meat and the half-and-half into the cooker. Spoon the turkey mixture over the pasta. Sprinkle with the cheese.

265- Rich French Onion Soup

6 large onions, chopped
1/2 cup butter or margarine
6 (10.5 ounce) cans condensed beef broth, undiluted

1 1/2 teaspoons Worcestershire sauce
3 bay leaves
10 slices French bread, toasted Shredded Parmesan and mozzarella cheeses

In a large skillet, saute onions in butter until crisp-tender. Transfer to an ungreased 5-qt. slow cooker. Add the broth, Worcestershire sauce and bay leaves.
Cover and cook on low for 5-7 hours or until the onions are tender. Discard bay leaves. Top each serving with French bread and cheeses.

266- Crabmeat and Asparagus Soup

1 (10 ounce) can asparagus tips, drained
2 (6 ounce) cans crabmeat, drained and
flaked
2 tablespoons fish sauce
1 tablespoon oyster sauce

1 cup chopped fresh spinach
1 cup diced firm tofu
2 teaspoons dried oregano
1 clove garlic, crushed

In a slow cooker, combine the asparagus, crabmeat, fish sauce, spinach, tofu, oregano and garlic. Fill with enough water to cover by about 2 inches. Cover, and cook on High for 45 minutes, or until you smell the aroma and the spinach has cooked down dramatically.

267- Marinated Pot Roast

1 cup dry white wine or beef broth
1/3 cup reduced-sodium soy sauce
1 tablespoon olive oil
4 garlic cloves, minced
2 green onions, thinly sliced
1 1/2 teaspoons ground ginger

1/4 teaspoon pepper
4 whole cloves
1 (4 pound) boneless beef top round
roast
5 teaspoons cornstarch
5 teaspoons cold water

In a gallon-size resealable plastic bag, combine the first eight ingredients. Cut roast in half; add to marinade. Seal bag and turn to coat; refrigerate overnight. Place roast and marinade in a 5-qt. slow cooker. Cover and cook on low for 8-10 hours or until meat is tender. remove roast to a serving platter and keep warm. Pour cooking juices into a 2-cup measuring cup; discard whole cloves In a saucepan, combine cornstarch and cold water until smooth; stir in 1-1/2 cups cooking juices. bring to a boil; cook and stir for 2 minutes or until thickened. Serve with the roast.

268- Flank Steak Roll-Up

1 (4 ounce) can mushroom stems and
pieces, undrained
2 tablespoons butter or margarine,
melted
1 (6 ounce) package seasoned stuffing
mix

1 3/4 pounds beef flank steak
1 (.75 ounce) packet dry brown gravy
mix
1/4 cup chopped green onion
1/4 cup dry red wine or beef broth

In bowl, toss the mushrooms, butter and dry stuffing mix. Spread over steak to within 1 in. of edges. Roll up jelly-roll style, starting with a long side; tie with kitchen string. Place in a slow cooker. Prepare gravy mix according to package directions; add onions and wine or broth. Pour over meat. Cover and cook on low for 8-10 hours. Remove meat to a serving platter and keep warm. Strain cooking juices and thicken if desired. Remove string from roll-up; slice and serve with gravy.

269- Wheat Salad

1 1/2 cups whole wheat berries
1 (8 ounce) package cream cheese, softened
1 (15.25 ounce) can crushed pineapple in juice, drained

2 tablespoons lemon juice
1 (3.4 ounce) package instant vanilla pudding mix
1 (8 ounce) tub frozen whipped topping, thawed

Soak wheat berries in a bowl of water for at least 5 hours or overnight. Drain and place in a slow cooker with enough water to cover by one inch. Cover, and cook on Low setting for 5 to 6 hours, until tender. Add more water if needed. When tender, drain, and rinse under cold water to chill. In a large bowl, stir together the cream cheese, pineapple and lemon juice. Stir in the dry pudding mix until smooth. Stir in the wheat berries until evenly coated. Fold in whipped topping just before serving. Refrigerate any leftovers.

270- Greek Chicken Pitas

1 medium onion, diced
3 cloves garlic, minced
1 pound skinless, boneless chicken breast halves - cut into strips
1 teaspoon lemon pepper
1/2 teaspoon dried oregano

1/4 teaspoon allspice
1/4 cup plain yogurt
1/4 cup sour cream
1/2 cup cucumber, peeled and diced
4 pita bread rounds, cut in half

Place onion and garlic in a slow cooker. Season chicken with lemon pepper, oregano, and allspice; place on top of onions. Cover, and cook on High for 6 hours. In a small bowl, stir together yogurt, sour cream, and cucumber. Refrigerate until chicken is done cooking. When chicken is done, fill pita halves with chicken, and top with the yogurt sauce.

271- Slow Cooker Veggie-Beef Soup with Okra

1 pound ground beef
1/4 cup onion, chopped
1 (14.5 ounce) can diced tomatoes, drained
1 (14.5 ounce) can Italian diced tomatoes, drained

1 (16 ounce) package frozen mixed vegetables
1 cup sliced fresh or frozen okra
2 potatoes, peeled and chopped
1 tablespoon ketchup salt and pepper to taste

In a skillet over medium heat, cook the ground beef and onion until beef is evenly brown and onion is tender. Drain grease. In a slow cooker, mix the beef and onion, diced tomatoes, Italian diced tomatoes, vegetables, okra, potatoes, ketchup, salt, and pepper. Pour in enough water to cover. Cover slow cooker, and cook 4 hours on Low.

272- Pumpkin Soup the Easy Way

1 tablespoon butter
1 cup chopped onion

2 teaspoons minced garlic
2 pounds cubed fully cooked ham

3 (29 ounce) cans pumpkin puree
1 (32 ounce) carton chicken broth
2/3 cup cream

1 teaspoon fresh thyme
1 teaspoon ground black pepper
1/2 teaspoon fresh rosemary

Melt the butter in a skillet over medium heat. Cook the onion and garlic in the butter until soft. Combine the onion, garlic, ham, pumpkin puree, chicken broth, cream, thyme, pepper, and rosemary in a slow cooker set to Low; cook 8 to 10 hours.

273- Slow Cooker Sauerkraut and Sausage

1 (20 ounce) can sauerkraut
1/4 cup brown sugar

1 1/2 pounds ground pork sausage
1 onion, sliced

In a medium bowl, combine the sauerkraut and brown sugar. then place in slow cooker. Arrange the sausage and onion over the sauerkraut. Cook on high for two hours, check for dryness, adding some water if necessary, then reduce to low setting, and cook on low for two more hours.

274- Slow Cooker Barbeque

1 (3 pound) boneless chuck roast
1 teaspoon garlic powder

1 teaspoon onion powder salt and pepper to taste
1 (18 ounce) bottle barbeque sauce

Place roast into slow cooker. Sprinkle with garlic powder and onion powder, and season with salt and pepper. Pour barbeque sauce over meat. Cook on Low for 6 to 8 hours. Remove meat from slow cooker, shred, and return to slow cooker. Cook for 1 more hour. Serve hot.

275- Honey Ribs

1 (10.5 ounce) can beef broth
3 tablespoons honey mustard
1/4 cup honey
1/2 cup water

1/4 cup honey barbeque sauce
1/4 cup soy sauce
1/4 cup maple syrup
3 pounds baby back pork ribs

In the crock of a slow cooker, mix together the beef broth, honey mustard, honey, water, barbeque sauce, soy sauce, and maple syrup. Slice ribs apart, leaving an even amount of meat on each side of the bone. Place them into the slow cooker so that they are covered by the sauce. If there is not enough sauce, you may add a little water or beef broth to compensate. Cover, and cook on High for 5 hours, or until the meat falls easily from the bones.

276- Harvey Ham Sandwiches

1 (6 pound) bone-in ham
1 (8 ounce) jar yellow mustard

1 pound brown sugar
24 dinner rolls, split

Place the ham in a large pot or slow cooker, and fill with enough water to cover. Bring to a boil, then reduce the heat to low, and simmer for 8 to 10 hours. Remove the meat from the water, and allow to cool. If it has cooked long enough, it will fall into pieces as you pick it up. Pull the ham apart into shreds once it is cool enough to handle. It doesn't have to be tiny shreds. Place the shredded ham into a slow cooker. Stir in the mustard and brown sugar, cover, and set to Low. Cook just until heated. Serve on dinner rolls. We don't use any other sandwich toppings with it, but that is a personal choice.

277- Pork Chops with Apples and Sweet Potatoes

4 (1 inch thick) boneless pork chops
2 medium sweet potatoes, peeled and
sliced 1/2 inch thick
1 medium onion, sliced
2 apples - peeled, cored and sliced

1 tablespoon brown sugar
1/2 teaspoon ground nutmeg
1/4 teaspoon salt
freshly ground black pepper to taste
1 (16 ounce) can sauerkraut, drained

Heat a skillet over medium-high heat and coat with cooking spray. Quickly brown the pork chops on each side. Set aside. Arrange sweet potato slices in the bottom of a 3 to 4 quart slow cooker. Cover with the onion slices, then the apple slices. Sprinkle brown sugar, nutmeg and salt over the apples, and grind a little pepper. Place the pork chops on top of the pile, and cover with sauerkraut. Cover, and cook on Low for about 5 hours. It can go an extra hour without drying out though. Serve pork and vegetables with juice from the slow cooker spooned over them.

278- Pork and Vinegar

6 carrots, peeled and cut in half
6 potatoes, washed but not peeled
1 (2 1/2 pound) pork shoulder roast
1 large white onion, sliced
3 cloves garlic, chopped

1 1/2 teaspoons crushed red pepper
flakes, or to taste
1 bay leaf
1 (15 ounce) can tomato sauce
3/4 cup distilled white vinegar salt and
pepper to taste

Place the carrots and potatoes into the bottom of a slow cooker, and place the pork roast on top. Add the onion, garlic, bay leaf, and red pepper flakes, and pour the tomato sauce and vinegar over everything. Set the cooker to Low, and cook for 8 hours. Season to taste with salt and pepper. Slice the pork, and serve with carrots, potatoes, and some of the sauce spooned over each portion.

279- Bold Vegan Chili

1 (12 ounce) package vegetarian burger
crumbles
3 (15.25 ounce) cans kidney beans
1 large red onion, chopped
4 stalks celery, diced
2 red bell peppers, chopped

4 bay leaves
2 tablespoons hot chili powder
3 tablespoons molasses
1 cube vegetable bouillon
1 tablespoon chopped fresh cilantro

1 teaspoon hot pepper sauce salt and
pepper to taste
1 cup water

3 tablespoons all-purpose flour
1 cup hot water

In a slow cooker combine vegetarian crumbles, kidney beans, onion, celery, bell pepper, bay leaves, chili powder, molasses, bouillon, cilantro, hot sauce, salt, pepper and 1 cup water. Cook on high for 3 hours. Dissolve flour in 1 cup hot water. Pour into chili and cook 1 more hour.

280- Drunken Sailors

1 (14 ounce) bottle ketchup
1 (12 ounce) bottle barbeque sauce
1/2 cup brown sugar
1/2 cup whiskey

1 (16 ounce) package kielbasa sausage,
sliced into 1/2 inch pieces
1 box toothpicks

Pour the ketchup and barbecue sauce into a slow cooker. Stir in the brown sugar, whiskey, and sausage. Set on Low, and cook for 6 hours. Serve hot with toothpicks.

281- Easy Green Chile Chicken Enchiladas

4 skinless, boneless chicken breast halves
2 (19 ounce) cans green enchilada sauce
24 corn tortillas

1 cup 2% shredded Mexican style cheese
1 large zucchini, shredded

Place the chicken breasts in a slow cooker along with one can of enchilada sauce. Cook on High until tender and no longer pink, about 3 hours. Shred using two forks and return to the slow cooker. Preheat an oven to 350 degrees F (175 degrees C). Grease a 9x13 inch baking dish. Pour the remaining can of enchilada sauce into a shallow dish. Dip tortillas in the sauce; fill each with 1/3 cup shredded chicken, a sprinkle of Mexican style cheese, and a bit of grated zucchini. Roll up and place in the prepared baking dish, seam side down. Top enchiladas with any leftover sauce and remaining cheese. Cover dish and bake in preheated oven for 20 minutes. Remove cover; continue to bake until the cheese has melted, and enchiladas are hot, about 10 additional minutes.

282- Pork Chops for the Slow Cooker

6 boneless pork chops
1/4 cup brown sugar
1 teaspoon ground ginger
1/2 cup soy sauce

1/4 cup ketchup
2 cloves garlic, crushed salt and pepper
to taste

Place pork chops in slow cooker. Combine remaining ingredients and pour over pork chops. Cook on Low setting for 6 hours, until internal temperature of pork has reached 160 degrees F (70 degrees C).

283- Fall French Onion Soup

4 large onions, thinly sliced
2 Granny Smith apples - peeled, cored
and chopped
1/2 cup butter, divided
2 tablespoons olive oil
4 cups chicken broth

1 1/2 cups apple cider
2 tablespoons brandy (optional)
1 tablespoon ground cinnamon
1 tablespoon white sugar
1/2 cup shredded Gouda cheese
6 French bread

Set a slow cooker on Low, and put in half of the butter to melt. Add the onions and apples; cover and cook on Low for 6 to 8 hours. After the cooking time is up and apples and onions are soft, pour in the brandy, chicken broth and apple cider. Set the slow cooker to High and cook for 1 to 2 hours, until simmering. Preheat the oven broiler. Mix together the cinnamon, sugar and remaining butter. Spread onto one side of each slice of bread. Place bread cinnamon side up on a baking sheet, and broil until toasted, about 3 minutes. Remove from the oven, flip the slices over so the cinnamon is on the bottom. Sprinkle Gouda cheese on the top and return to the broiler until the cheese is melted. Ladle soup into serving bowls and top with slices of toast, cheese side up to serve.

284- French Beef Stew

3 medium potatoes, peeled and cut into
1/2-inch cubes
2 pounds beef stew meat
4 medium carrots, sliced
2 medium onions, sliced
3 celery ribs, sliced
2 cups tomato juice

1 cup water
1/3 cup quick-cooking tapioca
1 tablespoon sugar
1 tablespoon salt
1 teaspoon dried basil
1/2 teaspoon pepper

Place the potatoes in a greased 5-qt. slow cooker. Top with the beef, carrots, onions and celery. in a bowl, combine the remaining ingredients. Pour over the vegetables. Cover and cook on low for 9-10 hours or until vegetables and beef are tender.

285- Delicious Beef Tongue Tacos

1 beef tongue
1/2 white onion, sliced
5 cloves garlic, crushed
1 bay leaf salt to taste
3 tablespoons vegetable oil

5 Roma tomatoes
5 serrano peppers salt to taste
1/2 onion, diced
2 (10 ounce) packages corn tortillas

Place the beef tongue in a slow cooker and cover with water. Add the onion slices, garlic, and bay leaf. Season with salt. Cover and cook on Low overnight or 8 hours. Remove the tongue and shred the meat into strands. Heat the oil in a skillet over medium heat. Cook the tomatoes and peppers in the hot oil until softened on all sides. Remove the tomatoes and peppers in a blender, keeping the oil on the heat; season with salt. Blend briefly until still slightly chunky. Cook the diced onion in the skillet until translucent; stir in the tomato mixture. Cook another

5 to 6 minutes. Build the tacos by placing shredded tongue meat into a tortilla and spooning salsa over the meat.

286- CB's Black Eyed Peas

4 slices bacon, chopped
1 pound dry black-eyed peas
6 cups water
1 onion, chopped

1 (14.5 ounce) can diced tomatoes, undrained
1 jalapeno pepper, finely chopped
1 clove garlic, minced
1 tablespoon chili powder salt to taste

Place the bacon in a large, deep skillet, and cook over medium heat, stirring occasionally, until evenly browned, about 10 minutes. Place the dried peas, water, onion, tomatoes, jalapeno pepper, garlic, and chili powder into a slow cooker, and stir to combine. Stir in the bacon and bacon grease, and set the cooker on High. Cook until peas are tender, about 4 hours. Season to taste with salt, and serve.

287- Italian Beef in a Bucket

3 1/2 pounds rump roast
1 (12 ounce) jar pickled mixed vegetables
1 (16 ounce) jar pepperoncini

1 (.7 ounce) package dry Italian- style salad dressing mix
1 (10.5 ounce) can beef broth

Place the roast in a 3 1/2 quart slow-cooker, and add the pickled mixed vegetables, pepperoncini, Italian dressing mix, and beef broth. Stir to blend, cover, and cook on low for 18 hours (yes, 18 hours - a light timer works well if you don't want to stay up until midnight to turn it on). To serve, remove roast from the slow cooker. If necessary, slice it for sandwiches, but it usually just falls apart. Place the pickled vegetables and pepperoncini in a bowl to serve along with the meat.

288- Slow Cooker Spare Ribs

1 (10.75 ounce) can condensed tomato soup
1 onion, chopped
3 cloves garlic, minced
1 tablespoon brown sugar

1 tablespoon Worcestershire sauce
2 tablespoons soy sauce
2 pounds pork spareribs
1 teaspoon cornstarch (optional)
1/4 cup cold water (optional)

Place ribs in a large stock pot, and cover with water. Bring to a boil, and cook for 15 minutes. In a mixing bowl, mix together soup, onion, garlic, brown sugar, Worcestershire sauce, and soy sauce. Remove ribs from water, and transfer to a slow cooker. Pour sauce over ribs. Cover, and cook on Low for 6 to 8 hours, or until ribs are tender. If sauce is too thin when cooking time is done, drain sauce from ribs, and pour into a sauce pan. Combine 1 teaspoon cornstarch with a small amount of cold water, stir into sauce, and bring sauce to boil. Cook until sauce has reached desired thickness.

289- Slow Cooker Barbequed Pork for Sandwiches

2 1/2 pounds boneless pork roast salt and
ground black pepper to taste
2 cups strong brewed coffee
2 tablespoons Worcestershire sauce
2 tablespoons bourbon whiskey
10 cloves garlic

3 cups beef broth
1 cup water
1 small onion, diced
1 pinch crushed red pepper flakes
2 (12 ounce) bottles barbeque sauce

Season the roast with salt and pepper. Place the seasoned roast, coffee, Worcestershire sauce, bourbon whiskey, garlic, beef broth, water, onion, and red pepper flakes in a slow cooker set to LOW. Cook 3 to 4 hours. Scoop garlic cloves out of the cooker and mash with a fork; return the mashed garlic to the slow cooker. Cook another 3 to 4 hours. Transfer roast to a large cutting board, and discard liquid. Shred the roast into strands using two forks, and return meat to the slow cooker. Stir in the barbeque sauce, and continue cooking on LOW for 1 to 3 hours.

290- Easy Marinated Mushrooms

2 cups soy sauce
2 cups water
1 cup butter

2 cups white sugar
4 (8 ounce) packages fresh mushrooms,
stems removed

In a medium saucepan over low heat, mix soy sauce, water and butter. Stir until the butter has melted, then gradually mix in the sugar until it is completely dissolved. Place mushrooms in a slow cooker set to low, and cover with the soy sauce mixture. Cook 8 to 10 hours, stirring approximately every hour. Chill in the refrigerator until serving.

291- Best Italian Sausage Soup

1 1/2 pounds sweet Italian sausage
2 cloves garlic, minced
2 small onions, chopped
2 (16 ounce) cans whole peeled tomatoes
1 1/4 cups dry red wine
5 cups beef broth
1/2 teaspoon dried basil

1/2 teaspoon dried oregano
2 zucchini, sliced
1 green bell pepper, chopped
3 tablespoons chopped fresh parsley
1 (16 ounce) package spinach fettuccine
pasta
salt and pepper to taste

In a large pot, cook sausage over medium heat until brown. Remove with a slotted spoon, and drain on paper towels. Drain fat from pan, reserving 3 tablespoons. Cook garlic and onion in reserved fat for 2 to 3 minutes. Stir in tomatoes, wine, broth, basil, and oregano. Transfer to a slow cooker, and stir in sausage, zucchini, bell pepper, and parsley. Cover, and cook on Low for 4 to 6 hours. Bring a pot of lightly salted water to a boil. Cook pasta in boiling water until al dente, about 7 minutes. Drain water, and add pasta to the slow cooker. Simmer for a few minutes, and season with salt and pepper before serving.

292- Hot Chicken Sandwiches II

1 (50 ounce) can whole cooked chicken, drained, bones and skin removed
2 (10.75 ounce) cans condensed cream of chicken soup

1 1/8 cups water
1 (8 ounce) package dry bread stuffing mix
6 hamburger buns, split

Shred chicken, and place in a large pot or slow cooker. Stir in soup and water. Stir in the seasoning mix from the stuffing, and then stir in the dry stuffing mix. Cook over medium heat until heated through. Spoon onto buns, and serve.

293- Italian Beef Hoagies

1 (4 pound) boneless sirloin tip roast, halved
2 (.7 ounce) packages Italian salad dressing mix

2 cups water
1 (16 ounce) jar mild pepper rings, undrained
18 hoagie buns, split

Place roast in a 5-qt. slow cooker. Combine the salad dressing mix and water; pour over roast. Cover and cook on low for 8 hours or until meat is tender. Remove meat; shred with a fork and return to slow cooker. Add pepper rings; heat through. Spoon 1/2 cup meat mixture onto each bun.

294- Great-Aunt Nina's Noodles and Chicken

2 carrots, sliced
2 onions, sliced
2 stalks celery, cut into 1 inch pieces
1 (4 pound) whole chicken
1 teaspoon salt
1/2 teaspoon ground black pepper
1/2 cup white wine

1/4 teaspoon dried basil
2 eggs, beaten
1/4 cup water
1 pinch salt
2 tablespoons shortening
1 cup all-purpose flour, or as needed
2 quarts low salt chicken broth

Place the carrots, onions and celery in the bottom of a slow cooker. Place the whole chicken on top of the vegetables and season with salt and pepper. Pour in the white wine and sprinkle basil over the top. Cover and cook on Low setting for 8 to 10 hours. In a medium bowl, stir together the eggs, water, salt, shortening and flour to form a stiff dough. After I've mixed in as much flour as possible using a fork, I knead the dough with my hand in the bowl to incorporate as much flour as possible. Let the dough rest for a few minutes. Roll the dough out on a well-greased board to 1/8 inch thickness. Use a pizza cutter or pie crust cutter to cut into strips about ½ inch wide and 3 inches long. Dust lightly with flour, and leave to dry for a few hours while the chicken cooks. When the chicken is done, remove the meat and vegetables to a platter. Transfer the juices to a large pot and stir in 2 quarts of chicken broth. Bring to a boil and add the noodles. Cook for about 10 minutes, until tender. Meanwhile, remove the meat from the chicken and shred. Discard bones and skin. When the noodles are done, return the vegetables to the pot and add shredded chicken meat. Serve.

295- Gram's Irish Stew

1 teaspoon vegetable oil
4 pounds cubed beef stew meat
2 teaspoons sage
10 potatoes, peeled and cubed
4 carrots, diced
1 (4 ounce) can sliced mushrooms, drained
1 small onion, chopped

1 teaspoon celery seed
1 teaspoon Worcestershire sauce
1 teaspoon ground black pepper
1 cube beef bouillon salt to taste
water to cover
1 tablespoon cornstarch, or as needed
1/4 cup warm water

Heat the oil in a skillet over medium-high heat. Add the beef to the oil and season with the sage; cook the beef until browned on all sides; drain. Place beef, potatoes, carrots, mushrooms, onion, celery seed, Worcestershire sauce, pepper, and beef bouillon in a slow cooker; season with salt. Pour enough water over the mixture to cover. Set slow cooker to HIGH and cover. Cook for 4 to 5 hours, stirring occasionally. Whisk together the cornstarch and warm water in a small bowl until smooth; stir through the stew. Allow the stew to cook until thickened, 15 to 20 minutes.

296- Smoked Paprika Goulash for the Slow Cooker

1 tablespoon vegetable oil
3 onions, sliced
3 cloves garlic, chopped
1/4 cup smoked Spanish paprika
2 teaspoons kosher salt
1 teaspoon coarsely ground black pepper
3 pounds lean beef stew meat, cut into 1-inch cubes

3 tablespoons vegetable oil, divided
1 1/2 cups water
1 (6 ounce) can tomato paste
1 (10 ounce) package egg noodles
1/2 cup sour cream (optional)
8 sprigs fresh parsley (optional)

Heat 1 tablespoon oil in a large skillet over medium-high heat. Cook and stir onions until they soften and begin to brown at the edges, 8 to 10 minutes. Add the garlic and cook for one minute. Transfer mixture to a slow cooker. Cover and set cooker to Low. Mix together paprika, salt, and pepper in a large bowl. Toss the meat cubes in the paprika mixture until evenly coated. Heat one tablespoon of the oil in the skillet over medium-high heat. Put a third of the beef cubes into the skillet and cook until nicely browned on all sides. Transfer to the slow cooker. Pour 2 tablespoons of water into the skillet and scrape the browned bits from the pan; pour liquid into the slow cooker. This prevents the paprika from burning when you brown the next batches of beef. Add another tablespoon of oil to the skillet and cook the next batch the same way; repeat for the third batch. Stir the tomato paste and the rest of the water into the slow cooker; cover. Cook on High for 4 to 5 hours (or on Low for 6 to 9 hours). Fill a large pot with lightly salted water and bring to a rolling boil over high heat. Stir in the egg noodles, and cook uncovered, stirring occasionally, until the noodles have cooked through, but are still firm to the bite, about 5 minutes. Drain. Serve goulash over noodles with a dollop of sour cream and a sprig of parsley.

297- Authentic, No Shortcuts and Louisiana Red Beans

1 pound dried red beans, soaked
overnight
10 cups water
1 pound andouille sausage, sliced into
rounds
1 large sweet onion, chopped
1 green bell pepper, chopped

1 jalapeno pepper, seeded and chopped
(optional)
8 cloves garlic, chopped
1 teaspoon ground black pepper
1 teaspoon Creole seasoning, or to taste
6 fresh basil leaves, chopped
1 ham hock
4 cups cooked rice

Place the beans and water into a slow cooker. Heat a skillet over medium-high heat. Brown
the sausage in the skillet; remove from the skillet with a slotted spoon and transfer to the slow
cooker. Reserve drippings. Add onion, green pepper, jalapeno pepper and garlic to the
drippings; cook and stir until tender, about 5 minutes. Transfer everything from the skillet to
the slow cooker. Season the mixture with pepper and Creole seasoning. Add the fresh basil
leaves and ham hock. Cover and cook on low for about 8 hours, or until beans are tender. If
the bean mixture seems too watery, take the lid off the slow cooker and set heat to High to
cook until they reach a creamy texture.

298- Dynamite

2 pounds ground beef
2 green bell peppers, seeded and diced
1 (1/4 inch x 3 inch) strip red bell pepper,
seeded and diced
1 medium yellow onion, chopped

1 medium red onion, chopped
2 (6 ounce) cans tomato paste
1 1/2 cups water
1 teaspoon red pepper flakes, or to taste
8 torpedo rolls, split

Place the ground beef in a large skillet over medium-high heat. Add the green pepper, red
pepper, yellow onion and red onion to the skillet, and cook until meat is evenly browned and
vegetables are tender. Drain excess grease from the pan. Transfer the mixture to a slow
cooker, and stir in tomato paste, water and red pepper flakes. Cover, and cook at the Low
setting for at least 4 hours. I usually let it go for 12. The longer it simmers, the spicier it gets!
Spoon into torpedo rolls and serve.

299- Stroganoff Soup

1 (16 ounce) package dry egg noodles
1 1/2 pounds round steak, cut into small
pieces
1 small yellow onion, diced

2 (10.75 ounce) cans condensed cream of
mushroom soup
2 2/3 cups water
1 (16 ounce) container sour cream
1 teaspoon steak sauce

Bring a large pot of lightly salted water to a boil. Add egg noodles and cook for 8 to 10
minutes, or until al dente; drain and rinse under hot water. In a slow cooker, combine the
soup, 2 2/3 cup (or 2 soup cans) of water, sour cream and steak sauce. Mix until smooth. Add
cooked steak pieces, onions and cooked noodles. Cook on low for 2 hours, or to desired taste

and consistency. In a large skillet, brown the round steak pieces with the onion to desired doneness.

300- Parmesan Chicken I

6 tablespoons butter
1 (1 ounce) package dry onion soup mix
1 cup converted long-grain white rice
1/4 cup grated Parmesan cheese for topping
6 skinless, boneless chicken breasts

1 1/2 cups milk
2 (10.75 ounce) cans condensed cream of mushroom soup
salt to taste
ground black pepper to taste

Mix together onion soup mix, milk, cream of mushroom soup, and rice in a medium bowl. Lay chicken breasts in the bottom of a lightly greased slow cooker. Place one tablespoon margarine on each chicken breast and pour soup mixture over all. Season with salt and pepper to taste and sprinkle with grated Parmesan cheese. Cook on Low for 8 to 10 hours, or on High for 4 to 6 hours.

301- Slow Cooker Potato Broccoli Soup

4 potatoes, peeled and cubed
2 potatoes, peeled and diced
1 head broccoli, diced
1 onion, minced
7 cups milk

2 tablespoons garlic powder
2 tablespoons minced fresh chives
2 cups instant potato flakes
1/4 cup dry bread crumbs

Combine the cubed potatoes, diced potatoes, broccoli, onion, milk, garlic powder, and chives in a slow cooker; cover, and cook on High for 4 hours. Stir the instant potato flakes and bread crumbs into the soup. Reduce heat to Low and simmer another 30 minutes. Serve hot.

302- Green Chile Beef Tacos

5 pounds boneless beef chuck roast
1 (1 ounce) packet taco seasoning mix

1 (16 ounce) jar green salsa
2 cups beef broth, or more if needed

Lay the chuck roast into the bottom of a slow cooker with a tight- fitting lid. Sprinkle the taco seasoning mix over the beef. Pour the green salsa over the beef, followed by the beef broth. Cook on Low for 4 hours. Add more beef broth if needed. Remove the beef from the slow cooker and shred with two forks. Return the shredded beef to the slow cooker; mix with the liquid. Serve hot.

303- Slow Cooker Sausage Florentine

1 pound Bob Evans® Original/Regular Recipe Sausage Roll
1 (10 ounce) package frozen chopped spinach, thawed and squeezed dry

1 (8 ounce) can sliced mushrooms, drained
6 eggs
3/4 cup milk

1/2 cup shredded Cheddar cheese

Spray interior of slow cooker with non-stick vegetable spray. In medium skillet over medium heat, crumble and cook sausage until brown. Place sausage in slow cooker. Add spinach and mushrooms. Stir to combine. In small bowl, beat eggs and milk until mixed. Pour over sausage mixture. Cover and cook on low 4 to 6 hours. Five minutes before serving, top with Cheddar cheese. Recover to melt cheese.

304- Slow-Cooked Round Steak

1/4 cup all-purpose flour
1/2 teaspoon salt
1/8 teaspoon pepper
2 pounds beef round steak, cut into serving-size pieces
6 teaspoons vegetable oil, divided

1 medium onion, thinly sliced
1 (10.75 ounce) can condensed cream of mushroom soup, undiluted
1/2 teaspoon dried oregano
1/4 teaspoon dried thyme

In a large resealable plastic bag, combine the flour, salt and pepper. Add beef, a few pieces at a time, and shake to coat. In a large skillet, brown meat on both sides in 4 teaspoons oil. Place in a 5-qt. slow cooker. In the same skillet, saute onion in remaining oil until lightly browned; place over beef. Combine the soup, oregano and thyme; pour over onion. Cover and cook on low for 7-8 hours or until meat is tender.

305- Tex-Mex Pork

1 (8 ounce) can tomato sauce
1 cup barbeque sauce
1 onion, chopped
2 (4 ounce) cans diced green chile peppers
1/4 cup chili powder

1 teaspoon ground cumin
1 teaspoon dried oregano
1/4 teaspoon ground cinnamon
2 1/2 pounds boneless pork loin roast, trimmed
1/2 cup chopped fresh cilantro

In a 3 quart or larger slow cooker, mix tomato sauce, barbeque sauce, onion, green chile peppers, chili powder, cumin, oregano, and cinnamon. Place pork in slow cooker, and spoon sauce over to coat. the meat. Cover, and cook on Low 8 to 10 hours, or until pork is tender. Remove pork to a cutting board. Using 2 forks, pull meat into shreds. Pour sauce into a serving dish; stir in cilantro and shredded pork.

306- Slow Cooker Collard Greens

4 bunches collard greens - rinsed, trimmed and chopped
1 pound ham shanks
4 pickled jalapeno peppers, chopped

1/2 teaspoon baking soda
1 teaspoon olive oil
ground black pepper to taste garlic powder to taste

Fill a large pot about 1/2 full with water. Place the ham shanks into the water, and as many of the greens as you can fit. Bring to a gentle boil. As soon as the greens begin wilting, start transferring the greens to the slow cooker. Alternate layers of greens with the ham shanks and jalapeno until the slow cooker is full. Stir in the baking soda, olive oil, pepper and garlic powder. Cover, and bring to a boil on High. Reduce heat to Low, and cook for 8 to 10 hours.

307- Slow Cooker Scalloped Potatoes with Ham

3 pounds potatoes, peeled and thinly sliced
1 cup shredded Cheddar cheese
1/2 cup chopped onion
1 cup chopped cooked ham

1 (10.75 ounce) can condensed cream of mushroom soup
1/2 cup water
1/2 teaspoon garlic powder
1/4 teaspoon salt
1/4 teaspoon black pepper

Place sliced potatoes in slow cooker. In a medium bowl, mix together shredded cheese, onion and ham. Mix with potatoes in slow cooker. Using the same bowl, mix together condensed soup and water. Season to taste with garlic powder, salt and pepper. Pour evenly over the potato mixture. Cover, and cook on High for 4 hours.

308- Slow Cooker Maple Country Style Ribs

1 1/2 pounds country style pork ribs
1 tablespoon maple syrup
1 tablespoon soy sauce
2 tablespoons dried minced onion
1/4 teaspoon ground cinnamon

1/4 teaspoon ground ginger
1/4 teaspoon ground allspice
1/2 teaspoon garlic powder
1 dash ground black pepper

Combine ribs, maple syrup, soy sauce, minced onion, cinnamon, ginger, allspice, garlic powder and pepper in a slow cooker. Cover and cook on Low for 7 to 9 hours.

309- Sausage Barley Soup

1 pound Italian sausage
1/2 cup diced onion
1 tablespoon minced garlic
1/2 teaspoon Italian seasoning
1 (48 fluid ounce) can chicken broth

1 large carrot, sliced
1 (10 ounce) package frozen chopped spinach
1/4 cup uncooked pearl barley

In a skillet over medium heat, cook the sausage, onion, and garlic until the sausage is evenly brown. Season with Italian seasoning. Remove from heat, and drain. In a slow cooker, mix the sausage mixture, chicken broth, carrot, spinach, and barley. Cover, and cook 4 hours on High or 6 to 8 hours on Low.

310- Montigott

2 (10.75 ounce) cans condensed tomato soup
2 (15 ounce) cans tomato sauce

2 (6 ounce) cans tomato paste
1 pound turkey sweet Italian sausages, casings removed

1 pound turkey hot Italian sausages,
casings removed
1 1/2 (16 ounce) packages mostaccioli
pasta

1/2 cup milk
2 (16 ounce) packages shredded
mozzarella cheese

Pour the tomato soup, tomato sauce and tomato paste into a slow cooker, and stir to blend. Crumble in the sweet and hot Italian sausages. Cover, and cook on low for 4 to 6 hours, stirring occasionally until the meat is cooked through, and the sauce is flavorful. When the tomato sauce is almost done, bring a large pot of lightly salted water to a boil. Add the mostaccoli pasta, and cook for 8 to 10 minutes, until tender. Drain and rinse. Preheat the oven to 375 degrees F (190 degrees C). Coat a 9x13 inch baking dish and an 8x8 inch baking dish with cooking spray. Layer the noodles and cheese in the two dishes to an even depth ending with cheese on the top, splash a little bit of the milk over each layer of cheese as you go except for the top layer. Bake for 15 minutes, or until cheese is melted and a little brown on the top. Cut into wedges, and spoon the sauce over them to serve.

311- Campbell's® Golden Chicken with Noodles

2 (10.75 ounce) cans Campbell's®
Condensed Cream of Chicken Soup
(Regular or 98% Fat Free)
1/2 cup water
1/4 cup lemon juice
1 tablespoon Dijon-style mustard

1 1/2 teaspoons garlic powder
8 large carrots, thickly sliced
8 skinless, boneless chicken breast halves
4 cups hot cooked egg noodles
Chopped fresh parsley

Stir the soup, water, lemon juice, mustard, garlic powder and carrots in a 3 1/2-quart slow cooker. Add the chicken and turn to coat. Cover and cook on LOW for 7 to 8 hours* or until the chicken is cooked through. Serve with the noodles. Sprinkle with the parsley.

312- Slow Cooker Beef Au Jus

3 pounds boneless beef rump roast
1 large onion, sliced
3/4 cup reduced-sodium beef broth

1 (1 ounce) package au jus gravy mix
2 cloves garlic, halved
1/4 teaspoon pepper

Cut roast in half. In a large nonstick skillet coated with nonstick cooking spray, brown meat on all sides over medium-high heat. Place onion in a 5-qt. slow cooker. Top with meat. Combine the broth, gravy mix, garlic and pepper; pour over meat. Cover and cook on low for 6-7 hours or until meat and onion are tender. Remove meat to a cutting board. Let stand for 10 minutes. Thinly slice meat and return to the slow cooker; serve with pan juices and onion.

313- Hot Buttered Apple Cider

1 (16 ounce) bottle apple cider
1/2 cup pure maple syrup
1/2 cup butter, softened
1/2 teaspoon ground nutmeg

1/2 teaspoon ground allspice
In slow cooker over low heat, cook apple
cider with maple syrup for
20 minutes or until steaming hot.

In a small bowl, combine butter, nutmeg and allspice. Mix well. Pour cider into mugs and top with a teaspoon of spice butter.

314- Slow Cooker Beef and Mushrooms

1 1/2 pounds cubed beef stew meat
1 (10.75 ounce) can condensed golden mushroom soup
1 (4.5 ounce) can sliced mushrooms, undrained

1 (1 ounce) package dry onion soup mix
1/4 cup red wine (optional)
1 pinch black pepper to taste
1 cup uncooked white rice
2 cups water

Combine the stew meat, mushroom soup, mushrooms with their liquid, and onion soup mix in the crock of a slow cooker. Pour in red wine, if desired. Season with pepper. Cook on Low for 8 to 10 hours, or on High for 4 to 6 hours. In the last half hour of cooking time, bring the rice and water to a boil in a saucepan over high heat. Reduce heat to medium-low, cover, and simmer until the rice is tender, and the liquid has been absorbed, 20 to 25 minutes.

315- Tender Barbecued Chicken

1 broiler/fryer chicken (3 to 4 pounds), cut up
1 medium onion, thinly sliced

1 medium lemon, thinly sliced
1 (18 ounce) bottle barbeque sauce*
3/4 cup regular cola

Place chicken in a slow cooker. Top with onion and lemon slices. Combine barbecue sauce and cola; pour over all. Cover and cook on low for 8-10 hours or until chicken juices run clear.

316- Classic Chulent

1/2 pound cubed beef brisket
6 potatoes, diced
1/4 cup dry kidney beans
1/2 cup barley
1 onion, chopped
2 cloves garlic, minced
2 tablespoons honey

1 tablespoon ketchup
1 tablespoon barbeque sauce
1 tablespoon soy sauce
1 tablespoon onion soup mix
1 tablespoon salt
1/4 teaspoon ground black pepper
1/2 teaspoon paprika

Combine the beef brisket, potatoes, kidney beans, barley, onion, garlic, honey, ketchup, barbeque sauce, soy sauce, onion soup mix, salt, pepper, and paprika in a 6-quart slow cooker. Cook on High for 1 hour. Then, turn to Low and continue cooking for another 7 hours.

317- Harvest Apple Cider

8 whole cloves
4 cups apple cider
4 cups pineapple juice

1/2 cup water
1 (3 inch) cinnamon stick
1 tea bag

Place cloves on a double thickness of cheesecloth; bring up corners of cloth and tie with kitchen string to form a bag. Place the remaining ingredients in a slow cooker; add spice bag. Cover and cook on low for 2 hours or until cider reaches desired temperature. Discard spice bag, cinnamon stick and tea bag before serving.

318- Slow Cooker Creamy Potato Soup

6 slices bacon, cut into 1/2 inch pieces
1 onion, finely chopped
2 (10.5 ounce) cans condensed chicken broth
2 cups water
5 large potatoes, diced

1/2 teaspoon salt
1/2 teaspoon dried dill weed
1/2 teaspoon ground white pepper
1/2 cup all-purpose flour
2 cups half-and-half cream
1 (12 fluid ounce) can evaporated milk

Place bacon and onion in a large, deep skillet. Cook over medium- high heat until bacon is evenly brown and onions are soft. Drain off excess grease. Transfer the bacon and onion to a slow cooker, and stir in chicken broth, water, potatoes, salt, dill weed, and white pepper. Cover, and cook on Low 6 to 7 hours, stirring occasionally. In a small bowl, whisk together the flour and half-and-half. Stir into the soup along with the evaporated milk. Cover, and cook another 30 minutes before serving.

319- German Lentil Soup

2 cups dried brown lentils, rinsed and drained
3 cups chicken stock
1 bay leaf
1 cup chopped carrots
1 cup chopped celery
1 cup chopped onion
1 cup cooked, cubed ham

1 teaspoon Worcestershire sauce
1/2 teaspoon garlic powder
1/4 teaspoon freshly grated nutmeg
5 drops hot pepper sauce
1/4 teaspoon caraway seed
1/2 teaspoon celery salt
1 tablespoon chopped fresh parsley
1/2 teaspoon ground black pepper

Place lentils in a 5 to 6 quart slow cooker. Add chicken stock, bay leaf, carrots, celery, onion, and ham. Season with Worcestershire sauce, garlic powder, nutmeg, hot pepper sauce, caraway seed, celery salt, parsley, and pepper. Cover, and cook on Low for 8 to 10 hours. Remove bay leaf before serving.

320- Slow Cooker Orange Chicken

1 pound skinless, boneless chicken breast halves
12 fluid ounces orange-flavored carbonated beverage

1/2 cup soy sauce
1 cup uncooked long grain white rice
2 cups water

Place the chicken in a slow cooker, and pour in the orange-flavored carbonated beverage and soy sauce. Cover slow cooker, and cook chicken on Low 5 to 6 hours. In a saucepan, bring the rice and water to a boil. Reduce heat to low, cover, and simmer 20 minutes. Serve cooked chicken over the rice.

321- Buffet Meatballs

1 cup grape juice
1 cup apple jelly
1 cup ketchup

1 (8 ounce) can tomato sauce
4 pounds frozen Italian meatballs

In a small saucepan, combine the juice, jelly, ketchup and tomato sauce. Cook and stir over medium heat until jelly is melted; remove from the heat. Place meatballs in a 5-qt. slow cooker. Pour sauce over the top and gently stir to coat. Cover and cook on low for 4 hours or until heated through.

322- Manhattan Clam Chowder

3 celery ribs, sliced
1 large onion, chopped
1 (14.5 ounce) can sliced potatoes, drained
1 (14.5 ounce) can sliced carrots, drained
2 (6.5 ounce) cans chopped clams
2 cups tomato juice

1 1/2 cups water
1/2 cup tomato puree
1 tablespoon dried parsley flakes
1 1/2 teaspoons dried thyme
1 teaspoon salt
1 bay leaf
2 whole black peppercorns

In a slow cooker, combine all ingredients; stir. Cover and cook on low for 8-10 hours or until the vegetables are tender. Remove bay leaf and peppercorns before serving.

323- Cola Beans

4 (28 ounce) cans baked beans, drained
1/2 pound bacon
1 cup brown sugar

1 (12 fluid ounce) can cola- flavored carbonated beverage

In a slow cooker, alternately layer the baked beans, bacon, and brown sugar. Pour in some of the cola with each layer, until all has been used. Cover, and cook 8 to 10 hours on Low or 4 to 6 hours on High.

324- Slow Cooker Borscht

1 pound beef stew meat, cut into
1/2 inch pieces
4 beets, peeled and chopped
1 (28 ounce) can diced tomatoes
2 potatoes, peeled and chopped
1 cup baby carrots, cut into 1/2 inch pieces

1 onion, chopped
3 cloves garlic, minced
2 cups beef broth, or more
1 (6 ounce) can tomato paste
6 tablespoons red wine vinegar
3 tablespoons brown sugar
1 1/2 teaspoons dried dill weed

1 tablespoon dried parsley
1 bay leaf
1 teaspoon salt

1/2 teaspoon ground black pepper
3 cups shredded green cabbage
1 cup sour cream, as garnish

Place beef, beets, tomatoes, potatoes, carrots, onion, and garlic in a slow cooker. Whisk together the beef broth, tomato paste, vinegar, brown sugar, dill weed, parsley, bay leaf, salt, and pepper. Pour mixture over the beef and vegetables, adding more broth to cover as needed. Cover and cook on Low for 8 1/2 hours, or High for 4 hours. Set heat to High, then stir in the shredded cabbage. Cover and continue cooking until the cabbage tender, about 30 minutes. Remove bay leaf. Serve in a bowl with a dollop of sour cream.

325- Patsy's Best Barbeque Beef

1 bunch celery, chopped
3 large onions, chopped
1 medium green bell pepper, chopped
1 1/4 cups ketchup
1/2 cup water
3 tablespoons barbeque sauce
3 tablespoons cider vinegar

1/8 teaspoon hot pepper sauce
2 teaspoons chili powder
2 tablespoons salt
1 teaspoon pepper
6 pounds boneless beef chuck roast, trimmed and chopped

In a large bowl, mix the celery, onions, green pepper, ketchup, water, barbeque sauce, vinegar, and hot pepper sauce. Season with chili powder, salt, and pepper. Place the roast in a slow cooker, and cover with the sauce mixture. Cover, and cook on Low for approximately 12 hours. Shred the meat with a fork. Increase cooking temperature to High, and continue cooking until most of the liquid has been reduced.

326- Egg Noodle Lasagna

6 1/2 cups uncooked wide egg noodles
3 tablespoons butter
1 1/2 pounds ground beef
2 1/4 cups spaghetti sauce
6 ounces process cheese (eg. Velveeta), cubed

3 cups shredded mozzarella cheese
Cook noodles according to package directions; drain. Add butter; toss to coat.

In a large skillet, cook beef over medium heat until no longer pink; drain. Spread a fourth of the spaghetti sauce into an ungreased 5- qt. slow cooker. Layer with a third of the noodles, a third of the beef, a third of the remaining sauce and a third of the cheeses. Repeat layers twice. Cover and cook on low for 4 hours or until cheese is melted and lasagna is heated through.

327- Middle Eastern White Beans

1 1/2 cups dried white kidney beans, soaked overnight
3 tablespoons tomato paste
1 tablespoon red pimento sauce

3 cloves garlic, chopped
3 medium onions, chopped
1 tablespoon lemon juice
1 teaspoon ground cumin

2 tablespoons olive oil salt and pepper to taste

1 (14.5 ounce) can beef broth

In a slow cooker combine the beans, tomato paste, pimento sauce, garlic, onions, cumin, lemon juice, olive oil, salt and pepper. Mix until the beans are coated. Pour in beef broth, and top off with enough water to completely cover the beans. Cover, and cook on High for 6 hours, or until the beans are tender and the liquid is thickened. It should not be soupy.

328- Slow Cooker Corned Beef-Style Brisket

1 small onion, minced
3 cloves garlic, minced
1/2 cup Dijon mustard
2 tablespoons apple cider vinegar
3 bay leaves, crumbled
8 whole black peppercorns, crushed
1 tablespoon pickling salt

1 teaspoon chopped fresh parsley
1 teaspoon celery seed
1 (4 pound) beef brisket
1 cup water
4 carrots, peeled and cut into 1- inch chunks
1/2 small head cabbage, sliced into strips

Stir together the onion, garlic, mustard, vinegar, bay leaves, peppercorns, salt, parsley, and celery seed in a bowl. Cover, and refrigerate for 24 hours. Rub the brisket with the mixture, wrap tightly, and refrigerate overnight. To cook the brisket, place it into a slow cooker along with the water. Cover, and cook on low for 5 hours. Add the carrots, and cabbage, and continue cooking until the brisket is tender, about 3 hours more.

329- Lauren's Cincinnati Chili

2 pounds extra lean ground beef
2 onions, finely chopped
1 quart water
4 cloves garlic, minced
1 teaspoon ground cumin
2 teaspoons ground cinnamon
1 1/2 teaspoons ground allspice
1 1/2 teaspoons ground cloves

1 1/2 teaspoons salt
2 teaspoons black pepper
1/2 teaspoon cayenne pepper
2 tablespoons apple cider vinegar
1 tablespoon Worcestershire sauce
2 bay leaves
1 (15 ounce) can tomato sauce
1/2 ounce unsweetened baking chocolate

Cook the beef and onion in a large skillet over medium high heat, breaking up beef into tiny pieces, just until meat is no longer pink. Drain and place in a large Dutch oven or slow cooker. Stir in the water, garlic, cumin, cinnamon, allspice, cloves, salt, pepper, cayenne pepper, cider vinegar, Worcestershire sauce, bay leaves, tomato sauce, and chocolate. Simmer over medium low heat for 3 to 5 hours.

330- Super Bowl Salsa Dip

1 (2 pound) loaf processed cheese, cubed
1 cup milk
1 (12 ounce) package ground pork sausage

1 white onion, chopped
1 (24 ounce) jar medium salsa
1/2 (15 ounce) can black beans, drained and rinsed

1 bunch green onions, chopped · 1 (12 ounce) package tortilla chips

In a slow cooker set to high heat, place the processed cheese and milk. Cover and, stirring occasionally, cook until the cheese has melted and is well blended with the milk. Place ground pork sausage in a medium skillet. Cook over medium high heat until evenly brown. Mix in white onion. Cook and stir until onion is translucent. Remove from heat and drain. Stir sausage mixture into the cheese mixture. Reduce heat to low. Mix in salsa and black beans. Continue cooking, stirring occasionally, approximately 1 hour. Garnish with green onions and serve with tortilla chips.

331- Southwest Style Creamy Corn Chowder

1/4 cup white sugar · 1 cup chicken broth
4 cups fresh corn kernels · 2 stalks celery, thinly sliced
1 (8 ounce) package cream cheese · 1 tablespoon minced garlic
1/2 cup shredded Mexican cheese blend · 2 slices bacon, cut into 1 inch pieces
1/2 cup 2% low-fat milk · 2 tablespoons ground black pepper

Place sugar, corn, cream cheese, Mexican cheese, milk, chicken broth, celery, garlic, bacon, and pepper into a slow cooker. Cook on High for 1 hour, then reduce heat to Low and cook for an additional 2 1/2 hours.

332- Sweet Pork for Burritos

3 pounds pork shoulder roast · 2 cups brown sugar
2 cups salsa · 1/2 (1.27 ounce) packet fajita seasoning
1 (12 fluid ounce) can or bottle cola- · 2 tablespoons taco seasoning mix
flavored carbonated beverage · 1 (7 ounce) can chopped green chilies

Place pork roast in the crock of a slow cooker, and add 4 cups water. Cook on High for 5 hours. Remove pork from the slow cooker and drain liquid. Cut the pork into 4 pieces, and set aside. Puree salsa in blender. Combine the pureed salsa, cola, brown sugar, fajita seasoning, taco seasoning, and green chilies in the crock of the slow cooker. Add the pork, and cook on High for an additional 3 hours. Remove the pork, and shred with 2 forks. Serve.

333- Spanish Chicken

2 pounds boneless chicken thighs · 5 large green bell peppers, cut into 2 inch
1 quart boiling water · pieces
1/2 teaspoon salt · 1 (8 ounce) jar chili sauce
5 onions, cut into 2 inch pieces · 1 (15 ounce) can tomato sauce
· 1 cup ketchup

Place chicken in a large slow cooker. Pour in enough boiling water to completely cover the chicken, and add 1/2 teaspoon salt. Cover, and set slow cooker to HIGH. Cook until the chicken meat turns white. Add the peppers and onions. Simmer until peppers and onions get a little tender, about 10 minutes. Stir in tomato sauce, chili sauce, and ketchup. Cover, set slow cooker to LOW, and cook for about 6 hours.

334- Roast Beef Hash Casserole

1 pound boneless beef roast
2 cups water
3 drops Worcestershire sauce
2 cups milk
1 (10.75 ounce) can condensed cream of chicken soup
1/2 cup shredded Cheddar cheese

2 cups frozen hash brown potatoes
1 tablespoon curry powder
1 tablespoon salt
1 teaspoon garlic powder
1 teaspoon seasoned salt
1/4 teaspoon paprika
1 pinch ground black pepper

Place the beef roast in a slow cooker with water and Worcestershire sauce. Cover, and cook 6 to 7 hours on Low. Remove beef from slow cooker, and shred. Preheat oven to 375 degrees F (190 degrees C). Mix milk and soup in a saucepan, and bring to a boil. Stir Cheddar cheese into the mixture until melted. Remove from heat, and mix in shredded beef and hash browns. Season with curry powder, salt, garlic powder, seasoned salt, paprika, and pepper. Transfer to a casserole dish. Bake 35 minutes in the preheated oven. Let stand 5 minutes before serving.

335- Brown Sugar Spice Cake

vegetable cooking spray
1 (10.75 ounce) can Campbell's®
Condensed Tomato Soup (Regular orB
Healthy Request®)
1/2 cup water
2 eggs

1 (18.25 ounce) package spice cake mix
1 1/4 cups hot water
3/4 cup packed brown sugar
1 teaspoon ground cinnamon vanilla ice cream

Spray the inside of a 4-quart slow cooker with the cooking spray. Combine the soup, water, eggs and cake mix in a medium bowl and mix according to the package directions. Pour the batter into the cooker. Stir the water, brown sugar and cinnamon in a small bowl. Pour over the batter. Cover and cook on HIGH for 2 hours or until a knife inserted in the center comes out clean. Spoon the cake into bowls, spooning the sauce from the bottom of the cooker. Serve warm with the ice cream.

336- Slow Cooker Squirrel and Veggies

1 onion, cut into chunks
2 cups baby carrots
4 large potatoes, cut into small chunks
1 large green bell pepper, cut into chunks
2 cloves garlic

4 cubes chicken bouillon salt and pepper to taste
3 squirrels - skinned, gutted, and cut into pieces
water to cover
2 tablespoons flour

Place the onion, carrots, potatoes, bell pepper, garlic, chicken bouillon, salt, and pepper in a slow cooker. Lay the squirrel meat on top of the vegetable mixture. Pour enough water over the mixture to cover completely. Cover and cook on HIGH 6 hours. Stir the flour into the mixture and cook another 2 hours.

337- Sausage Pepper Sandwiches

5 (4 ounce) links Italian sausage
1 medium green pepper, cut into
1-inch pieces
1 large onion, cut into 1 inch pieces

1 (8 ounce) can tomato sauce
1/8 teaspoon pepper
6 hoagie or submarine sandwich buns, split

In a large skillet, brown sausage links over medium heat. Cut into 1/2-inch slices; place in a slow cooker. Stir in the peppers, onion, tomato sauce and pepper. Cover and cook on low for 8 hours or until sausage is no longer pink and vegetables are tender. Use a slotted spoon to serve on buns.

338- Slow Cooker Chili II

1 pound ground beef
3/4 cup diced onion
3/4 cup diced celery
3/4 cup diced green bell pepper
2 cloves garlic, minced
2 (10.75 ounce) cans tomato puree
1 (15 ounce) can kidney beans with
liquid
1 (15 ounce) can kidney beans, drained

1 (15 ounce) can cannellini beans with
liquid
1/2 tablespoon chili powder
1/2 teaspoon dried parsley
1 teaspoon salt
3/4 teaspoon dried basil
3/4 teaspoon dried oregano
1/4 teaspoon ground black pepper
1/8 teaspoon hot pepper sauce

Place the beef in a skillet over medium heat, and cook until evenly brown. Drain grease. Place the beef in a slow cooker, and mix in onion, celery, green bell pepper, garlic, tomato puree, kidney beans, and cannellini beans. Season with chili powder, parsley, salt, basil, oregano, black pepper, and hot pepper sauce. Cover, and cook 8 hours on Low.

339- Slow Cooker Apple Butter

12 pounds Golden Delicious apples -
peeled, cored and sliced
1/2 cup apple cider vinegar
3 cups white sugar

1 cup brown sugar
1 tablespoon ground cinnamon
1/4 teaspoon ground cloves
1 teaspoon ground allspice

Place apples and vinegar into a large slow cooker, and place lid on top. Set on High, and cook for 8 hours, then turn to Low, and continue cooking 10 hours more. After 18 hours, stir in white sugar, brown sugar, cinnamon, clove, and allspice, and cook 4 hours more.

340- Fragrant Lemon Chicken

1 apple - peeled, cored and quartered
1 stalk celery with leaves, chopped

1 (3 pound) whole chicken salt to taste
ground black pepper to taste

1 onion, chopped
1/2 teaspoon dried rosemary, crushed

1 lemon, zested and juiced
1 cup hot water

Rub salt and pepper into the skin of the chicken, and then place apple and celery inside the chicken. Place chicken in slow cooker. Sprinkle chopped onion, rosemary, and lemon juice and zest over chicken. Pour 1 cup hot water into the slow cooker. Cover, and cook on High for 1 hour. Switch to Low, and cook for 6 to 8 hours, basting several times.

341- Hearty Wild Rice

1 pound ground beef
1/2 pound bulk pork sausage
6 celery ribs, diced
2 (10.5 ounce) cans condensed beef broth, undiluted
1 1/4 cups water

1 medium onion, chopped
1 cup uncooked wild rice
1 (4 ounce) can mushroom stems and pieces, drained
1/4 cup soy sauce

In a large skillet, cook beef and sausage over medium heat until no longer pink; drain. Transfer to a 5-qt. slow cooker. Add the celery, broth, water, onion, rice, mushrooms and soy sauce; mix well. Cover and cook on high for 1 hour. Reduce heat to low; cover and cook for 4 hours or until the rice is tender.

342- Hot Crab Dip II

1/2 cup milk
1/3 cup salsa
3 (8 ounce) packages cream cheese

1 pound imitation crabmeat, flaked
1 cup chopped green onions
1 (4 ounce) can diced green chiles

In a small bowl, combine milk and salsa. Coat a slow cooker with non-stick cooking spray. Transfer the milk and salsa mixture into the slow cooker. Stir in cream cheese, crab, onions, and chilies. Cover and cook on low for 3 to 4 hours, stirring every 30 minutes.

343- Mensaf (Jordanian Lamb Stew)

4 tablespoons olive oil
2 pounds boneless lamb shoulder, cut into 2 inch pieces
8 cups water

2 cups uncooked white rice
1/4 cup pine nuts
6 pita bread rounds
1 cup salted goat's milk (jameed el-kasih)

Place 1 tablespoon olive oil into a pressure cooker over medium- high heat. Add the lamb and cook until evenly browned on all sides. Remove the lamb. Add cooking rack; place lamb on rack. Pour in 4 cups water. Close cover securely; place pressure regulator on vent pipe. Bring cooker to full pressure over high heat. Reduce heat to medium-high; cook for 40 minutes. (Pressure regulator should maintain a slow steady rocking motion; adjust heat if needed.) Remove pressure cooker from heat, and allow pressure to drop on its own. Remove lamb, separate meat from bones, and keep warm. Discard bones. Pour pan broth into a bowl, and set aside. Meanwhile, place remaining four cups water, 1 tablespoon olive oil, and rice into a saucepan; bring to a boil over medium-high heat. Stir, reduce heat, cover, and simmer until all moisture is absorbed, about 20 minutes. Place remaining 2 tablespoons olive oil into a skillet over medium heat. Stir in the pine nuts; cook and stir until deep brown, about 5 minutes. Pour 2 cups of the reserved broth into a large pan. Pour in the goat's milk. Add the lamb to the milk mixture. Simmer over medium heat allowing the lamb to absorb some of the liquid, about 30 minutes. To serve, arrange the pita bread over the bottom of a large platter. Spoon rice over the bread. Place the lamb on top of the rice, and drizzle with any remaining milk mixture. Sprinkle pine nuts over the top.

344- Beef Barley Lentil Soup

1 pound lean ground beef
1 medium onion, chopped
2 cups cubed red potatoes (1/4 inch pieces)
1 cup chopped celery
1 cup diced carrots
1 cup dry lentils, rinsed

1/2 cup medium pearl barley
8 cups water
2 teaspoons beef bouillon granules
1 teaspoon salt
1/2 teaspoon lemon-pepper seasoning
2 (14.5 ounce) cans stewed tomatoes

In a nonstick skillet, cook beef and onion over medium heat until meat is no longer pink; drain. Transfer to a 5-qt. slow cooker. Layer with the potatoes, celery, carrots, lentils and barley. Combine the water, bouillon, salt and lemon-pepper; pour over vegetables. Cover and cook on low for 6 hours or until vegetables and barley are tender. Add the tomatoes; cook 2 hours longer.

345- Budget-Friendly Hearty Winter Soup

2 sweet potatoes, peeled and chopped
1/2 head cabbage, coarsely chopped
1 cup chopped carrots
1 pound turkey bratwurst, sliced
1/2 teaspoon salt

1/2 teaspoon dried thyme
1/2 teaspoon dried rosemary
1/2 teaspoon ground white pepper
1/2 cup dry white wine
3 cups chicken broth

Place the sweet potatoes, cabbage, and carrots into a slow cooker, then place the bratwurst slices on top of the vegetables. Sprinkle with the salt, thyme, rosemary, and pepper. Pour the wine and chicken broth over the vegetables. Cook on Low until the sweet potatoes are easily pierced with a fork, 5 to 6 hours.

346- Smoky Bean Stew

1 (16 ounce) package miniature smoked sausage links
1 (16 ounce) can baked beans
2 cups frozen cut green beans
2 cups frozen lima beans
1/2 cup packed brown sugar

1/2 cup thinly sliced fresh carrots
1/2 cup chopped onion
1/2 cup ketchup
1 tablespoon cider vinegar
1 teaspoon prepared mustard

In a 3-qt. slow cooker, combine all ingredients. cover and cook on high for 4-5 hours or until vegetables are tender.

347- Easy Slow Cooker Pork Chops

4 (1 inch thick) pork chops
1 tablespoon vegetable oil
1 cup sliced onions
2 tablespoons chicken soup base

1 (20 ounce) can apple pie filling
2 large sweet potatoes, peeled and cut into large chunks

In a large skillet, heat oil over medium-high heat. Season pork chops with salt and pepper, and then brown them in the hot skillet. Remove from heat. Spray the inside surface of a slow cooker with cooking spray. Arrange sliced onions in the bottom, and place pork chops on top of onions. Sprinkle with chicken base, and top with apple pie filling. Cook on Low for 5 to 6 hours, adding sweet potatoes during the last 1 1/2 hours of cooking.

348- Easy Slow Cooker Chicken

4 skinless, boneless chicken breast halves
1 (10.75 ounce) can condensed cream of chicken soup
1 (10.75 ounce) can condensed cream of mushroom soup

1 (10.75 ounce) can condensed cream of celery soup
1 cup white rice

Cut chicken breasts into large chunks. Place the chicken breasts, cream of chicken soup, cream of mushroom soup, cream of celery soup and the rice in a slow cooker. Cook on high for 3 hours or low for 4 hours.

349- Outrageous Warm Chicken Nacho Dip

1 (14 ounce) can diced tomatoes with green chile peppers (such as RO*TEL®), drained
1 (1 pound) loaf processed cheese food (such as Velveeta®), cubed
2 large cooked skinless, boneless chicken breast halves, shredded

1/3 cup sour cream
1/4 cup diced green onion
1 1/2 tablespoons taco seasoning mix
2 tablespoons minced jalapeno pepper, or to taste (optional)
1 cup black beans, rinsed and drained

Place the diced tomatoes, processed cheese, chicken meat, sour cream, green onion, taco seasoning, and jalapeno pepper into a slow cooker. Cook on High, stirring occasionally until the cheese has melted and the dip is hot, 1 to 2 hours. Stir in the black beans, and cook 15 more minutes to reheat.

350- Creamy Bratwurst Stew

4 medium potatoes, cubed
2 medium carrots, coarsely chopped

2 celery ribs, chopped
1 cup chopped onion

3/4 cup chopped green pepper
2 pounds fresh bratwurst links, cut into
1-inch slices
1/2 cup chicken broth
1 teaspoon salt

1 teaspoon dried basil
1/2 teaspoon pepper
2 cups half-and-half cream
3 tablespoons cornstarch
1 tablespoon cold water

In a 5-qt. slow cooker, combine the potatoes; carrots, celery, onion and green pepper. Top with bratwurst slices. Combine the broth, salt, basil and pepper; pour over top. Cover and cook on low for 7 hours or until vegetables are tender and sausage is no longer pink. Stir in cream. Combine cornstarch and water until smooth; stir into stew. Cover and cook on high for 30 minutes or until gravy is thickened.

351- Slow-Cooked Orange Chicken

1 (3 pound) broiler-fryer chicken, cut up
and skin removed
3 cups orange juice
1 cup chopped celery
1 cup chopped green pepper
1 (4 ounce) can mushroom stems and
pieces, drained

4 teaspoons dried minced onion
1 tablespoon minced fresh parsley
1/2 teaspoon salt
1/4 teaspoon pepper
3 tablespoons cornstarch
3 tablespoons cold water
Hot cooked rice

Combine the first nine ingredients in a slow cooker. Cover and cook on low for 4 hours or until meat juices run clear. Combine cornstarch and water until smooth; stir into cooking juices. Cover and cook on high for 30-45 minutes or until thickened. Serve over rice if desired.

352- Creole Chicken I

8 chicken thighs
1/4 pound cooked ham, cut into one inch
cubes
1 (16 ounce) can diced tomatoes
1 green bell pepper, chopped
6 green onions, chopped
1 (6 ounce) can tomato paste

1 teaspoon salt
2 dashes hot pepper sauce
2 cups water
1 cup uncooked long grain white rice
1/2 pound Polish sausage, sliced
diagonally

In a slow cooker, place the chicken, ham, tomatoes, bell pepper, green onions, tomato paste, salt, and hot pepper sauce. Cover, and cook on Low for 4 to 5 hours. Combine water and rice in a medium saucepan. Bring to a boil. Reduce heat, cover, and simmer for 20 minutes. Mix the cooked rice and sausage into the slow cooker. Cover, and cook on High for 15 to 20 minutes, or until the sausage is heated through.

353- Slow Cooker Ground Beef

2 pounds ground beef
1/2 cup chopped onion
1 1/2 cups ketchup

1/4 cup SPLENDA® No Calorie
Sweetener, Granulated
1/4 cup white vinegar

1/4 cup prepared yellow mustard
1/2 teaspoon celery seed
3/4 teaspoon Worcestershire sauce

1/2 teaspoon ground black pepper
3/4 teaspoon salt

Place the ground beef and onion in a large skillet over medium-high heat. Cook, stirring to crumble, until beef is browned. Drain. Transfer the beef and onion to a slow cooker and stir in the ketchup, SPLENDA® Granulated Sweetener, vinegar and mustard. Season with celery seed, Worcestershire sauce, pepper and salt. Cover and simmer on Low setting for a few hours before serving.

354- Slow Cooker Beef Stroganoff I

1 pound cubed beef stew meat
1 (10.75 ounce) can condensed golden mushroom soup
1/2 cup chopped onion

1 tablespoon Worcestershire sauce
1/4 cup water
4 ounces cream cheese

In a slow cooker, combine the meat, soup, onion, Worcestershire sauce and water.
Cook on Low setting for 8 hours, or on High setting for about 5 hours. Stir in cream cheese just before serving.

355- Seasoned Short Ribs

1 1/2 cups tomato juice
1/2 cup maple syrup
1/4 cup chopped onion
3 tablespoons cider vinegar
1 tablespoon Worcestershire sauce
1 tablespoon Dijon mustard
2 teaspoons minced garlic

1/4 teaspoon ground cinnamon
1/4 teaspoon ground cloves
4 pounds beef short ribs
1 teaspoon pepper
1 tablespoon cornstarch
2 tablespoons cold water

In a small bowl, combine the first nine ingredients; set aside. Cut ribs into serving-size pieces; place on a broiler pan. Sprinkle with pepper. Broil 4-6 in. from the heat for 3-5 minutes on each side or until browned; drain on paper towels. Place ribs in a 5-qt. slow cooker; top with tomato juice mixture. Cover and cook on low for 6-7 hours or until meat is tender. In a small bowl, combine cornstarch and cold water until smooth. Pour 1 cup cooking liquid into a small saucepan; skim off fat. Bring to a boil; stir in cornstarch mixture. Return to a boil; cook and stir for 2 minutes or until thickened. Serve over ribs.

356- Rustic Slow Cooker Stew

3 pounds beef stew meat salt and pepper to taste
2 (14 ounce) cans beef broth
1 (10.5 ounce) can condensed beef consomme
2 cups Burgundy wine

1 cup water
1 teaspoon ground mustard seed
1 teaspoon dried thyme
5 red potatoes, cut into chunks
1/2 pound baby carrots
1/2 pound pearl onions, peeled

2 tablespoons cornstarch (optional)   1 tablespoon water (optional)

Season the beef with salt and pepper, and place in a skillet over medium heat. Cook until evenly brown, and drain. In a slow cooker, mix the beef broth, condensed beef consomme, wine, water, mustard, and thyme. Place beef into the liquid, and stir in the potatoes, carrots, and onions. Cover, and cook 6 hours on Low or 4 hours on High. If you prefer a thick stew, mix the cornstarch and water together and stir into the slow cooker about 30 minutes before the end of the cooking time. Stir occasionally until thickened.

357- Slow Cooked Squirrel

2 squirrels - skinned, gutted, and cut into   4 onions, sliced
pieces   2 cups water
4 large potatoes, quartered   1/4 medium head cabbage
1 pound carrots, chopped   1 teaspoon salt
1 green bell pepper, chopped   1 teaspoon ground black pepper

In a slow cooker, place the squirrel meat, potatoes, carrots, green bell pepper, onions, water, cabbage, salt and ground black pepper. Cover and cook on low setting for 8 hours.

358- Shipwreck Stew

2 pounds ground beef   5 large potatoes, cubed
2 (10.75 ounce) cans condensed tomato   2 (15.25 ounce) cans kidney beans,
soup   undrained
2 medium onions, chopped

Crumble the ground beef into a large skillet over medium-high heat. Cook and stir until browned. Drain grease, and transfer beef to a slow cooker. Mix in the tomato soups (undiluted), onions, potatoes, and beans. Cover, and cook on the Low setting for 4 to 5 hours, until stew is thick and potatoes are tender.

359- Slow Cooker Lasagna II

1 (16 ounce) package lasagna noodles   1/2 cup grated Parmesan cheese
1 pound lean ground beef   1 (8 ounce) container ricotta cheese
1 1/2 (26 ounce) jars spaghetti sauce   2 eggs
2 cups shredded mozzarella cheese   2 cups shredded mozzarella cheese

Fill a large pot with lightly salted water and bring to a rolling boil over high heat. Once the water is boiling, stir in the lasagna noodles, and return to a boil. Cook the pasta uncovered, stirring occasionally, until the pasta is slightly tender but not cooked through, about 7 minutes. Drain well in a colander set in the sink. Cook and stir ground beef in a large skillet over medium-high heat until beef is browned; drain, then stir in sauce. Set aside. Combine 2 cups of mozzarella cheese, Parmesan cheese, ricotta cheese, and eggs in a separate bowl. Pour about 1/2 cup of the sauce mixture in the bottom of a slow cooker and cover with a layer of noodles. Sprinkle about 1/4 of the cheese mixture over the noodles, then ladle about 1/4 of the remaining sauce over the cheese. Repeat layering, ending with a layer of sauce and topping with the remaining 2 cups of mozzarella cheese. Cook on High setting for 2 to 3 hours, or on Low setting for 8 to 9 hours.

360- Marinated Chicken Wings

20 whole chicken wings*
2 cups soy sauce
1/2 cup white wine or chicken broth
1/2 cup vegetable oil

2 cloves garlic cloves, minced
2 tablespoons sugar
2 teaspoons ground ginger

Cut chicken wings into three sections; discard wing tips. Place wings in a large resealable heavy-duty plastic bag or 12-in. x 9-in. x 2-in. baking dish. In a bowl, combine remaining ingredients; mix well. Pour half of the sauce over chicken; turn to coat. Seal or cover the chicken and remaining sauce; refrigerate overnight. Drain chicken, discarding the marinade. Place chicken in a 5-qt. slow cooker; top with reserved sauce. Cover and cook on low for 3-1/2 to 4 hours or until chicken juices run clear. Transfer wings to a serving dish; discard cooking juices.

361- GrannyLin's Barbeque Ribs Made Easy

1 large onion, sliced
1 (4 pound) package country style pork ribs

Salt and ground black pepper
1 (18 ounce) bottle barbeque sauce
1/2 cup water

Preheat the oven's broiler and set the oven rack about 6 inches from the heat source. Set slow cooker on Medium, add the sliced onions and cover. Place the ribs on a baking sheet, season with salt and ground black pepper, and place under the preheated broiler until brown, about 5 minutes. Place the browned ribs into the preheated slow cooker with the onion. Cover and cook for 4 hours. After 4 hours, pour the entire bottle of barbeque sauce over the ribs and onions, pour water into the barbeque sauce bottle, shake and pour into the slow cooker to prevent sticking. Stir gently to combine the water and barbeque sauce. Cover and cook until tender, about another 4 hours.

362- Kyle's Favorite Beef Stew

3 pounds cubed beef stew meat
1/4 cup all-purpose flour
1/2 teaspoon salt
3 tablespoons olive oil
3 tablespoons Worcestershire sauce
1 pound carrots, peeled and cut into 2-inch pieces
4 large potatoes, cubed
1 tablespoon dried parsley
1 1/2 teaspoons ground black pepper

2 cups boiling water
2 (1 ounce) envelopes onion soup mix
3 tablespoons butter
3 large onions, quartered
2 tablespoons minced garlic
1/2 cup burgundy wine
2 (6 ounce) packages fresh button mushrooms, halved
1/4 cup warm water
3 tablespoons cornstarch

Toss the beef, flour, and salt in a sealable bag until the beef is coated. Heat the oil in a large skillet over medium-high heat. Combine the beef and Worcestershire sauce in the skillet; cook until the beef is evenly browned on all sides; transfer to a slow cooker, but do not clean the skillet. Add the carrots, potatoes, parsley, and pepper to the slow cooker. Combine the boiling water and soup mix in a small bowl; add to slow cooker. Melt the butter in the skillet over medium-high heat. Cook the onion and garlic in the melted butter until soft; transfer the onion and garlic to the slow cooker and return the skillet to the heat. Combine the wine and mushrooms to the skillet; cook until the mushrooms begin to absorb the wine; pour the mixture into the slow cooker. Place the cover on the slow cooker and set to High; cook for one hour. Reduce heat to Low and cook until the beef is fork-tender, 6 to 8 hours. Whisk together the warm water and cornstarch; stir into the stew; cook uncovered until stew thickens, about 15 minutes.

363- Five Star Venison Stew

2 pounds cubed venison
1/2 (16 ounce) bottle French salad dressing (such as Wishbone®) seasoned salt to taste
1 pinch salt and black pepper to taste (optional)
2 tablespoons all-purpose flour
1/4 cup vegetable oil
1 (6 ounce) can tomato paste
2 (14 ounce) cans beef broth
2/3 cup water
3 tablespoons brown sugar
1 tablespoon Worcestershire sauce

1/4 teaspoon mustard powder
1/4 teaspoon paprika
1 clove garlic, minced
1 (1 ounce) package dry onion soup mix
4 potatoes, peeled and cut into 1- inch pieces
4 carrots, peeled and cut in chunks
3 stalks celery, sliced
1 large onion, chopped
1 (10 ounce) package frozen peas, thawed
1 (10 ounce) package frozen Brussels sprouts, thawed (optional)

Combine the venison and French salad dressing in a non-metallic bowl until the venison is evenly coated. Cover the bowl with plastic wrap and marinate in the refrigerator overnight. Remove the venison from the marinade, squeeze off excess, and place the venison cubes into a clean bowl. Discard the remaining marinade. Season the venison with seasoned salt, salt, and pepper; sprinkle with the flour and toss to coat. Heat the vegetable oil in a large skillet over medium-high heat. Add the venison cubes, and cook until golden brown on all sides, about 10 minutes. While the venison cubes are browning, whisk together the tomato paste and beef broth in a slow cooker until the tomato paste has dissolved. Stir in the water, brown sugar, Worcestershire sauce, mustard powder, paprika, garlic, onion soup mix, potatoes, carrots, celery, chopped onion, peas, Brussels sprouts, and the browned venison cubes. Cover and cook on Low until the venison, potatoes, and carrots are tender, 10 to 12 hours.

364- Andy's Spicy Green Chile Pork

1 white onion, chopped salt and pepper to taste
2 1/2 pounds pork shoulder roast

1 (16 ounce) jar green salsa (such as Frontera®)
1/2 cup chopped fresh cilantro
2 serrano chile peppers, or to taste

Layer the chopped onion into the bottom of a slow cooker. Season the pork shoulder with salt and pepper; place atop the chopped onion. Pour the green salsa over the pork. Sprinkle the the cilantro over the salsa and pork. Drop the serrano chile peppers into the slow cooker. Cook on Low until the meat falls apart easily, about 8 hours. Gently remove the pork to a cutting board. Strain and discard about half the remaining liquid from the slow cooker, reserving the rest. Discard the onions, peppers, and cilantro if desired. Shred the pork shoulder with a pair of forks. Mix the pork with the reserved liquid from the slow cooker to serve.

365- Parmesan Red Potatoes

4 medium unpeeled red potatoes, quartered
1/3 cup grated Parmesan cheese

3 teaspoons garlic powder
1 (14.5 ounce) can chicken broth
2 tablespoons minced fresh parsley

Place potatoes in a 6-qt. pressure cooker. Sprinkle with Parmesan cheese and garlic powder; add broth. Close cover securely; place pressure regulator on vent pipe. Bring cooker to full pressure over high heat. Reduce heat to medium-high; cook for 6 minutes. (Pressure regulator should maintain a slow steady rocking motion; adjust heat if needed.) Remove from the heat; immediately cool according to manufacturer's directions until pressure is completely reduced. Sprinkle with parsley.

366- Mother's Pot Roast

2 1/2 pounds tip round roast
1 (15 ounce) can tomato sauce
1 onion, cut into thin strips

2 bay leaves
3 tablespoons all-purpose flour salt and
pepper to taste

Spray slow cooker with non-stick cooking spray. Place meat in pot with fat side up. Pour tomato sauce over roast. Place onion rings over all. Toss in bay leaves. Cover and cook 1 hour on high. After 1 hour reduce heat to low and cook 6 to 8 more hours. Carefully lift meat out of pot and remove to a warm platter. Pour drippings through strainer into medium sized saucepan and discard material in strainer. Whisk in flour to liquid. Cook, stirring constantly over medium heat until thickened. Season to taste with salt and pepper, serve alongside roast.

367- Unbelievably Easy Slow Cooker Black Forest Cake

1/2 cup butter
1 (8 ounce) can crushed pineapple,
drained and juice reserved

1 (21 ounce) can cherry pie filling
1 (18.25 ounce) package chocolate cake
mix

Melt the butter in a small saucepan, and mix with reserved juice from the can of pineapple. Set the mixture aside. Spread the crushed pineapple in a layer on the bottom of a slow cooker. Spoon the cherry pie filling in an even layer on top of the pineapple, and empty the dry cake mix into the slow cooker on top of the cherry filling. Stir the butter and pineapple juice mixture, and pour it over the dry cake mix. Set the slow cooker to Low, and cook for 3 hours.

Spoon the dessert into bowls, and let cool about 5 minutes to cool the hot pie filling before eating.

368- Spicy Chipotle Black-Eyed Peas

2 tablespoons olive oil
1 tablespoon balsamic vinegar
1 cup chopped orange bell pepper
1 cup chopped celery
1 cup chopped carrot
1 cup chopped onion
1 teaspoon minced garlic
2 (16 ounce) packages dry black- eyed peas
4 cups water

4 teaspoons vegetable bouillon base (such as Better Than Bouillon® Vegetable Base)
1 (7 ounce) can chipotle peppers in adobo sauce, chopped, sauce reserved
2 teaspoons liquid mesquite smoke flavoring
2 teaspoons ground cumin
1/2 teaspoon ground black pepper

Heat the olive oil and balsamic vinegar in a skillet; cook and stir the orange bell pepper, celery, carrot, onion, and garlic in the hot oil until the onion is translucent, 5 to 8 minutes. Transfer the mixture to a slow cooker; mix in the black-eyed peas, water, and vegetable base, stirring to dissolve the vegetable base. Stir in the chipotle peppers, about 1 tablespoon of the reserved adobo sauce (or to taste), liquid smoke, cumin, and black pepper. Cook in the slow cooker on Low until the black-eyed peas are very tender and the flavors are blended, about 8 hours.

369- Mushroom Wild Rice

2 1/4 cups water
1 (10.5 ounce) can condensed beef consomme, undiluted
1 (10.5 ounce) can condensed French onion soup, undiluted

3 (4 ounce) cans mushroom stems and pieces, drained
1/2 cup butter or margarine, melted
1 cup uncooked brown rice
1 cup uncooked wild rice

In a slow cooker, combine all ingredients; stir well. Cover and cook on low for 7-8 hours or until rice is tender.

370- Slow Cooker Sweet and Sour Pork Chops

1 large onion, cut into 1-inch cubes
1 large carrot, peeled and diced
2 stalks celery, cut into 1/2 inch pieces
1 small green bell pepper, cut into 1 inch pieces
1 (4 ounce) jar whole mushrooms, drained
1 cup canned diced pineapple in juice, drain juice and reserve

2 1/2 pounds large boneless pork chops or cubed pork loin
1 cup reserved pineapple juice from the can
2 tablespoons sherry wine
2 tablespoons apple cider vinegar
2 tablespoons low-sodium soy sauce
1 teaspoon cornstarch
2 tablespoons brown sugar
1/4 teaspoon ground white pepper

1/4 teaspoon minced fresh ginger root
1/4 teaspoon mustard powder
1/4 teaspoon minced garlic

1 pinch salt and ground black pepper to taste
2 dashes hot pepper sauce, or to taste
1 (6 ounce) can tomato paste

Place the onions in the bottom of a 5 quart slow cooker. Layer carrots over the onions, followed by layers of celery, mushrooms, and pineapple. Season pork chops with salt and pepper. Place them on top of the vegetables. If you like, you may brown them in a hot skillet first. In a medium bowl, stir together the pineapple juice, sherry, cider vinegar, and soy sauce. Stir in the cornstarch until dissolved. Mix in the brown sugar, white pepper, ginger, mustard powder, garlic, salt, pepper, hot pepper sauce and tomato paste. Pour this over the pork chops and vegetables. The sauce will taste less sharp after a few hours in the slow cooker. Cover, and cook on Low for 6 to 8 hours, or on High for 3 to 4 hours.

371- Bandito Beans

1 pound mild pork sausage
1 (15 ounce) can wax beans, drained
1 (15 ounce) can cut green beans, drained
1 (15 ounce) can lima beans, drained
1 (15 ounce) can black beans, drained
1/2 (28 ounce) can barbeque baked beans, with liquid

1 (15 ounce) can chili beans, with liquid
1 (6 ounce) can tomato paste
1 cup packed light brown sugar
1/4 cup barbeque sauce
1 small green bell pepper, diced
1 small yellow onion, diced
1 teaspoon fennel seed

Place sausage in a skillet over medium heat, and cook until evenly brown. Drain grease, and transfer sausage to a slow cooker. Into the slow cooker with the sausage, mix wax beans, green beans, lima beans, and black beans. Mix in baked beans with liquid and chili beans with liquid. Stir in the tomato paste, brown sugar, barbeque sauce, green bell pepper, onion, and fennel seed. Cover slow cooker. Cook on Low at least 5 hours.

372- Beef Barley Vegetable Soup

1 (3 pound) beef chuck roast
1/2 cup barley
1 bay leaf
2 tablespoons oil
3 carrots, chopped
3 stalks celery, chopped
1 onion, chopped
1 (16 ounce) package frozen mixed vegetables

4 cups water
4 cubes beef bouillon cube
1 tablespoon white sugar
1/4 teaspoon ground black pepper
1 (28 ounce) can chopped stewed tomatoes
salt to taste
ground black pepper to taste

In a slow cooker, cook chuck roast until very tender (usually 4 to 5 hours on High, but can vary with different slow cookers). Add barley and bay leaf during the last hour of cooking. Remove meat, and chop into bite-size pieces. Discard bay leaf. Set beef, broth, and barley aside. Heat oil in a large stock pot over medium-high heat. Saute carrots, celery, onion, and frozen mixed vegetables until tender. Add water, beef bouillon cubes, sugar, 1/4 teaspoon pepper, chopped stewed tomatoes, and beef/barley mixture. Bring to boil, reduce heat, and simmer 10 to 20 minutes. Season with additional salt and pepper to taste.

373- Slow Cooker Nacho Chicken and Rice Wraps

2 (10.75 ounce) cans Campbell's® Condensed Cheddar Cheese Soup
1 cup water
2 cups Pace® Picante Sauce
1 1/4 cups uncooked regular long- grain white rice
2 pounds skinless, boneless chicken breasts, cut into cubes
10 flour tortillas (10-inch)

Stir the soup, water, picante sauce, rice and chicken in a 4-quart slow cooker. Cover and cook on LOW for 7 to 8 hours or until chicken is cooked through. Spoon about 1 cup chicken mixture down the center of each tortilla. Fold the tortilla around the filling.

374- Sunday Chicken Supper

4 medium carrots, cut into 2-inch pieces
1 medium onion, chopped
1 celery rib, cut into 2 inch pieces
2 cups fresh green beans (2-inch pieces)
5 small red potatoes, quartered
1 (3 pound) broiler/fryer chicken cut up
4 bacon strips, cooked and crumbled
1 1/2 cups hot water
2 teaspoons chicken bouillon granules
1 teaspoon salt
1/2 teaspoon dried thyme
1/2 teaspoon dried basil
1 pinch pepper

In a 5-qt. slow cooker, layer the first seven ingredients in order listed. In a bowl, combine the remaining ingredients; pour over the top. Do not stir. Cover and cook on low for 6-8 hours or until vegetables are tender and chicken juices run clear. Remove chicken and vegetables. Thicken juices for gravy if desired.

375- Slow Cooker Sausage Vegetable Soup

1 pound Bob Evans® Original/Regular Recipe Sausage Roll
3 (14.5 ounce) cans reduced sodium chicken broth
1 (20 ounce) package Bob Evans® Home Fries diced potatoes
1 (16 ounce) package frozen mixed vegetables
1 (8 ounce) can tomato sauce

In medium skillet over medium heat, crumble and cook sausage until brown. Place in slow cooker. Add remaining ingredients. Cover and cook on low 6 to 8 hours.

376- Slow Cooker Teriyaki Pork Tenderloin

2 tablespoons olive oil
2 pounds pork tenderloin
1/2 cup teriyaki sauce
1 cup chicken broth
1/4 cup brown sugar
4 cloves garlic, chopped
3 fresh red chile pepper, finely chopped
1/2 large onion, sliced

1/4 teaspoon black pepper

Heat the olive oil in a skillet over medium-high heat. Brown tenderloins on all sides, about 10 minutes. Meanwhile, mix together teriyaki sauce, chicken broth, and brown sugar in a bowl. Stir in garlic, red chile pepper, onion, and black pepper. Put browned tenderloins into slow cooker, cover with the teriyaki sauce mixture. Cook on High for about 4 hours, turning 2 to 3 times during the cooking time to ensure even doneness. Remove tenderloins from the slow cooker and let rest for 5 minutes before slicing. If desired, spoon liquid over slices when serving.

377- Red Bean Vegetable Soup

3 large sweet red peppers
3 celery ribs, chopped
2 medium onions, chopped
4 (16 ounce) cans red kidney beans,
rinsed and drained
4 cups chicken broth

2 bay leaves
1/2 teaspoon salt
1/2 teaspoon Cajun seasoning
1/2 teaspoon pepper
1/4 teaspoon hot pepper sauce

In a 5-qt. slow cooker, combine the peppers, celery, onions and beans. Stir in the remaining ingredients. Cover and cook on low for 6 hours or until vegetables are tender. Discard bay leaves before serving.

378- Mijo's Slow Cooker Shredded Beef

5 pounds chuck roast
3 cloves garlic, crushed
1 tablespoon paprika
1 tablespoon celery salt
1 tablespoon garlic powder
1 tablespoon dried parsley
1/2 tablespoon ground black pepper
1/2 tablespoon chili powder
1/2 tablespoon cayenne pepper
1/2 teaspoon seasoned salt

1/2 teaspoon mustard powder
1/2 teaspoon dried tarragon
4 fluid ounces beer
1 1/2 tablespoons Worcestershire sauce
4 tablespoons hot pepper sauce
2 teaspoons liquid smoke flavoring
1 large onion, chopped
1 green bell pepper, chopped
2 jalapeno chile peppers, chopped

Using a sharp knife, poke several 1 inch deep holes in the roast. Insert the garlic slivers into the holes. In a small bowl, combine the paprika, celery salt, garlic powder, parsley, ground black pepper, chili powder, cayenne pepper and seasoned salt. Mix together well and rub over the meat. In a separate small bowl, combine the beer OR cola, Worcestershire sauce, hot pepper sauce and liquid smoke and mix well. Place the roast in a slow cooker and pour this mixture over the meat. Add the onion, green bell pepper and jalapeno chile peppers to the slow cooker. Cook on low setting for 10 hours, or more, if desired.

379- Mediterranean Fish Soup

1 onion, chopped
1/2 green bell pepper, chopped
2 cloves garlic, minced
1 (14.5 ounce) can diced tomatoes, drained
2 (14 ounce) cans chicken broth
1 (8 ounce) can tomato sauce
2 1/2 ounces canned mushrooms
1/4 cup sliced black olives
1/2 cup orange juice
1/2 cup dry white wine
2 bay leaves
1 teaspoon dried basil
1/4 teaspoon fennel seed, crushed
1/8 teaspoon ground black pepper
1 pound medium shrimp - peeled and deveined
1 pound cod fillets, cubed

Place onion, green bell pepper, garlic, tomatoes, chicken broth, tomato sauce, mushrooms, olives, orange juice, wine, bay leaves, dried basil, fennel seeds, and pepper into a slow cooker. Cover, and cook on low 4 to 4 1/2 hours or until vegetables are crisp tender. Stir in shrimp and cod. Cover. Cook 15 to 30 minutes, or until shrimp are opaque. Remove and discard bay leaves. Serve.

380- Super Easy Slow Cooker Chicken

1 (10.75 ounce) can condensed low fat cream of chicken and herbs soup
1 (4 ounce) can mushroom pieces, drained
1/2 red onion, chopped
1 1/2 pounds skinless, boneless chicken breast halves - cut into strips
1 dash Marsala wine

Combine soup, mushroom pieces, onion, chicken, and wine in slow cooker. Cook on Low setting for 2 1/2 to 3 hours.

381- Lemon Salmon Soup

2 pounds potatoes, peeled and cubed
1 pound salmon fillets water to cover
2 tablespoons butter
1 tablespoon lemon zest
1 1/2 teaspoons salt
ground black pepper to taste
1 pinch dried oregano
1 pinch dried thyme
1 pinch dried basil
2 cups milk

Layer the potatoes and salmon into the bottom of a slow cooker. Pour enough water into the slow cooker to cover. Add the butter, lemon zest, salt, pepper, oregano, thyme, and basil. Loosely cover and cook on Low for 4 to 5 hours. Stir in the milk and cover tightly; cook another 1 to 2 hours.

382- Old Fashioned Beef Stew

2 pounds cubed beef stew meat
4 cups boiling water
1 tablespoon lemon juice
1 teaspoon Worcestershire sauce
1 clove garlic, crushed
1 onion, diced
1 bay leaf
1 tablespoon salt

1 teaspoon sugar
1/2 teaspoon ground black pepper
1/2 teaspoon paprika
1/8 teaspoon ground allspice

6 potatoes, cubed
2 carrots, sliced
1/2 cup whole kernel corn

In a slow cooker, combine the stew meat, boiling water, lemon juice, Worcestershire sauce and garlic. Stir in the onion, bay leaf, salt, sugar, ground pepper, paprika and allspice. Add the potatoes, carrots and corn. Cook on HIGH for 2 hours. Switch the slow cooker to LOW and cook for another 3 1/2 hours. Remove bay leaves before serving.

383- Savory Chicken Sandwiches

4 bone-in chicken breast halves
4 chicken thighs
1 envelope onion soup mix
1/4 teaspoon garlic salt

1/4 cup prepared Italian salad dressing
1/4 cup water
14 hamburger buns, split

Remove skin from chicken if desired. Place chicken in a 5-qt. slow cooker. Sprinkle with soup mix and garlic salt. Pour dressing and water over chicken. Cover and cook on low for 8-9 hours. Remove chicken; cool slightly. Skim fat from cooking juices. Remove chicken from bones; cut into bite-size pieces and return to slow cooker. Serve with a slotted spoon on buns.

384- Sausage Spanish Rice

1 pound fully cooked kielbasa or Polish sausage, cut into 1/4-inch slices
2 (14.5 ounce) cans diced tomatoes, undrained
2 cups water
1 1/2 cups uncooked parboiled (converted) rice

1 cup salsa
1 medium onion
1/2 cup chopped green pepper
1/2 cup chopped sweet red pepper
1 (4 ounce) can chopped green chilies
1 (1.25 ounce) package taco seasoning

In a slow cooker, combine all ingredients; stir to blend. Cover and cook on low for 5-6 hours or until rice is tender.

385- Slow Cooker Kielbasa and Beer

2 pounds kielbasa sausage, cut into 1 inch pieces

1 (12 fluid ounce) can or bottle beer
1 (20 ounce) can sauerkraut, drained

In a slow cooker combine sausage, beer and sauerkraut. Cook on low for 5 to 6 hours, until the meat is tender and plump.

386 - Slow Cooker Chicken Mole

1 cup chopped onion
1/3 cup golden raisins

1/3 cup currants
2 cloves garlic, minced

1 1/2 teaspoons ancho chile powder
2 tablespoons toasted sesame seeds
3/4 teaspoon ground cumin
3/4 teaspoon ground cinnamon
5 teaspoons cocoa powder
1/4 teaspoon hot pepper sauce, or to taste

1 (14.5 ounce) can diced tomatoes
1 cup tomato sauce
1 cup chicken broth
3 pounds skinless, boneless chicken
breast halves
1/4 cup slivered almonds, for garnish

Place the onion, raisins, currants, garlic, chile powder, sesame seeds, cumin, cinnamon, cocoa powder, hot sauce, tomatoes, tomato sauce, and chicken broth into a slow cooker; stir to mix. Add the chicken breasts, and stir to cover with sauce. Cover and cook on Low 6 hours, then increase heat to High, and continue cooking until the chicken is tender, about 3 hours more. Or cook on Low for 11 to 12 hours. Once the chicken is tender, remove, shred, and stir it back into the mole. Serve sprinkled with slivered almonds.

387- Bourbon Barbecue Slow Cooker Beans

1 (16 ounce) package dry 15 bean mix for
soup
1 bay leaf
1 pound bacon
1 pound ground beef
1 pound kielbasa sausage, sliced
1 onion, chopped
1 green bell pepper, chopped
1 red bell pepper, chopped

2 (10.5 ounce) cans chicken broth
1 (16 ounce) bottle hickory flavored
barbeque sauce (such as Open Pit®)
1 1/2 teaspoons Worcestershire sauce
1/3 cup honey
1/4 cup real maple syrup
2/3 cup bourbon whiskey
3 tablespoons coarse-grain mustard

Rinse the beans, and place in a very large pot. Cover beans with water, add the bay leaf, and bring to a boil. Simmer until all of the water is absorbed, 45 minutes to 1 hour. Remove the bay leaf. Place the chopped bacon in a large, deep skillet; cook over medium-high heat, stirring, until evenly browned, about 5 minutes. Drain the bacon on a paper towel-lined plate. Return the skillet to the heat, and add the ground beef; cook until the beef is cooked through and browned, about 5 minutes. Drain fat. Combine the beans, bacon, ground beef, sliced kielbasa, onion, green pepper, red pepper, chicken broth, barbeque sauce, Worcestershire sauce, honey, maple syrup, bourbon, and mustard in the crock of a slow cooker, and stir well to combine. Turn the slow cooker to Low heat, and cook until the beans are tender, 8 to 10 hours.

388- Julie's Sheperd's Pie

3 medium potatoes, coarsely chopped
1 cup coarsely chopped fresh cauliflower
1/2 cup milk
1 beef bouillon cube
1/4 cup warm water
1 pound beef stew meat, cut into small
pieces

3 strips bacon, chopped
3/4 cup chopped carrot
1/4 cup chopped onion
2 cloves garlic, minced
1 tomato, chopped
1/2 cup shredded Cheddar cheese

Bring a pot of water to a boil; add the potatoes and cauliflower and cook at a boil until soft, about 20 minutes. Drain and transfer to a large bowl. Pour the milk over the mixture and mash with a potato masher until smooth. Crumble the beef bouillon cube into the water; whisk until the bouillon is dissolved. Pour into a slow cooker. Add the stew meat, bacon, carrot, onion, garlic, and tomato to the slow cooker. Spread the mashed cauliflower and potato mixture over the meat and vegetable mixture. Sprinkle the Cheddar cheese over the top. Set the slow cooker to Low and cook for 8 hours, or, if you prefer, at High for 4 hours.

389- Molly's Chicken

3 1/2 pounds chicken drumsticks, skin removed
1/2 cup soy sauce

1/4 cup packed brown sugar
2 cloves garlic, minced
1 (8 ounce) can tomato sauce

Place drumsticks in a slow cooker. In a medium bowl, stir together soy sauce, brown sugar, garlic, and tomato sauce. Pour sauce over chicken. Cover, and cook on Low heat 8 hours.

390- Slow Cooker Garlic Mashed Potatoes

2 pounds red potatoes, diced with peel
1/4 cup water
1/4 cup butter
1 1/4 teaspoons salt

1/2 teaspoon garlic powder
1/4 teaspoon ground black pepper
1/2 cup milk, or as needed

Place the potatoes, water, and butter into a slow cooker. Season with salt, garlic powder, and pepper. Cover, and cook on Low for 7 hours, or High for 4 hours. Mash potatoes with a masher or electric beater, adding the desired amount of milk to achieve a creamy consistency. Keep warm on low until serving.

391- Pork Barbeque

1/2 cup white wine
1 teaspoon white pepper
2 teaspoons liquid smoke flavoring
4 cloves garlic
2 teaspoons freshly ground black pepper
2 tablespoons hot pepper sauce
3 tablespoons Worcestershire sauce
5 pounds boneless pork chops

2 tablespoons barbeque sauce
2 medium onions, finely chopped
1 medium green bell pepper, finely chopped
1 medium red bell pepper, finely chopped
1 medium yellow bell pepper, finely chopped

In a bowl, mix the wine, white pepper, liquid smoke, garlic, black pepper, pepper sauce, and Worcestershire sauce. Place pork in a slow cooker, and cover with the sauce mixture. Cover, and cook 4 to 5 hours on Low, or until the meat shreds easily. Shred the pork with a fork. Mix in the barbeque sauce, onion, green bell pepper, red bell pepper, and yellow bell pepper. Continue cooking 30 minutes, or until vegetables are tender. Place pork in a strainer to remove excess liquid, pushing down with a large spoon to extract as much moisture as possible. Liquid may be reserved as a dipping sauce.

392- Shredded French Dip

1 (3 pound) boneless beef chuck roast, trimmed
1 (10.5 ounce) can condensed French onion soup, undiluted
1 (10.5 ounce) can condensed beef consomme, undiluted

1 (10.5 ounce) can condensed beef broth, undiluted
1 teaspoon beef bouillon granules
8 French or Italian rolls, split

Halve roast and place in a 3-qt. slow cooker. Combine the soup, consomme, broth and bouillon; pour over roast. Cover and cook on low for 6-8 hours or until meat is tender. Remove meat and shred with two forks. Serve on rolls. Skim fat from cooking juices and serve as a dipping sauce.

393- Slow Cooker Thai Peanut Pork

2 red bell pepper, seeded and sliced into strips
4 (8 ounce) boneless pork loin chops
1/2 cup teriyaki sauce
1/4 cup creamy peanut butter
2 tablespoons rice vinegar

1 teaspoon crushed red pepper flakes
2 cloves garlic, minced
1/2 cup chopped green onions
1/4 cup chopped roasted peanuts
2 limes, cut into wedges

Coat a slow cooker with cooking spray. Place the bell pepper strips and pork chops into the slow cooker. Pour the teriyaki sauce, vinegar, red pepper flakes, and garlic over the pork chops. Cover and cook on Low until the pork is very tender, 8 to 9 hours. Once tender, remove the pork from the slow cooker, and whisk in the peanut butter until smooth. Return the pork to the slow cooker, and cook 10 minutes more. Pour into a serving dish and sprinkle with green onions and peanuts to garnish. Decorate with lime wedges to serve.

394- Creamy Chipped Beef Fondue

1 1/3 cups milk
2 (8 ounce) packages cream cheese, softened
3 (2.5 ounce) packages thinly sliced dried beef, chopped

1/4 cup chopped green onions
2 teaspoons ground mustard
1 (1 pound) loaf French bread, cubed

In a saucepan, heat milk and cream cheese over medium heat; stir until smooth. Stir in beef, onions and mustard; heat through. Transfer to a fondue pot or slow cooker; keep warm. Serve with bread cubes.

395- Slow Cooker Apple Crisp

1 cup all-purpose flour
1/2 cup light brown sugar
1/2 cup white sugar

1/2 teaspoon ground cinnamon
1/4 teaspoon ground nutmeg
1 pinch salt

1/2 cup butter, cut into pieces
1 cup chopped walnuts
1/3 cup white sugar, or to taste
1 tablespoon cornstarch
1/2 teaspoon ground ginger

1/2 teaspoon ground cinnamon
6 cups apples - peeled, cored and chopped
2 tablespoons lemon juice

Mix flour, brown sugar, 1/2 cup of white sugar, 1/2 teaspoon cinnamon, nutmeg, and salt together in a bowl. Combine butter with the flour mixture using fingers or a fork until coarse crumbs form. Stir in walnuts and set aside. Whisk together 1/3 cup sugar, cornstarch, ginger, and 1/2 teaspoon cinnamon. Place the apples in a slow cooker, stir in the cornstarch mixture; toss with lemon juice. Sprinkle the walnut crumb topping on top. Cover and cook on High for 2 hours or Low for 4 hours, until apples are tender. Partially uncover the slow cooker to allow the topping to harden, about 1 hour.

396- Creamy Vegetable Soup

1 onion, chopped
1/4 cup butter, melted
3 sweet potatoes, peeled and diced
3 zucchini, chopped
1 1/2 cups fresh broccoli, chopped
3 (14 ounce) cans chicken broth

2 potatoes, peeled and shredded
1/2 teaspoon celery seed
2 teaspoons salt
1 teaspoon ground cumin
2 cups milk

In a slow cooker stir together the onion, butter or margarine, sweet potatoes, zucchini and broccoli. Pour in the chicken broth and stir. Add the potatoes, celery seed, salt and ground cumin and stir. Cover and cook on low for 8 to 10 hours. Add the milk and cook for 30 minutes to 1 hour. Serve.

397- Slow Cooker Party Mix

4 cups Wheat Chex® cereal
4 cups Cheerios® cereal
3 cups pretzel sticks
1 (12 ounce) can salted peanuts

1/4 cup butter or margarine, melted
2 tablespoons grated Parmesan cheese
1 teaspoon celery salt
1/2 teaspoon seasoned salt

In a 5-qt. slow cooker, combine cereals, pretzels and peanuts. Combine butter, Parmesan cheese, celery salt and seasoned salt; drizzle over cereal mixture and mix well. Cover and cook on low for up to 3 hours, stirring every 30 minutes. Serve warm or at room temperature.

398- Beer Chops II

1 onion, chopped
2 pork chops butterfly cut

1 (12 fluid ounce) can or bottle beer
2 cubes chicken bouillon

Arrange chopped onions in bottom of slow cooker. Lay butterfly chops on top, separating if you wish. Pour in beer and drop in chicken bouillon cubes. Cook on low for 6 to 8 hours.

399- Lazy Golumbkis

1 pound ground beef
1 onion, diced
1 cup uncooked white rice
1 small head cabbage, shredded

1 (28 ounce) can canned tomato sauce
1 tablespoon chopped fresh parsley
salt and pepper to taste

In a slow cooker, combine ground beef, onion, rice and cabbage. Pour in tomato sauce. Season with parsley, salt and pepper. Mix well, and cook on low, for 6 to 8 hours.

400- Hearty Beef Vegetable Stew

1 (28 ounce) can crushed tomatoes, undrained
3 tablespoons quick-cooking tapioca
2 tablespoons dried basil
1 tablespoon sugar
1/2 teaspoon salt
1/8 teaspoon pepper

1 1/2 pounds red potatoes, cut into 1-inch cubes
3 medium carrots, cut into 1-inch slices
1 medium onion, chopped
1/2 cup chopped celery
1 1/2 pounds lean chuck roast, cut into 1-inch cubes
2 teaspoons canola oil

In a bowl, combine the tomatoes, tapioca, basil, sugar, salt and pepper; let stand for 15 minutes. Place the potatoes, carrots, onion and celery in a 5-qt. slow cooker. In a large nonstick skillet, brown meat in oil over medium heat. Drain and transfer meat to slow cooker. Pour tomato mixture over the top. Cover and cook on high for 5-6 hours or until meat and vegetables are tender.

401- Country Cooking Slow Cooker Neck Bones

3 pounds pork neck bones
1 small onion, chopped
3 cloves garlic, minced, or more to taste
1 teaspoon salt (optional)

1 teaspoon dried thyme leaves
1 tablespoon distilled white vinegar
4 cups water

Place the neck bones into a slow cooker. Sprinkle in the onion, garlic, salt, and thyme leaves. Pour in the vinegar and water. Cover and cook on High until the meat is tender, about 4 hours.

402- Campbell's® Slow-Cooker Chicken and

1 1/2 pounds skinless, boneless chicken breasts, cut into 1-inch pieces
2 medium Yukon Gold potatoes, cut into 1-inch pieces
2 cups whole baby carrots
2 stalks celery, sliced

2 (10.75 ounce) cans Campbell's® Condensed Cream of Chicken Soup (Regular or 98% Fat Free)
1 cup water
1 teaspoon dried thyme leaves, crushed
1/4 teaspoon ground black pepper
2 cups all-purpose baking mix

2/3 cup milk

Place the chicken, potatoes, carrots and celery into a 6-quart slow cooker. Stir the soup, water, thyme and black pepper in a small bowl. Pour the soup mixture over the chicken and vegetables. Cover and cook on LOW for 7 to 8 hours* or until the chicken is cooked through. Stir the baking mix and milk in a medium bowl. Spoon the batter over the chicken mixture. Turn the heat to HIGH. Tilt the lid to vent and cook for 30 minutes or until the dumplings are cooked in the center.

403- Southwestern Style Fifteen Bean Soup

1 (8 ounce) package 15 bean soup mix
12 cups water
1 pound bacon
2 (4 ounce) cans canned green chile peppers, chopped

1 tablespoon chili powder
1 tablespoon crushed red pepper flakes
1 onion, chopped
2 cloves garlic, minced

Rinse and sort the beans in the mix. Place them in a slow cooker on low setting with the water. Cook overnight. The next morning, add the ham, chile peppers, chili powder, crushed red pepper, onion and garlic and continue to cook on low for 8 hours.

404- Shredded Beef Sandwiches

3 pounds beef stew meat, cut into
1 inch cubes
3 medium green peppers, diced
2 large onions, diced
1 (6 ounce) can tomato paste
1/2 cup packed brown sugar

1/4 cup cider vinegar
3 tablespoons chili powder
2 teaspoons salt
2 teaspoons Worcestershire sauce
1 teaspoon ground mustard
14 sandwich buns, split

In a 6-qt. slow cooker, combine the beef, green peppers and onions. In a small bowl, combine tomato paste, brown sugar, vinegar, chili powder, salt, Worcestershire sauce and mustard. Stir into meat mixture. Cover and cook on high for 7-8 hours or until meat is tender. Skim fat from cooking juices. Shred beef, using two forks. With a slotted spoon, place about 1/2 cup beef mixture on each bun.

405- Rice Pudding in a Slow Cooker

1 cup uncooked glutinous white rice
1 cup white sugar
2 (12 fluid ounce) cans evaporated milk

1 teaspoon vanilla extract
1 ounce cinnamon stick
1 teaspoon ground nutmeg

Place the rice, sugar, evaporated milk, vanilla, cinnamon stick, and nutmeg into a slow cooker. Cover, and cook on Low for 1 1/2 hours, stirring occasionally. Remove cinnamon stick, and serve warm.

406- Slow Cooker Chicken Tortilla Soup

1 (10.75 ounce) can Campbell's®
Condensed Cream of Chicken Soup
(Regular or 98% Fat Free)
1 (10.75 ounce) can Campbell's®
Condensed Fiesta Nacho Cheese Soup

2 (10.75 ounce) cans milk*
1 (4 ounce) can chopped green chilies
2 skinless, boneless chicken breasts
halves, cooked and diced
tortilla chips

Mix soups, milk, chilies and chicken in 3 1/2-qt. slow cooker. Cover and cook on LOW 5 to 6 hours. Place a few tortilla chips in each serving bowl. Ladle hot soup over chips. Serve immediately.

407- Savory Pork Stew

1 tablespoon extra virgin olive oil
2 pounds cubed pork stew meat salt to
taste
ground black pepper to taste garlic
powder to taste
2 tablespoons cornstarch, or as needed
8 red potatoes
1 green bell pepper, chopped
1 red bell pepper, chopped

1 sweet onion, diced
1 (11 ounce) can whole kernel corn
1 (14 ounce) can stewed tomatoes
1 (10.75 ounce) can cream of mushroom
soup
1 1/4 cups milk
1 (14 ounce) can beef broth
1 tablespoon Italian seasoning

Heat the olive oil in a skillet over medium heat. Sprinkle pork on all sides with salt, pepper, and garlic powder, and lightly coat with cornstarch. Place pork in the skillet, and cook until lightly browned but not done. Transfer to a slow cooker. Place potatoes, green bell pepper, red bell pepper, onion, and corn in the slow cooker. In a bowl, mix the tomatoes, cream of mushroom soup, milk, broth, and Italian seasoning. Pour into the slow cooker. Cover, and cook 1 hour on High. Reduce heat to Low, and continue cooking at least 1 hour.

408- Slow Cooker Corned Beef and Cabbage

4 large carrots, peeled and cut into
matchstick pieces
10 baby red potatoes, quartered
1 onion, peeled and cut into bite- sized
pieces

4 cups water
1 (4 pound) corned beef brisket with
spice packet
6 ounces beer
1/2 head cabbage, coarsely chopped

Place the carrots, potatoes, and onion into the bottom of a slow cooker, pour in the water, and place the brisket on top of the vegetables. Pour the beer over the brisket. Sprinkle on the spices from the packet, cover, and set the cooker on High. Cook the brisket for about 8 hours. An hour before serving, stir in the cabbage and cook for 1 more hour.

409- Uncle Bob's Soybean Bread

1 cup bread flour
2 cups warm water (110 degrees F)
1 (.25 ounce) package active dry yeast
1/2 cup dried soybeans

1 1/2 teaspoons salt
3 cups bread flour
2 tablespoons quinoa
1 tablespoon olive oil

In a large bowl or crock pot, dissolve yeast and 1 cup flour in water. Cover with plastic wrap or a pot lid and let stand for 2 hours. Coarsely grind the soybeans in a food processor or blender. Stir soy beans and 1 cup flour into the yeast mixture. Let stand for 2 hours. Stir in the salt and remaining flour, 1/2 cup at a time, beating well after each addition. When the dough has pulled together, turn it out of the slow cooker and knead 1 1/2 tablespoons quinoa into the dough. Form into a loaf and place in a lightly greased 9x5 inch loaf pan. Sprinkle the remaining quinoa on top of the loaf. Brush or drizzle on the olive oil. Cover and let rise until loaf is just above the top of the loaf pan. Meanwhile, preheat oven to 400 degrees F (200 degrees C). Bake in preheated oven for 45 minutes, or until loaf sounds hollow when tapped on the bottom. Let cool before slicing.

410- Slow Cooked Venison

1 tablespoon olive oil
1/2 onion, diced
2 teaspoons minced garlic
1 pound boneless venison roast
1/2 cup ketchup
1/4 cup Worcestershire sauce

1/4 cup soy sauce
1/4 cup chile-garlic sauce
1/4 teaspoon liquid smoke
1/3 cup water
2 teaspoons salt
1 tablespoon pepper

Heat olive oil in a skillet over medium heat. Stir in onion and cook until softened, about 3 minutes. Stir in garlic and cook 2 more minutes until softened. Place venison roast into a slow cooker, and sprinkle with onion mixture. Stir together ketchup, Worcestershire sauce, soy sauce, chile-garlic sauce, water, salt, and pepper. Pour over the venison. Cover and cook on Low until tender and no longer pink, 4 to 5 hours.

411- All Day Apple Butter

5 1/2 pounds apples - peeled, cored and finely chopped
4 cups white sugar

2 teaspoons ground cinnamon
1/4 teaspoon ground cloves
1/4 teaspoon salt

Place the apples in a slow cooker. In a medium bowl, mix the sugar, cinnamon, cloves and salt. Pour the mixture over the apples in the slow cooker and mix well. Cover and cook on high 1 hour. Reduce heat to low and cook 9 to 11 hours, stirring occasionally, until the mixture is thickened and dark brown. Uncover and continue cooking on low 1 hour. Stir with a whisk, if desired, to increase smoothness. Spoon the mixture into sterile containers, cover and refrigerate or freeze.

412- Sweet-n-Sour Kielbasa

2 pounds kielbasa sausage, cut into 1/4-inch slices
1 (12 ounce) bottle tomato-based chili sauce (such as Heinz®)

1 (12 ounce) jar red currant jelly
1 tablespoon crushed red pepper flakes
1/2 cup water

Stir the sausage slices, chili sauce, red currant jelly, red pepper flakes, and water together in a slow cooker, cover, and set the cooker to Low. Cook at least 4 hours, stirring once every hour.

413- V-Eight Vegetable Beef Soup

1 pound lean ground beef
48 ounces tomato-vegetable juice cocktail

2 (16 ounce) packages frozen mixed vegetables

Place ground beef in a Dutch oven or slow cooker. Cook over medium-high heat until evenly brown. Drain excess fat, and crumble. Add juice cocktail and mixed vegetables. In a Dutch oven, simmer for 30 minutes. In a slow cooker, cook 1 hour on High. Then reduce heat to Low and simmer 6 to 8 hours.

414- Chicken With Orange Sauce

1 broiler/fryer chicken (3 to 4 pounds), cut up
2 tablespoons vegetable oil
1 large onion, halved and sliced
1/2 medium green pepper, julienned

1/2 medium sweet yellow pepper, julienned
1 garlic clove, minced
1/2 teaspoon grated orange peel
2 1/2 cups water

Orange Sauce:
2 tablespoons cornstarch
3/4 cup orange juice
1/4 cup sherry, or chicken broth
1/4 cup teriyaki sauce

3 tablespoons brown sugar
1 tablespoon butter or margarine
1/4 teaspoon ground ginger
1/2 cup slivered almonds, toasted

In a pressure cooker, brown chicken in oil over medium-high heat; drain. Remove chicken to a 30-in. x 18-in. piece of heavy-duty foil. Top with onion, peppers, garlic and orange peel. Wrap tightly. Place on a rack in pressure cooker; add water. Close over securely; place pressure regulator on vent pipe. Bring cooker to full pressure over high heat. Reduce heat to medium-high; cook for 12 minutes. (Pressure regulator should maintain a slow steady rocking motion; adjust heat if needed.) Immediately cool according to manufacturer's directions until pressure is completely reduced. In a small saucepan, combine cornstarch and orange juice until smooth. Stir in the sherry or broth, teriyaki sauce, brown sugar, butter and ginger. Bring to a boil; cook and stir for 1 minute or until thickened. Remove chicken and vegetables to a serving platter. Top with sauce; sprinkle with almonds.

415- Potato Minestrone

2 (14.5 ounce) cans chicken broth
1 (28 ounce) can crushed tomatoes
1 (16 ounce) can kidney beans, rinsed
and drained
1 (15 ounce) can garbanzo beans
(chickpeas)
1 (14.5 ounce) can beef broth
2 cups frozen cubed hash brown
potatoes, thawed
1 tablespoon dried minced onion

1 tablespoon dried parsley flakes
1 teaspoon salt
1 teaspoon dried oregano
1/2 teaspoon garlic powder
1/2 teaspoon dried basil
1/2 teaspoon dried marjoram
1 (10 ounce) package frozen chopped
spinach, thawed and drained
2 cups frozen peas and carrots, thawed

In a slow cooker, combine the first 13 ingredients. Cover and cook on low for 8 hours. Stir in the spinach, peas and carrots; heat thorough.

416- Mom's Easy Roast

1 (3 pound) bottom round roast salt and
pepper to taste
2 medium baking potatoes, quartered

4 carrots, cut into thirds
1 (1 ounce) envelope dry onion soup mix
1 cup water

Season the roast with salt and pepper, and place in the bottom of a slow cooker. Sprinkle half of the onion soup mix over it, and pour in half of the water. Put in the potatoes, followed by carrots. Season with the remaining soup mix, then pour in the rest of the water. Cover, and cook on High for 6 to 8 hours.

417- Slow-Cooked Tamale Casserole

1 pound ground beef
1 egg
1 1/2 cups milk
3/4 cup cornmeal
1 (15.25 ounce) can whole kernel corn,
drained
1 (14.5 ounce) can diced tomatoes,
undrained

1 (2.25 ounce) can sliced ripe olives,
drained
1 (1.25 ounce) package chili seasoning
mix
1 teaspoon seasoned salt
1 cup shredded Cheddar cheese

In a skillet, cook beef over medium heat until no longer pink; drain. In a bowl, combine the egg, milk and cornmeal until smooth. Add corn, tomatoes, olives, chili seasoning, seasoned salt and beef. Transfer to a greased slow cooker. Cover and cook on high for 3 hours and 45 minutes. Sprinkle with cheese; cover and cook 15 minutes longer or until cheese is melted.

418- All-Day Apple Butter

5 1/2 pounds apples - peeled, cored and
finely chopped

4 cups sugar
2 teaspoons ground cinnamon

1/4 teaspoon ground cloves   1/4 teaspoon salt

Place apples in a slow cooker. Combine sugar, cinnamon, cloves and salt; pour over apples and mix well. Cover and cook on high for 1 hour. Reduce heat to low; cover and cook for 9-11 hours or until thickened and dark brown, stirring occasionally (stir more frequently as it thickens to prevent sticking). Uncover and cook on low 1 hour longer. If desired, stir with a wire whisk until smooth. Spoon into freezer containers, leaving 1/2-in. headspace. Cover and refrigerate or freeze.

419- Tangy Slow Cooker Pork Roast

1 large onion, sliced
2 1/2 pounds boneless pork loin roast
1 cup hot water
1/4 cup white sugar
3 tablespoons red wine vinegar
2 tablespoons soy sauce

1 tablespoon ketchup
1/2 teaspoon black pepper
1/2 teaspoon salt
1/4 teaspoon garlic powder
1 dash hot pepper sauce, or to taste

Arrange onion slices evenly over the bottom of the slow cooker, and then place the roast on top of the onion. In a bowl, mix together water, sugar, vinegar, soy sauce, ketchup, black pepper, salt, garlic powder, and hot sauce; pour over roast. Cover, and cook on Low for 6 to 8 hours, or on High for 3 to 4 hours.

420- Slow Cooker Beef Stew IV

3 pounds cubed beef stew meat
1/4 cup all-purpose flour
1/2 teaspoon salt, or to taste
3 tablespoons olive oil
1 cup baby carrots
4 large potatoes, cubed
1 tablespoon dried parsley
1 teaspoon ground black pepper

2 cups boiling water
1 (1 ounce) package dry onion soup mix
3 tablespoons butter
3 onions, sliced
1/4 cup red wine
1/4 cup warm water
2 tablespoons all-purpose flour

Place meat in a large plastic bag. Combine 1/4 cup flour with 1/2 teaspoon salt; pour into the bag with the meat, and shake to coat. Heat olive oil in a large skillet over medium-high heat. Add stew meat, and cook until evenly browned on the outside. Transfer to a slow cooker along with the carrots, potatoes, parsley, and pepper. In a small bowl, stir together 2 cups of boiling water and dry soup mix; pour into the slow cooker. In the same skillet, melt butter and saute onions until softened; remove to the slow cooker. Pour red wine into the skillet, and stir to loosen browned bits of food on the bottom. Remove from heat, and pour into the slow cooker. Cover, and cook on High for 30 minutes. Reduce heat to Low, and cook for 6 hours, or until meat is fork tender. In a small bowl or cup, mix together 2 tablespoons flour with 1/4 cup warm water. Stir into stew, and cook uncovered for 15 minutes, or until thickened.

421- Spicy Slow Cooker Mac-n-Cheese

2 (11 ounce) cans condensed
Cheddar cheese soup
2 3/4 cups water
1 (16 ounce) package uncooked shell
pasta

1/2 pound andouille sausage, sliced into
rounds
1 cup sour cream
1 cup shredded Cheddar cheese
1 cup shredded mozzarella cheese
salt and black pepper to taste

Stir the condensed soup and water together in a slow cooker until smooth. Add the shell pasta
and andouille sausage. Set the slow cooker to High; cook 2 hours, stirring frequently to
prevent sticking. Once the pasta is tender, stir in the sour cream, Cheddar, and mozzarella
until the cheeses melt. Season to taste with salt and pepper. Remove from heat, and allow to
rest 15 minutes before serving.

422- Bob's Slow Cooker Braciole

2 (26 ounce) jars marinara sauce
2 eggs, beaten
1/2 cup dry bread crumbs
1 (1 1/2-pound) flank steak, pounded to
1/4 inch

1 teaspoon kosher salt ground black
pepper
5 slices bacon
1 cup shredded Italian cheese blend
2 tablespoons vegetable oil

Pour the marinara sauce into the slow cooker and set on High to warm. Combine the eggs and
the breadcrumbs in a small bowl. Sprinkle both sides of the meat with salt and pepper. Pat the
breadcrumb mixture over one side of the flank steak, leaving about a one inch border around
edges. Top breadcrumbs with the bacon slices; sprinkle with shredded cheese. Starting from
one long side, tightly roll flank steak into a log. Use string or toothpicks to secure the log in 4
or 5 places. Heat oil in a heavy skillet. Sear the stuffed flank steak in the hot oil until well
browned on all sides, about 10 minutes. Transfer the meat to the warm sauce in the slow
cooker. Spoon sauce over meat to cover. Turn slow cooker to Low; cook meat until very
tender, 6 to 8 hours. Remove string/toothpicks before slicing. Serve with marinara.

423- Cabbage Rolls II

12 leaves cabbage
1 cup cooked white rice
1 egg, beaten
1/4 cup milk
1/4 cup minced onion
1 pound extra-lean ground beef

1 1/4 teaspoons salt
1 1/4 teaspoons ground black pepper
1 (8 ounce) can tomato sauce
1 tablespoon brown sugar
1 tablespoon lemon juice
1 teaspoon Worcestershire sauce

Bring a large pot of water to a boil. Boil cabbage leaves 2 minutes; drain. In large bowl,
combine 1 cup cooked rice, egg, milk, onion, ground beef, salt, and pepper. Place about 1/4
cup of meat mixture in center of each cabbage leaf, and roll up, tucking in ends. Place rolls in
slow cooker. In a small bowl, mix together tomato sauce, brown sugar, lemon juice, and
Worcestershire sauce. Pour over cabbage rolls. Cover, and cook on Low 8 to 9 hours.

424- Hot Mint Malt

6 chocolate-covered peppermint patties
5 cups milk

1 teaspoon vanilla extract
6 tablespoons whipped topping

Combine the peppermint patties, milk, and vanilla extract in a slow cooker set to LOW. Cook 2 hours. Transfer the mixture to a blender and blend until frothy. Pour into 6 mugs; top each with 1 tablespoon of whipped topping.

425- Taco Bean Dip

2 (11.5 ounce) cans condensed bean with bacon soup
1 (1 ounce) package taco seasoning mix

8 ounces sour cream
1/4 cup salsa
1/2 cup shredded Cheddar cheese

Place the soup, seasoning mix, sour cream, and salsa in a slow cooker and mix together. Top with cheese and heat on low until cheese melts, about 1 hour.

426- It's Chili by George!!

2 pounds lean ground beef
1 (46 fluid ounce) can tomato juice
1 (29 ounce) can tomato sauce
1 (15 ounce) can kidney beans, drained and rinsed
1 (15 ounce) can pinto beans, drained and rinsed
1 1/2 cups chopped onion

1/4 cup chopped green bell pepper
1/8 teaspoon ground cayenne pepper
1/2 teaspoon white sugar
1/2 teaspoon dried oregano
1/2 teaspoon ground black pepper
1 teaspoon salt
1 1/2 teaspoons ground cumin
1/4 cup chili powder

Place ground beef in a large, deep skillet. Cook over medium-high heat until evenly brown. Drain, and crumble.In a large pot over high heat combine the ground beef, tomato juice, tomato sauce, kidney beans, pinto beans, onions, bell pepper, cayenne pepper, sugar, oregano, ground black pepper, salt, cumin and chili powder. Bring to a boil, then reduce heat to low. Simmer for 1 1/2 hours. (Note: If using a slow cooker, set on low, add ingredients, and cook for 8 to 10 hours.)

427- Slow Cooker Chicken Creole

4 skinless, boneless chicken breast halves
salt and pepper to taste
Creole-style seasoning to taste
1 (14.5 ounce) can stewed tomatoes, with liquid
1 stalk celery, diced

1 green bell pepper, diced
3 cloves garlic, minced
1 onion, diced
1 (4 ounce) can mushrooms, drained
1 fresh jalapeno pepper, seeded and chopped

Place chicken breasts in slow cooker. Season with salt, pepper, and Creole-style seasoning to taste. Stir in tomatoes with liquid, celery, bell pepper, garlic, onion, mushrooms, and jalapeno pepper. Cook on Low for 10 to 12 hours, or on High for 5 to 6 hours.

428- Hamburger Salad

1 pound ground beef	3/4 cup brown sugar
1 pound bacon	1/2 cup white sugar
1 cup chopped onion	1 teaspoon mustard powder
1/2 cup ketchup	1 (15 ounce) can baked beans with pork
2 tablespoons white vinegar	3 (15 ounce) cans pinto beans, drained

Fry the bacon in a large skillet over medium heat until crisp, turning as needed. Remove to paper towels and drain off the grease from the skillet . Crumble the ground beef into the same skillet; cook and stir over medium heat until evenly browned. Add the onions and cook just until wilted. Transfer the beef, onions and bacon to a slow cooker, crumbling the bacon as you put it in. Pour in the baked beans and pinto beans. Stir in the ketchup, vinegar, brown sugar, white sugar and mustard powder. Cover and heat on Low setting for 5 to 6 hours before serving.

429- Steak Burritos

2 flank steaks (1 pound each)	1 1/2 cups shredded Monterey
2 (1.25 ounce) packages taco seasoning	Jack cheese
1 medium onion, chopped	1 1/2 cups chopped, seeded plum
1 (4 ounce) can chopped green chilies	tomatoes
1 tablespoon vinegar	3/4 cup sour cream
10 (8 inch) flour tortillas	

Cut steaks in half; rub with taco seasoning. Place in a slow cooker coated with nonstick cooking spray. Top with onion, chilies and vinegar. Cover and cook on low for 8-9 hours or until meat is tender. Remove steaks and cool slightly; shred meat with two forks. (Turn to page 51 for a tip on shredding meat.) Return to slow cooker; heat through. Spoon about 1/2 cup meat mixture down the center of each tortilla. Top with cheese, tomato and sour cream. Fold ends and sides over filling.

430- Wildfire BBQ Beef on Buns

3 pounds chuck roast or round steak	1/2 cup apricot preserves
1 small onion, thinly sliced	2 tablespoons Dijon mustard
1 cup Bob Evans® Wildfire BBQ Sauce	12 rolls or buns

Place beef and onion into slow cooker. Combine Wildfire sauce, preserves and mustard and pour into slow cooker. Cover and heat on low for 8 to 10 hours or until meat is tender. Remove meat and shred with 2 forks. Combine shredded meat with sauce and serve on buns.

431- Slow Cooker Ham and Beans

1 pound dried great Northern beans,
soaked overnight
1/2 pound cooked ham, chopped
1/2 cup brown sugar
1 tablespoon onion powder

1 tablespoon dried parsley
1/2 teaspoon garlic salt
1/2 teaspoon black pepper
1/4 teaspoon cayenne pepper water to
cover

Combine the beans, ham, brown sugar, onion powder, parsley, garlic salt, black pepper, and cayenne pepper in a slow cooker. Pour enough water into the slow cooker to cover the mixture by about 2 inches. Set slow cooker to Low; simmer 12 hours, stirring occasionally.

432- Chicken Paprika

4 bone-in chicken breast halves, with
skin
1 medium onion, chopped
2 tablespoons all-purpose flour
1 cup chicken broth
1 tablespoon tomato paste

1 clove garlic, minced
1 tablespoon paprika
1/2 teaspoon salt
1/2 teaspoon dried thyme
1 dash hot pepper sauce
1 cup sour cream

Place chicken in a pressure cooker; top with onion. In a small bowl, combine flour and broth until smooth. Whisk in the tomato paste, garlic, paprika, salt, thyme and hot pepper sauce. Pour over the chicken. Close cover securely; place pressure regulator on vent pipe. Bring cooker to low pressure over high heat. Reduce heat to medium- high; cook for 12 minutes. (Pressure regulator should maintain a slow steady rocking motion or release of steam; adjust heat if needed.) Remove from the heat. Immediately cool according to manufacturer's directions until pressure is completely reduced. Remove chicken and keep warm. Stir sour cream into cooking juices; serve over chicken.

433- SwansonB® Slow-Cooker Chicken Cacciatore

1 3/4 cups SwansonB® Chicken
Broth (regular, Natural GoodnessB
„ÿ or Certified Organic)
1 teaspoon garlic powder
2 (14.5 ounce) cans diced Italian- style
tomatoes

4 cups mushrooms, cut in half
2 large onions, chopped
3 pounds chicken parts, skin removed
10 cups hot cooked spaghetti, cooked
without salt

Mix broth, garlic powder, tomatoes, mushrooms and onions in 3 1/2-quart slow cooker. Add chicken and turn to coat. Cover and cook on LOW 7 to 8 hours* or until done. Serve over spaghetti.

434- Charley's Slow Cooker Mexican Style Meat

1 (4 pound) chuck roast
1 teaspoon salt

1 teaspoon ground black pepper
2 tablespoons olive oil

1 large onion, chopped
1 1/4 cups diced green chile pepper
1 teaspoon chili powder

1 teaspoon ground cayenne pepper
1 (5 ounce) bottle hot pepper sauce
1 teaspoon garlic powder

Trim the roast of any excess fat, and season with salt and pepper. Heat olive oil in a large skillet over medium-high heat. Place meat in hot skillet, and brown meat quickly on all sides. Transfer the roast to a slow cooker, and sprinkle onion over meat. Season with chile peppers, chili powder, cayenne pepper, hot pepper sauce, and garlic powder. Add enough water to cover 1/3 of the roast. Cover, and cook on High for 6 hours, checking to make sure there is always at least a small amount of liquid in the bottom. Reduce heat to Low, and continue cooking for 2 to 4 hours, or until meat is totally tender and falls apart.

435- Savory Cheese Soup

3 (14.5 ounce) cans chicken broth
1 small onion, chopped
1 large carrot, chopped
1 celery rib, chopped
1/4 cup chopped sweet red pepper
2 tablespoons butter or margarine
1 teaspoon salt

1/2 teaspoon pepper
1/3 cup all-purpose flour
1/3 cup cold water
1 (8 ounce) package cream cheese, cubed
and softened
2 cups shredded Cheddar cheese
1 (12 fluid ounce) can beer (optional)

Optional toppings: croutons, popcorn, cooked crumbled bacon, sliced green onions
In a slow cooker, combine the first eight ingredients. Cover and cook on low for 7-8 hours. Combine flour and water until smooth; stir into soup. Cover and cook on high 30 minutes longer or until soup is thickened. Stir in cream cheese and cheddar cheese until blended. Stir in beer if desired. Cover and cook on low until heated through. Serve with desired toppings.

436- Slim's Bad Attitude Nacho Sauce

7 (15 ounce) jars nacho cheese dip
3 pounds ground beef
3 (1.25 ounce) packages dry
Mexican or taco seasoning

1 yellow onion, diced
1 teaspoon chili powder
4 (10 ounce) cans diced tomatoes with
green chilies, drained water (optional)

Pour the cheese sauce into a large slow cooker. Cover, and set to High. Place a large skillet over medium heat. Cook the ground beef until completely browned; stir in the taco seasoning. Reserving the fat in the skillet, use a slotted spoon to transfer the beef to the slow cooker and stir into the cheese. Return the skillet to medium heat. Combine the onion and chili powder in the skillet; cook until the onion softens. Stir in the tomatoes with green chiles. Add to the cheese mixture and stir through. If sauce is too thick, stir in up to 1/2 cup water.

437- Sweet and Sour Meatballs

1 (12 fluid ounce) can or bottle chile
sauce
2 teaspoons lemon juice

9 ounces grape jelly
1 pound lean ground beef
1 egg, beaten

1 large onion, grated salt to taste

Whisk together the chili sauce, lemon juice and grape jelly. Pour into slow cooker and simmer over low heat until warm. Combine ground beef, egg, onion and salt. Mix well and form into 1 inch balls. Add to sauce and simmer for 1 1/2 hours.

438- Slow Cooker Buffalo Brisket

1 teaspoon olive oil
1 (3 pound) buffalo brisket
1 small onion, chopped
2 teaspoons chopped garlic

1 teaspoon dried basil salt and pepper to taste
2 cups chicken broth
1 cup water

Lightly coat the inside of a slow cooker with olive oil and place the brisket in the bottom of the cooker. Sprinkle in the onion, garlic, and basil; season with salt and pepper. Pour the chicken broth and water. Cook on LOW, covered, until brisket is tender, 6 to 10 hours, basting meat several times to moisten.

439- Vegetable Beef Stew

3/4 pound lean beef stew meat, cut into 1/2-inch cubes
2 teaspoons canola oil
1 (14.5 ounce) can beef broth
1 (14.5 ounce) can stewed tomatoes, cut up
1 1/2 cups peeled and cubed butternut squash
1 cup frozen corn, thawed

6 dried apricot or peach halves, quartered
1/2 cup chopped carrot
1 teaspoon dried oregano
1/4 teaspoon salt
1/4 teaspoon pepper
2 tablespoons cornstarch
1/4 cup water
2 tablespoons minced fresh parsley

In a nonstick skillet, brown beef in oil over medium heat. Transfer to a slow cooker. Add the broth, tomatoes, squash, corn, apricots, carrot, oregano, salt and pepper. Cover and cook on high for 5-6 hours or until vegetables and meat are tender. Combine cornstarch and water until smooth; stir into stew. Cover and cook on high for 30 minutes or until gravy is thickened. Stir in parsley.

440- Slow Cooker Pork Cacciatore

2 tablespoons olive oil
1 onion, sliced
4 boneless pork chops
1 (28 ounce) jar pasta sauce
1 (28 ounce) can diced tomatoes
1 green bell pepper, seeded and sliced into strips

1 (8 ounce) package fresh mushrooms, sliced
2 large cloves garlic, minced
1 teaspoon Italian seasoning
1/2 teaspoon dried basil
1/2 cup dry white wine
4 slices mozzarella cheese

In a large skillet, brown chops over medium-high heat. Transfer to slow cooker. In the same pan, cook onion in oil over medium heat until browned. Stir in mushrooms and bell pepper, and cook until these vegetables are soft. Mix in pasta sauce, diced tomatoes, and white wine. Season with Italian seasoning, basil, and garlic. Pour over pork chops in slow cooker. Cook on Low for 7 to 8 hours. To serve, place a slice of cheese over each chop, and cover with sauce.

441- Beer Beef Stew II

2 tablespoons vegetable oil
3 1/2 pounds beef stew meat, cut into 1
1/2 inch pieces
1 cup all-purpose flour
2 large potatoes, chopped
1 cup chopped carrots
3/4 cup chopped celery

3/4 cup chopped onion
3 cloves garlic, chopped
1 tablespoon dried basil
1 tablespoon dried thyme
1 cup chili sauce
1 cup beer
1/4 cup brown sugar

Heat the oil in a skillet over medium heat. Place the beef stew meat and flour in a large resealable plastic bag, and shake to coat. Transfer coated meat to the skillet, and cook about 1 minute, until browned. Mix the potatoes, carrots, celery, onion, and garlic in a slow cooker. Place browned beef over the vegetables, and season with basil and thyme. In a bowl, mix the chili sauce, beer, and brown sugar, and pour over meat in the slow cooker. Cover slow cooker, and cook 8 hours on Low or 2 hours on High.

442- Cream of Leek Soup

4 bacon strips, diced
3 medium leeks (white portion only),
sliced
1 medium onion, chopped
4 large potatoes, peeled and sliced

4 cups chicken broth
2 cups half-and-half cream
2 tablespoons minced fresh parsley
salt and pepper to taste

In a pressure cooker, cook bacon over medium heat until crisp. Remove with a slotted spoon to paper towels. In the drippings, saute leeks and onion until tender. Add potatoes and broth. Close cover securely; place pressure regulator on vent pipe.Bring cooker to full pressure over high heat. Reduce heat to medium-high and cook for 5 minutes. (Pressure regulator should maintain a slow steady rocking motion; adjust heat if needed.) Remove from the heat. Immediately cool according to manufacturer's directions until pressure is completely reduced. Uncover; cool soup slightly. In a blender, process soup in batches until smooth. return all to the pan. Add cream and parsley; heat through over medium-low heat (do not boil). Season with salt and pepper. Garnish with bacon.

443- Jeanne's Slow Cooker Spaghetti Sauce

1 (28 ounce) can crushed tomatoes
1 (28 ounce) can diced tomatoes
1 (6 ounce) can tomato paste
1 (10 ounce) can tomato sauce

1/2 pound turkey kielbasa, chopped
1/4 cup extra light olive oil
3 onions, chopped
6 yellow squash, diced

1 small green bell pepper, minced
3 cloves garlic, pressed
1/2 pound extra lean ground beef
1/2 pound extra-lean ground turkey
breast
5 bay leaves

15 whole black peppercorns
1 1/2 teaspoons dried basil
1 teaspoon dried marjoram
2 teaspoons dried thyme
1/2 teaspoon dried oregano

In a slow cooker, combine crushed tomatoes, diced tomatoes, tomato paste, tomato sauce, and kielbasa. Set slow cooker to High. Heat olive oil in a large, deep skillet over medium heat. Cook onions, squash, green pepper, and garlic in oil until onions are translucent. Transfer vegetables to the slow cooker. Place ground beef and ground turkey in a large, deep skillet. Cook over medium-high heat until evenly brown. Drain, crumble finely, and transfer to slow cooker. Season with bay leaves, peppercorns, basil, marjoram, thyme, and oregano. Cover, and cook on High for 2 hours. Remove lid, and cook 1 hour more.

444- Cheese Dip II

1 (2 pound) loaf processed cheese, cubed
1 1/2 pounds ground beef
2/3 cup water

1 (1.25 ounce) package taco seasoning mix
1 (16 ounce) jar picante sauce

Melt processed cheese in a slow cooker set for high heat. Stir occasionally to avoid burning. Place ground beef in a large skillet. Cook over medium high heat until evenly brown. Drain beef, and mix in water and taco seasoning mix. Cook and stir 2 to 4 minutes. Stir seasoned beef into the melted processed cheese. Mix in salsa. Cook and stir until well blended. Serve warm.

445- Hungarian Goulash II

2 pounds beef chuck roast, cubed
1 large onion, diced
1/2 cup ketchup
2 tablespoons Worcestershire sauce
1 tablespoon brown sugar

2 teaspoons salt
2 teaspoons Hungarian sweet paprika
1/2 teaspoon dry mustard
1 1/4 cups water, divided
1/4 cup all-purpose flour

Place beef in slow cooker, and cover with onion. In a medium bowl, stir together ketchup, Worcestershire sauce, brown sugar, salt, paprika, mustard, and 1 cup water. Pour mixture over beef and onions. Cover, and cook on Low for 9 to 10 hours, or until meat is tender. Mix 1/4 cup water with flour to form a paste, and stir into goulash. Cook on High for 10 to 15 minutes, or until sauce thickens.

446- Slow Cooker Pepper Steak

2 pounds beef sirloin, cut into 2 inch
strips
garlic powder to taste
3 tablespoons vegetable oil

1 cube beef bouillon
1/4 cup hot water
1 tablespoon cornstarch
1/2 cup chopped onion

2 large green bell peppers, roughly
chopped
1 (14.5 ounce) can stewed tomatoes, with
liquid

3 tablespoons soy sauce
1 teaspoon white sugar
1 teaspoon salt

Sprinkle strips of sirloin with garlic powder to taste. In a large skillet over medium heat, heat
the vegetable oil and brown the seasoned beef strips. Transfer to a slow cooker. Mix bouillon
cube with hot water until dissolved, then mix in cornstarch until dissolved. Pour into the slow
cooker with meat. Stir in onion, green peppers, stewed tomatoes, soy sauce, sugar, and salt.
Cover, and cook on High for 3 to 4 hours, or on Low for 6 to 8 hours.

447- Slow-Cooked Pork Barbecue

1 (3 pound) boneless pork loin roast
1 1/2 teaspoons seasoned salt
1 teaspoon garlic powder

1 cup barbecue sauce
1 cup regular cola
8 sandwich rolls, split

Cut roast in half; place in a slow cooker. Sprinkle with seasoned salt and garlic powder. Cover
and cook on low for 4 hours or until meat is tender. Remove meat; skim fat from cooking
juices. Shred meat with a fork and return to the slow cooker. Combine barbecue sauce and
cola; pour over meat. Cover and cook on high for 1-2 hours or until sauce is thickened. Serve
on rolls.

448- Chicken and Two Bean Chili

2 chicken breasts, cut into chunks
1 tablespoon olive oil
1/3 red onion, chopped
3 cloves garlic, minced
1 (15 ounce) can black beans, drained
1 (14.5 ounce) can great Northern beans,
drained
2 (14.5 ounce) cans diced tomatoes with
green chile peppers
1 (14 ounce) can tomato sauce
1/2 cup chicken stock

1/2 cup brown sugar
1/2 cup frozen corn
1/4 cup white vinegar
3 tablespoons chili powder
3 tablespoons ground cumin
2 tablespoons dried cilantro
Dash of salt
1 pinch cayenne pepper
1/2 green bell peppers, diced
1/2 red bell pepper, diced
1/2 yellow bell pepper, diced

Fill a large pot with lightly-salted water and bring to a boil. Boil the chicken until no longer
pink in the center and the juices run clear, 7 to 10 minutes. Drain the chicken and place in a
slow cooker. Heat the olive oil in a skillet over medium heat. Brown the onion and garlic in
the hot oil, 5 to 7 minutes; scrape into the slow cooker. Add the black beans, great Northern
beans, tomatoes with green chiles, tomato sauce, chicken stock, brown sugar, corn, vinegar,
chili powder, cumin, cilantro, salt, and cayenne pepper to the slow cooker. Cook on High until
the beans are tender, 3 to 4 hours. Stir the diced green, red, and yellow bell peppers into the
chili and cook another 20 minutes.

449- Slow Cooker Carrot Chicken

4 pounds skinless, boneless chicken
breast meat
1 medium head cabbage, quartered
1 pound carrots, cut into 1 inch pieces
water to cover

4 cubes chicken bouillon
1 teaspoon poultry seasoning
1/4 teaspoon Greek-style seasoning
2 tablespoons cornstarch
1/4 cup water

Rinse chicken and place in slow cooker. Rinse cabbage and place on top of chicken, then add carrots. Add enough water to almost cover all. Add bouillon cubes and sprinkle liberally with poultry seasoning. Add Greek seasoning to taste (as you would salt and pepper). Cook on low for 8 hours OR on high for 4 hours. To Make Gravy: When you're nearly ready to eat, pour off some of the juice and place in a saucepan. Bring to a boil. Dissolve cornstarch in about 1/4 cup water (depending on how thick you like your gravy). Add to saucepan and simmer all together until thick. If desired, season with additional Greek seasoning. Serve gravy over chicken and potatoes, if desired.

450- Warm Fruit Compote

2 (29 ounce) cans sliced peaches, drained
2 (29 ounce) cans pear halves, drained
and sliced
1 (20 ounce) can pineapple chunks,
drained

1 (15 ounce) can apricot halves, drained
and sliced
1 (21 ounce) can cherry pie filling

In a 5-qt. slow cooker, combine the peaches, pears, pineapple and apricots. Top with pie filling. Cover and cook on high for 2 hours or until heated through. Serve with a slotted spoon.

451- Bavarian Style Meatballs

12 fluid ounces tomato-based chili sauce
1 (16 ounce) can whole cranberry sauce
27 ounces Bavarian-style sauerkraut,
undrained

1 cup water
1 cup packed brown sugar
1 (16 ounce) package frozen meatballs

In a medium size mixing bowl, combine chili sauce, cranberry sauce, sauerkraut, water, and brown sugar. Mix well. Pour sauce and meatballs in a slow cooker, stir. Cook, covered, at a medium temperature for 4 hours. Stir occasionally to coat meatballs.

452- Easy Slow Cooker Meatballs

1 1/2 pounds ground beef
1 1/4 cups Italian seasoned bread crumbs
1/4 cup chopped fresh parsley
2 cloves garlic, minced
1 medium yellow onion, chopped

1 egg, beaten
1 (28 ounce) jar spaghetti sauce
1 (16 ounce) can crushed tomatoes
1 (14.25 ounce) can tomato puree

In a bowl, mix the ground beef, bread crumbs, parsley, garlic, onion, and egg. Shape the mixture into 16 meatballs. In a slow cooker, mix the spaghetti sauce, crushed tomatoes, and tomato puree. Place the meatballs into the sauce mixture. Cook on Low for 6 to 8 hours.

453- Spicy Beef Vegetable Stew

1 pound ground beef
1 cup chopped onion
1 (30 ounce) jar meatless spaghetti sauce
3 1/2 cups water
1 (16 ounce) package frozen mixed
vegetables

1 (10 ounce) can diced tomatoes and
green chilies
1 cup sliced celery
1 teaspoon beef bouillon granules
1 teaspoon pepper

In a skillet over medium heat, cook beef and onion until meat is no longer pink; drain. Transfer to a slow cooker. Stir in the remaining ingredients. Cover and cook on low for 8 hours or until the vegetables are tender.

454- Slow Cooker Balsamic Beef and Onions

1 tablespoon olive oil
1 large yellow onion, quartered and
sliced
1 1/2 pounds boneless beef rump roast
4 cloves garlic, thinly sliced

1/4 cup balsamic vinegar, or more to
taste
3 tablespoons tomato paste
1/2 cup water
salt and pepper to taste

Drizzle olive oil into the bottom of a slow cooker, and arrange half the onion slices over the oil. Lay the beef roast on top of the onion, and sprinkle the rest of the onion slices and the garlic around the roast. Sprinkle the balsamic vinegar, tomato paste, and water around the roast. Cover the slow cooker, set to High, and cook until the meat is tender, about 6 hours. Shred the meat into bite-size pieces with two forks, and season with salt and pepper. Serve with the juices from the slow cooker.

455- Sour Cream Pork Chops

6 pork chops
salt and pepper to taste garlic powder to
taste
1/2 cup all-purpose flour
1 large onion, sliced 1/4 inch thick

2 cubes chicken bouillon
2 cups boiling water
2 tablespoons all-purpose flour
1 (8 ounce) container sour cream

Season pork chops with salt, pepper, and garlic powder, and then dredge in 1/2 cup flour. In a skillet over medium heat, lightly brown chops in a small amount of oil. Place chops in slow cooker, and top with onion slices. Dissolve bouillon cubes in boiling water and pour over chops. Cover, and cook on Low 7 to 8 hours. Preheat oven to 200 degrees F (95 degrees C). After the chops have cooked, transfer chops to the oven to keep warm. Be careful, the chops are so tender they will fall apart. In a small bowl, blend 2 tablespoons flour with the sour cream; mix into meat juices. Turn slow cooker to High for 15 to 30 minutes, or until sauce is slightly thickened. Serve sauce over pork chops.

456- Slow-Cooked, Texas-Style Beef Brisket

8 pounds untrimmed beef brisket
1 cup strong black coffee
1 (14 ounce) bottle ketchup
1 (12 fluid ounce) can cola carbonated beverage

3 tablespoons Worcestershire sauce
3 tablespoons prepared yellow mustard
2 tablespoons liquid smoke flavoring
2 tablespoons brown sugar, packed

Place the beef brisket in a large slow cooker with the fat side up. Pour the coffee over the meat. Cook the brisket on LOW for 24 hours. Meanwhile, stir together the ketchup, cola beverage, Worcestershire sauce, mustard, liquid smoke, and brown sugar in a bowl until well blended. Refrigerate until needed. After 24 hours, remove and discard any fat from the brisket. Use a fork to pull apart and shred the meat. Pour the sauce over the meat, stirring to coat evenly, and cook 1 hour longer.

457- Barbecued Country Ribs

1/3 cup all-purpose flour
1/4 teaspoon garlic powder
1/4 teaspoon salt
1/8 teaspoon pepper
1 1/2 pounds boneless country- style ribs, cut into 2-inch chunks

1 tablespoon vegetable oil
1 cup hot water
1/2 cup ketchup
1/4 teaspoon chili powder
1/8 teaspoon hot pepper sauce
1 small onion, halved and sliced

In a large resealable plastic bag, combine the flour, garlic powder, salt and pepper. Add rib pieces; shake to coat. In a pressure cooker, brown meat on all sides in oil; drain. Combine the water, ketchup, chili powder and hot pepper sauce; pour over ribs. Add onion. Close cover securely; place pressure regulator on vent pipe. Bring cooker to full pressure over high heat. Reduce heat to medium-high and cook for 15 minutes. (Pressure regulator should maintain a slow steady rocking motion; adjust heat if needed.) Remove from the heat; allow pressure to drop on its own. Skim fat from sauce if necessary and serve with ribs if desired.

458- Apple Butter IV

6 (16 ounce) jars applesauce
6 cups apple juice
8 cups white sugar

2 tablespoons ground cinnamon
2 teaspoons ground cloves
2 teaspoons ground nutmeg

In a Dutch oven or slow cooker, bring to a boil the applesauce and apple juice. Reduce heat and simmer 1 hour. In a small bowl, mix the sugar, cinnamon, cloves and nutmeg. Stir the mixture into the simmering applesauce. Continue simmering 2 hours more, creating a thick, rich butter. Ladle the apple butter into sterile jars and refrigerate.

459- Cranberry Pot Roast

3 cups beef broth
1 cup water
2 (14.5 ounce) cans cranberry sauce
1 (4 pound) beef chuck roast

salt and ground black pepper to taste
3 tablespoons all-purpose flour
2 tablespoons vegetable oil
1 large sweet onion, chopped

Bring the beef broth and water to a boil in a saucepan over high heat. Stir in the cranberry sauce until dissolved. Pour the sauce into a slow cooker set to High. Meanwhile, season the beef roast with salt and pepper, then sprinkle evenly with the flour. Heat the vegetable oil in large skillet over medium heat. Cook the roast in the hot oil until brown on all sides, about 2 minutes per side. Transfer the roast to the slow cooker along with the chopped onion. Cook until the roast easily pulls apart with a fork, about 4 hours.

460- The Ultimate Chili

1 pound lean ground beef salt and
pepper to taste
3 (15 ounce) cans dark red kidney beans
3 (14.5 ounce) cans Mexican-style stewed
tomatoes
2 stalks celery, chopped
1 red bell pepper, chopped

1/4 cup red wine vinegar
2 tablespoons chili powder
1 teaspoon ground cumin
1 teaspoon dried parsley
1 teaspoon dried basil
1 dash Worcestershire sauce
1/2 cup red wine

In a large skillet over medium-high heat, cook ground beef until evenly browned. Drain off grease, and season to taste with salt and pepper. In a slow cooker, combine the cooked beef, kidney beans, tomatoes, celery, red bell pepper, and red wine vinegar. Season with chili powder, cumin, parsley, basil and Worcestershire sauce. Stir to distribute ingredients evenly. Cook on High for 6 hours, or on Low for 8 hours. Pour in the wine during the last 2 hours.

461- Slow Cooker Venison Chili for the Big Game

1 pound boneless venison steak, cubed
1 pound pork sausage
1 onion, chopped
2 cloves garlic, minced
1 (6 ounce) can tomato paste hot pepper
sauce to taste
salt and ground black pepper to taste

1 (15.5 ounce) can cannellini beans,
drained
1 (10 ounce) can diced tomatoes with
green chiles
3 tablespoons chili powder, or to taste
1 cup shredded Cheddar cheese for
garnish

Place the venison and sausage in a large skillet and cook, breaking up with a wooden spoon as necessary, over medium heat until no longer pink and evenly browned. Drain grease. Stir in the onions and garlic, and cook until aromatic, about 3 minutes. Drain, and mix in the tomato paste. Season to taste with hot pepper sauce, salt, and pepper. Pour the cannellini beans and tomatoes into a slow cooker. Stir in the venison mixture. Cover, and cook 8 to 10 hours on Low, or 5 hours on High. Sprinkle each serving with shredded Cheddar cheese.

462- Slow Cooker Clam Chowder

1 (6 ounce) can minced clams
4 slices bacon, cut into small pieces
3 potatoes, peeled and cubed
1 cup chopped onion
1 carrot, grated

1 (10.75 ounce) can condensed cream of mushroom soup
1/4 teaspoon ground black pepper
2 (12 fluid ounce) cans evaporated milk

In a small bowl, drain the clams and reserve the juice. Add water to the juice as needed to total 1 3/4 cups liquid. Cover the clams and put in refrigerator for later. In a slow cooker combine the bacon, potatoes, onion, carrot, soup, ground black pepper, evaporated milk and reserved clam juice with water. Cover and cook on low setting for 9 to 11 hours OR on high setting for 4 to 5 hours. Add the clams and cook on high setting for another hour.

463- Spicy Seafood Stew

2 pounds potatoes, peeled and diced
1 pound carrots, sliced
1 (26 ounce) jar spaghetti sauce
2 (6 ounce) jars sliced mushrooms, drained
1 1/2 teaspoons ground turmeric
1 1/2 teaspoons minced garlic

1 teaspoon cayenne pepper
3/4 teaspoon salt
1 1/2 cups water
1 pound sea scallops
1 pound uncooked medium shrimp, peeled and deveined

In a 5-qt. slow cooker, combine the first eight ingredients. Cover and cook on low for 4-1/2 to 5 hours or until potatoes are tender. Stir in the water, scallops and shrimp. Cover and cook for 15-20 minutes or until scallops are opaque and shrimp turn pink.

464- Slow-Cooked German Short Ribs

2 tablespoons all-purpose flour
1 teaspoon salt
1/8 teaspoon ground black pepper
3 pounds beef short ribs
2 tablespoons olive oil
1 slice onion, sliced
1/2 cup dry red wine
1/2 cup chile sauce

3 tablespoons packed brown sugar
3 tablespoons vinegar
1 tablespoon Worcestershire sauce
1/2 teaspoon dry mustard
1/2 teaspoon chili powder
2 tablespoons all-purpose flour
1/4 cup water

In a small bowl, combine 2 tablespoons flour, salt, and pepper. Coat the short ribs with the flour mixture. In a large skillet, heat the olive oil over medium-high heat. Brown short ribs in olive oil. In a slow cooker, combine onions, wine, chili sauce, brown sugar, vinegar, Worcestershire sauce, mustard, and chili powder. Mix thoroughly. Transfer the short ribs from the skillet to the slow cooker. Cover, and cook on Low for 6 to 8 hours. Remove ribs, and turn the slow cooker control to High. Mix the remaining 2 tablespoons of flour with 1/4 cup water, and stir into the sauce. Cook for 10 minutes, or until slightly thickened.

465- Luscious Lima Bean Soup II

3 slices bacon
4 cups frozen lima beans
1 (15 ounce) can butter beans, undrained
2 potatoes, diced
2 stalks celery, chopped
2 small onions, chopped

3 carrots, sliced
1/4 cup butter
1/2 tablespoon dried marjoram
1 teaspoon salt
1/2 teaspoon pepper
3 (14 ounce) cans chicken broth

Cook the bacon in a skillet over medium heat until evenly brown and crisp. Drain and crumble. In a slow cooker, mix the cooked bacon, lima beans, butter beans and liquid, potatoes, celery, onions, carrots, and butter. Season with marjoram, salt, and pepper. Pour in the chicken broth. Cover slow cooker, and cook soup 7 hours on Low.

466- The Sarge's Goetta - German Breakfast Treat

3 quarts water
2 tablespoons salt
2 teaspoons ground black pepper
5 cups steel cut oats

2 pounds ground beef
2 pounds ground pork sausage
2 large onions, finely chopped
1/4 cup cooking oil

Bring water, salt, and pepper to boil in a slow cooker set to High. Stir in steel cut oats, cover, and cook 90 minutes. In a large bowl, mix beef, pork, and onions. Stir into the oat mixture, and reduce heat to Low. Cover, and continue cooking 3 hours, stirring occasionally. Transfer the mixture to a medium baking pan, and cool until semi- solid. Turn out onto wax paper, and chill 1 hour in the refrigerator, or until firm. Heat oil in a large, heavy skillet over medium high heat. Cut the refrigerated mixture into thin slices. Cook slices one at a time in the heated oil until evenly brown.

467- Roast Beef and Gravy

1 (3 pound) boneless beef chuck roast
2 (10.75 ounce) cans condensed cream of mushroom soup, undiluted

1/3 cup sherry, wine or beef broth
1 envelope onion soup mix

Cut roast in half; place in a slow cooker. In a bowl, combine the remaining ingredients; pour over roast. Cover and cook on low for 8-9 hours or until meat is tender.

468- Diego's Special Beef Stew

1 pound cubed beef stew meat
1 tablespoon all-purpose flour
2 tablespoons olive oil
2 teaspoons butter
1 medium yellow onion, thinly sliced
1/4 cup red wine
1 beef bouillon cube

1 cup hot water
1 large potato, cubed
1/2 cup baby carrots
1/2 teaspoon rosemary
1/2 teaspoon dried thyme
1/2 tablespoon garlic powder
1/2 teaspoon ground black pepper

1/4 cup water   2 dashes Worcestershire sauce

Place cubed beef and flour in a resealable plastic bag. Seal and shake to evenly coat beef with flour. Heat the oil in a skillet over medium heat, and brown beef on all sides. Transfer to a slow cooker. Melt the butter in the skillet over medium heat, and cook onion until tender. Transfer to the slow cooker with the beef. Pour wine into the skillet to deglaze, then pour wine into slow cooker. Dissolve the beef bouillon cube in 1 cup hot water, and pour into slow cooker. Place potato and carrots in slow cooker, and season with rosemary, thyme, garlic powder, and pepper. Mix in remaining water and Worcestershire sauce. Add more water if needed to cover all ingredients. Cover slow cooker, and cook stew 7 to 8 hours on Low.

469- Better Slow Cooker Robust Chicken

1 1/2 pounds skinless, boneless chicken breast halves - cut into 1 inch strips
2 tablespoons bacon bits
1/4 cup chopped green olives
1 (14.5 ounce) can diced tomatoes, drained

1 (4.5 ounce) can sliced mushrooms, drained
1 (1.25 ounce) envelope dry chicken gravy mix
1/2 cup red wine
3 tablespoons Dijon mustard
1/4 cup balsamic vinegar

In a slow cooker, combine the chicken, bacon bits, olives, tomatoes, mushrooms, gravy mix, wine, mustard, and vinegar. Mix together. Cover slow cooker, and cook on Low setting for 6 to 8 hours.

470- Easiest Pot Roast Ever

3 pounds beef roast
6 potatoes
1 1/2 cups baby carrots
1 yellow onion

2 stalks celery
3 cubes beef bouillon
1/2 cup water

Cut up potatoes, onions, and celery in to fairly large chunks and place in a slow cooker. Put roast on top of vegetables. Place 3 bouillon cubes randomly on top of roast and pour in water. Cover, and cook on low for 6 to 8 hours or High for 4 to 5 hours.

471- Slow Cooker Chicken Pot Pie Stew

4 large skinless, boneless chicken breast halves, cut into cubes
10 medium red potatoes, quartered
1 (8 ounce) package baby carrots
1 cup chopped celery
2 (26 ounce) cans condensed cream of chicken soup

6 cubes chicken bouillon
2 teaspoons garlic salt
1 teaspoon celery salt
1 tablespoon ground black pepper
1 (16 ounce) bag frozen mixed vegetables

Combine the chicken, potatoes, carrots, celery, chicken soup, chicken bouillon, garlic salt, celery salt, and black pepper in a slow cooker; cook on High for 5 hours. Stir the frozen mixed vegetables into the slow cooker, and cook 1 hour more.

472- Hash Brown Casserole for the Slow Cooker

2 cups sour cream
1 (10.75 ounce) can condensed cream of mushroom soup, undiluted
2 cups shredded processed cheese
1/2 cup chopped onion

1/4 teaspoon salt
1/4 teaspoon pepper
1 (32 ounce) package frozen hash brown potatoes, thawed

In a large bowl, stir together the sour cream, cream of mushroom soup, cheese, onion, salt and pepper. Gradually mix in the hash browns until evenly coated. Coat the inside of a slow cooker with cooking spray or butter. Spoon the hashbrown mixture into the slow cooker. Cover, and cook on High for 1 1/2 hours, then reduce heat to Low, and cook for an additional 2 1/2 hours.

473- Cream of Mushroom and Soy Sauce Pork Chops

1/4 cup brown sugar
6 pork chops
1 (5 ounce) bottle soy sauce

1 (10.75 ounce) can condensed cream of mushroom soup

Rub brown sugar into pork chops. Place chops in shallow dish and pour soy sauce over. Cover and refrigerate. Allow to marinate for one hour. Pour the cream of mushroom soup into the crock of a slow cooker. Remove chops from the soy sauce and place on top of soup. Cover, and cook on Low until very tender, 6 to 8 hours.

474- Cocktail Meatballs III

3 pounds ground beef
2 (1 ounce) packages dry onion soup mix
3 slices white bread
2 tablespoons half-and-half

1 (28 ounce) bottle ketchup
1 cup packed dark brown sugar
2 tablespoons Worcestershire sauce

Preheat oven to 350 degrees F (175 degrees C). Remove the crusts from the white bread and tear into small bread crumbs. In a medium size mixing bowl, combine beef, soup mix, white bread crumbs and half-and-half cream. Roll mixture into 1 inch balls and arrange in 9x13 inch baking dishes (as many baking dishes as it takes or bake the meatballs in shifts). Bake 10 to 15 minutes; or until browned. In a slow cooker with the temperature set to high, mix together ketchup, brown sugar and Worcestershire sauce. Cook until the mixture comes to a boil, then reduce temperature to low until you are ready to serve the meatballs. Place the meatballs in the sauce and serve.

475- Mexican Style Shredded Pork

1 (3 pound) boneless pork loin roast, cut into 2 inch pieces
1/2 teaspoon salt
2 (4 ounce) cans diced green chile peppers
3 cloves garlic, crushed
1/4 cup chipotle sauce
3 1/4 cups water, divided
1 1/2 cups uncooked long grain white rice
1/4 cup fresh lime juice
1/4 cup chopped cilantro

Place the roast in a slow cooker, and season with salt. Place chile peppers and garlic on top of roast. Pour in the chipotle sauce and 1/2 cup water. Cover, and cook 7 hours on Low.
In a pot, bring remaining 2 3/4 cups water and rice to a boil. Mix in the lime juice and cilantro. Reduce heat to low, cover, and simmer 20 minutes. Remove roast from the slow cooker, and use two forks to shred. Return pork to the slow cooker, and allow to sit 15 minutes to absorb some of the liquid. Serve over the cooked rice.

476- Vegetarian Buffalo Chicken Dip

1 (8 ounce) package seasoned chicken-style vegetarian strips (such as Morningstar Farms® Chik'n Strips), diced
2 (8 ounce) packages reduced fat cream cheese, softened
1 (16 ounce) bottle reduced-fat ranch salad dressing
1 (12 fluid ounce) bottle hot buffalo wing sauce (such as Frank's® REDHOT Buffalo Wing Sauce)
1 cup Colby-Monterey Jack cheese blend

Place the diced vegetarian chicken strips, cream cheese, ranch dressing, and buffalo wing sauce into a slow cooker. Cook on Low, stirring occasionally, until the cheese has melted and the dip is hot, 1 to 2 hours. Stir in the shredded cheese and serve.

477- Anna's Amazing Easy Pleasy Meatballs over

2 (10.75 ounce) cans condensed cream of celery soup
2 (10.5 ounce) cans condensed French onion soup
1 (16 ounce) container sour cream
6 pounds frozen Italian-style meatballs
2 (16 ounce) packages uncooked egg noodles
1/2 cup butter

In a large slow cooker, mix together the cream of celery soup, French onion soup, and sour cream. Stir in the meatballs. Cook on high heat for 3-4 hours. Bring a large pot of lightly salted water to a boil. Add pasta and cook for 8 to 10 minutes or until al dente; drain. In a large bowl, toss the pasta with butter. Serve meatballs and sauce over the cooked pasta.

478- Crock Pot Cheesy Mushroom Chicken

6 skinless, boneless chicken breast halves
1 (10.75 ounce) can condensed cream of
chicken soup
1 (10.75 ounce) can condensed cream of
mushroom soup
1/2 cup cooking sherry

1 teaspoon minced garlic
1 teaspoon celery flakes
1/2 teaspoon paprika
1/2 cup grated Parmesan cheese
1 (8 ounce) can mushroom pieces,
drained

Place the chicken breasts into a slow cooker. Whisk the cream of chicken soup, cream of mushroom soup, sherry, garlic, celery flakes, and paprika in a mixing bowl. Stir in the Parmesan cheese and mushroom pieces; pour over the chicken. Cook on Low for 8 hours until the chicken is tender, and the sauce has reduced slightly.

479- Bean and Beef Shaloupias

1 pound pinto beans, boiled according to
package directions
2 cubes beef bouillon water to cover
1 1/2 pounds ground beef
1/4 teaspoon salt

1/4 teaspoon ground black pepper
1/2 onion, diced
10 (6 inch) corn tortillas
3 cups shredded Mexican-style cheese

In slow cooker, combine boiled pinto beans with bouillon cubes and enough water to almost fill cooker. Let simmer on Low setting for 8 hours. In a large skillet, brown beef with salt, pepper and onion. Drain well and set aside. Assemble as follows: Top each tortilla with beef mixture, cheese and a ladel of beans with juice from slow cooker. Top with preferred garnishes as desired and serve.

480- Sweet N Sour Beans

8 bacon strips, diced
2 medium onions, halved and thinly
sliced
1 cup packed brown sugar
1/2 cup cider vinegar
1 teaspoon salt
1 teaspoon ground mustard
1/2 teaspoon garlic powder
1 (28 ounce) can baked beans, undrained

1 (16 ounce) can kidney beans, rinsed
and drained
1 (15.5 ounce) can pinto beans, rinsed
and drained
1 (15 ounce) can lima beans, rinsed and
drained
1 (15.5 ounce) can black-eyed
peas, rinsed and drained

In a large skillet, cook bacon over medium heat until crisp. Remove with slotted spoon to paper towels. Drain, reserving 2 tablespoons drippings. Saute onions in the drippings until tender. Add brown sugar, vinegar, salt, mustard and garlic powder. Bring to a boil. In a 5-qt. slow cooker, combine beans and peas. Add onion mixture and bacon; mix well. Cover and cook on high for 3-4 hours or until heated through.

481- Nacho Rice Dip

1 (6.8 ounce) package Spanish rice and vermicelli mix
2 tablespoons butter or margarine
2 cups water
1 (14.5 ounce) can diced tomatoes, undrained

1 pound ground beef
1 pound process American cheese, cubed
1 (14.5 ounce) can stewed tomatoes
1 (8 ounce) jar process cheese sauce
Tortilla chips

In a large saucepan, cook rice mix in butter until golden. Stir in water and diced tomatoes; bring to a boil. Reduce heat; cover and simmer for 15-20 minutes or until rice is tender. Meanwhile, in a skillet, cook beef until no longer pink. Drain andadd to the rice. Stir in cheese, stewed tomatoes and cheese sauce; cook and stir until cheese is melted. Transfer to a slow cooker; cover and keep warm on low. Serve with tortilla chips.

482- Pork Chops to Live For

2 tablespoons shortening
4 pork chops
1 egg, beaten
1/2 cup all-purpose flour

1 large onion, sliced
2 (10.75 ounce) cans condensed cream of mushroom soup
2 cups milk

Melt shortening in a large skillet over medium-high heat. Dip pork chops in beaten egg, then dredge in flour. Cook in hot skillet, turning once to brown both sides. Place pork chops into a slow cooker, and arrange sliced onions over meat. Pour soup and milk over the meat and onions. Cover, and cook on High for 4 to 5 hours, or on Low for 8 to 10 hours.

483- Slow-Cooked Sirloin

1 (1 1/2-pound) boneless beef sirloin steak
1 medium onion, cut into 1-inch chunks
1 medium green bell pepper, cut into 1 inch pieces
1 (14.5 ounce) can reduced- sodium beef broth

1/4 cup Worcestershire sauce
1/4 teaspoon dill weed
1/4 teaspoon dried thyme
1/4 teaspoon pepper
1 dash crushed red pepper flakes
2 tablespoons cornstarch
2 tablespoons water

In a large nonstick skillet coated with nonstick cooking spray, brown beef on both sides. Place onion and green pepper in a 3-qt. slow cooker. Top with beef. Combine the broth, Worcestershire sauce, dill, thyme, pepper and pepper flakes; pour over beef. Cover and cook on high for 3-4 hours or until meat reaches desired doneness and vegetables are crisp-tender. Remove beef and keep warm. Combine cornstarch and water until smooth; gradually stir into cooking juices. Cover and cook about 30 minutes longer or until slightly thickened. Return beef to the slow cooker; heat through.

484- Barbecued Beans

1 pound dry navy beans
1 pound sliced bacon, cooked and
crumbled
1 (32 fluid ounce) bottle tomato juice
1 (8 ounce) can tomato sauce
2 cups chopped onion

2/3 cup packed brown sugar
1 tablespoon soy sauce
2 teaspoons garlic salt
1 teaspoon Worcestershire sauce
1 teaspoon ground mustard

Place beans in a 3-qt. saucepan; cover with water. Bring to a boil; boil for 2 minutes. Remove from the heat; let stand for 1 hour. Drain beans and discard liquid. In a 5-qt. slow cooker, combine remaining ingredients; mix well. Add the beans. Cover and cook on high for 2 hours. Reduce heat to low and cook 8-10 hours longer or until beans are tender.

485- Homemade Potato Soup

6 medium white potatoes, peeled and
chopped
2 onions, chopped
1 carrot, peeled and diced
3 stalks celery, diced
1 tablespoon oil-packed minced garlic
4 cubes chicken bouillon

1 quart water
1 tablespoon parsley flakes
1 tablespoon salt-free herb seasoning
blend
1 tablespoon Italian seasoning
1 1/2 cups soy milk
2 cups chopped broccoli

In a slow cooker, place the potatoes, onions, carrot, celery, oil- packed garlic, and bouillon cubes. Pour in the water, and season with parsley, herb seasoning blend, and Italian seasoning. Cover slow cooker, and cook soup 3 to 4 hours on High, or 10 to 12 hours on Low. Stir in soy milk during the final 30 minutes of cook time. Place broccoli over boiling water in a pot fitted with a steamer basket, and steam 5 minutes, or until tender but firm. Spoon into the soup to serve.

486- Trout Chowder

1 medium onion, chopped
1 tablespoon butter or margarine
2 cups milk
1 cup Ranch salad dressing
1 pound skinless, boneless trout fillets
1 (10 ounce) package frozen broccoli
cuts, thawed

1 cup cubed or shredded Cheddar cheese
1 cup cubed or shredded
Monterey Jack cheese
1/4 teaspoon garlic powder
Paprika

In a skillet, saute onion in butter until tender. Transfer to a slow cooker; add milk, dressing, fish, broccoli, cheeses and garlic powder. Cover and cook on high for 1-1/2 to 2 hours or until soup is bubbly and fish flakes easily with a fork. Sprinkle with paprika if desired.

487- Slow Cooker Macaroni and Cheese I

1/2 pound elbow macaroni
4 cups shredded Cheddar cheese,
divided
1 (12 fluid ounce) can evaporated milk

1 1/2 cups milk
2 eggs
1 teaspoon salt
1/2 teaspoon ground black pepper

Coat the inside of the slow cooker with cooking spray. In a large bowl, beat eggs with fresh and evaporated milks. Mix in uncooked macaroni and 3 cups shredded cheese. Transfer to slow cooker, and sprinkle remaining cheese on top. Cook on low for 5 to 6 hours. Do not stir or remove lid while cooking.

488- Slow Cooker Buffalo Chicken Sandwiches

4 skinless, boneless chicken breast halves
1 (17.5 fluid ounce) bottle buffalo wing
sauce, divided

1/2 (1 ounce) package dry ranch salad
dressing mix
2 tablespoons butter
6 hoagie rolls, split lengthwise

Place the chicken breasts into a slow cooker, and pour in 3/4 of the wing sauce and the ranch dressing mix. Cover, and cook on Low for 6 to 7 hours. Once the chicken has cooked, add the butter, and shred the meat finely with two forks. Pile the meat onto the hoagie rolls, and splash with the remaining buffalo wing sauce to serve.

489- Currant Jelly Wiener Sauce

1 cup red currant jelly
1 cup prepared Dijon-style mustard
1/4 cup ketchup

3/4 cup brown sugar
4 (16 ounce) packages little smokie
sausages

In a slow cooker over medium low heat, mix the red currant jelly, Dijon-style mustard, ketchup and brown sugar. Place little smokie sausages into the mixture and simmer at least 2 hours before serving with toothpicks.

490- Chicken and Rice Soup II

1/2 cup chopped celery
1 pound boneless chicken breast halves,
cooked and diced
3 (14.5 ounce) cans chicken broth
1/2 cup water

2 cups frozen mixed vegetables
3/4 cup converted long-grain white rice
1 tablespoon dried parsley
2 teaspoons lemon and herb seasoning

Combine celery, chicken pieces, chicken broth, water, mixed vegetables, rice, parsley and herb seasoning in a slow cooker. Cover, and cook on low 6 to 8 hours. If soup is too thick, add more water to dilute and allow 15 minutes of additional cooking time.

491- Slow Cooker Chicken with Mushroom Wine Sauce

1 (10.75 ounce) can condensed cream of mushroom soup
1 teaspoon dried minced onion
1 teaspoon dried parsley
1/4 cup white wine
1/4 teaspoon garlic powder
1 tablespoon milk
1 (4 ounce) can mushroom pieces, drained
salt and pepper to taste
4 boneless, skinless chicken breast halves

In a slow cooker, mix together the soup, onion, parsley, wine, garlic powder, milk, and mushroom pieces. Season with salt and pepper. Place chicken in the slow cooker, covering with the soup mixture. Cook on Low setting for 5 to 6 hours, or on High setting for 3 to 4 hours.

492- Hobo Beef and Vegetable Soup

1 (32 fluid ounce) container beef broth, or more if needed
3 carrots, cut into bite-size pieces
1 large stalk celery, cut into bite- size pieces
1 1/2 tablespoons chopped fresh parsley
1/2 teaspoon celery seed
2 bay leaves
1 pound lean ground beef
1 onion, chopped
1 clove garlic, minced, or to taste
1 (14.5 ounce) can stewed tomatoes
2 potatoes, peeled and cut into bite-size pieces
1 (15.25 ounce) can whole kernel corn, drained
1 (15 ounce) can green beans, drained
1 (15 ounce) can peas, drained

Stir the beef broth, carrots, celery, parsley, celery seed, and bay leaves into a slow cooker set on High, cover, and cook until the vegetables are tender, about 2 hours. Place the ground beef, onion, and garlic into a skillet over medium heat. Cook, stirring frequently to break the beef into small pieces, until the onion is translucent and the beef is browned and no longer shows pink areas, 10 to 15 minutes. Drain off fat, and stir the stewed tomatoes into the beef mixture. Bring to a boil over medium heat, and cook, stirring frequently, until the tomatoes are broken up into small pieces. Stir the potatoes, corn, green beans, and peas into the soup in the slow cooker, and add the beef mixture. Stir everything together, cover, and set the slow cooker on High. Cook for 4 hours.

493- Easy Slow Cooker Chicken Wings

5 1/2 pounds chicken wings, split and tips discarded
1 (12 fluid ounce) can or bottle chile sauce
1/4 cup fresh lemon juice
1/4 cup molasses
2 tablespoons Worcestershire sauce
3 drops hot pepper sauce
1 tablespoon salsa
2 1/2 teaspoons chili powder
1 teaspoon garlic powder
2 teaspoons salt

Place chicken in slow cooker. In a medium bowl combine the chile sauce, lemon juice, molasses, Worcestershire sauce, hot pepper sauce, salsa, chili powder, garlic powder and salt.

Mix together and pour mixture over chicken. Cook in slow cooker on Medium Low setting for 5 hours.

494- Busy Day Barbeque Brisket

1 tablespoon dried thyme leaves
1 tablespoon paprika
2 teaspoons freshly ground black pepper
2 teaspoons salt
1 teaspoon onion powder
1/2 teaspoon garlic powder

1/2 teaspoon cayenne pepper
1/2 teaspoon ground cumin
3 pounds beef brisket, trimmed of fat
1/2 teaspoon liquid smoke flavoring
2 tablespoons Worcestershire sauce
1 1/2 cups barbeque sauce

Combine thyme, paprika, pepper, salt, onion powder, garlic powder, cayenne, and cumin in a small bowl; set aside. Rub brisket all over with liquid smoke, then rub with spice mixture. Pour Worcestershire and barbeque sauces into a slow cooker; place beef on top. Cover, and cook on LOW 8 to 10 hours, until fork tender.

495- Apricot Glazed Pork Roast

1 (10.5 ounce) can Campbell's®
Condensed Chicken Broth
1 (18 ounce) jar apricot preserves

1 large onion, chopped
2 tablespoons Dijon-style mustard
4 pounds boneless pork loin roast

Mix broth, preserves, onion and mustard in 3 1/2-qt. slow cooker. Cut pork to fit. Add to cooker. Cover and cook on LOW 8 to 9 hr.* or until done.

496- Hearty Beef Stew

1 pound cubed beef stew meat
1/4 cup all-purpose flour
1 tablespoon paprika salt and pepper to taste
2 cups beef broth
1 1/2 tablespoons teriyaki sauce
1 onion, chopped

3 carrots, sliced
1 stalk celery, sliced
2 potatoes, cubed
1/2 pound mushrooms, quartered
2 cloves garlic, minced
1 bay leaf

Place beef stew meat into a slow cooker. In a small bowl, mix together flour, paprika, salt, and pepper; sprinkle over beef stew meat, stirring to coat. Stir in beef broth, teriyaki sauce, onion, carrots, celery, potatoes, mushrooms, garlic and bay leaf. Cover, and cook on Low 6 hours, stirring occasionally.

497- Jenny's Cuban-Style Slow-Cooker Chicken

1 large onion, chopped
6 cloves garlic, chopped
1/2 green bell pepper, chopped
8 small whole peeled potatoes

1 (8 ounce) can tomato sauce
1/2 cup dry white wine
1/2 tablespoon cumin
1 leaf fresh sage

salt and pepper to taste   2 pounds chicken leg quarters

In a medium bowl, combine onion, garlic, bell pepper, and potatoes. Stir in tomato sauce and wine; season with cumin, sage leaf, and salt and pepper. Place chicken legs in slow cooker, and pour mixture over chicken. Cover, and cook on Low heat until juices run clear, about 6 to 8 hours.

498- Slow Cooker Sweet and Tangy Chicken

2 (18 ounce) bottles barbeque sauce   1 onion, chopped
1 (15 ounce) can pineapple chunks   2 cloves garlic, minced
1 green bell pepper, chopped   8 boneless, skinless chicken breast halves

In a large bowl, mix together barbecue sauce, pineapple with juice, green bell pepper, onion, and garlic. Arrange 4 of the chicken breasts in the bottom of a slow cooker. Pour half of the barbecue sauce over the chicken. Place remaining chicken in slow cooker, and pour remaining sauce over the top. Cover, and cook on Low for 8 to 9 hours.

499- Slower Cooker Meatloaf

2 pounds lean ground beef   3 tablespoons dry onion soup mix
2 eggs, beaten   3 tablespoons steak seasoning
3 tablespoons ketchup   3 tablespoons ketchup

In a medium bowl, mix together the ground beef, eggs, 3 tablespoons ketchup, onion soup mix and steak seasoning using your hands. Pat lightly into the bottom of a slow cooker. Spread remaining ketchup over the top. Cover, and cook for 6 to 8 hours on Low, or 4 hours on High.

500- Hot Caramel Apples

4 large tart apples, cored   1/4 cup butter
1/2 cup apple juice   8 caramels
1/2 cup packed brown sugar   1/4 teaspoon ground cinnamon
12 red-hot candies   Whipped cream

Peel about 3/4 in. off the top of each apple; place in a 3-qt. slow cooker. Pour juice over apples. Fill the center of each apple with 2 tablespoons of sugar, three red-hots, 1 tablespoon butter and two caramels. Sprinkle with cinnamon. Cover and cook on low for 4-6 hours or until the apples are tender. Serve immediately with whipped cream if desired.

Table Of Contents

62 - Slow Cooker Pumpkin Soup

63 - Cheesy Italian Tortellini

64 - Slow-Cooked Short Ribs

65 - Warm Mexican Corn Dip

66 - Shredded Barbecue Beef

67 - Texas Black Bean Soup

68 - Shredded Beef

69 - Slow Cooker Posole with Pork and Chicken

70 - Fruity Pork Chops

71 - Candied Kielbasa

72 - Craig's Mystic Wings

73 - Chicken Broth in a Slow Cooker

74 - Slow Cooker Blackberry Pork Tenderloin

75 - Slow Cooker Venison Stroganoff Meal

76 - Original Homemade Italian Beef

77 - Slow-Cooked White Chili

78 - Authentic Cochinita Pibil (Spicy Mexican Pulled Pork)

79 - Italian Turkey Sandwiches

80 - Slow Cooker Chicken Cacciatore

81 - Hearty Pasta Tomato Soup

82 - Barbecue Pork On Buns

83 - Hamburger Soup II

84 - Slow Cooker Tamale Pie

85 - Wassail Punch

86 - Chops With Fruit Stuffing

87 - Kevin's Sausage Dip

88 - Cheesy Taco Dip

89 - October Dinner Fondue

90 - Slowly Deviled Beef

91 - Simple Slow Cooker Meatloaf

92 - BBQ Pork for Sandwiches

93 - Sweet Barbeque Beans

94 - Cantonese Dinner

95 - Salmon with Spinach Sauce

96 - Slow Cooker Chile Verde

97 - Ten Bean Soup II

98 - Apple Butter I

99 - Chicken Delicious

100 - Slow Cooker Squirrel and Liver

101 - Daria's Slow Cooker Beef Stroganoff

102 - Sauerkraut-Stuffed Slow-Cooked Pork Roast

103 - Creamy Slow Cooker Marsala Pork

104 - Barbecue Chicken Wings

105 - Slow Cooker Chicken Curry with Quinoa

106 - Citrus Pork Roast

107 - Hot Crab Spread

108 - Slow Cooker Lime Chicken with Rice

109 - Colorado Buffalo Chili

110 - Our Favorite Olive Beef

111 - Slow Cooker Sausage with Sauce

112 - Keon's Slow Cooker Curry Chicken

113 - Easy Slow Cooker Ham

114 - Pork Chops a la Slow Cooker

115 - Pork Chalupas

116 - Slow Cooker Venison Stroganoff

117 - Melt-In-Your-Mouth Meat Loaf

118 - Hungarian Noodle Side Dish

119 - Italian Beef Hoagies

120 - Slow Cooker Macaroni and Cheese II

121 - Slow Cooker Mussaman Curry

122 - Spicy Beef Curry Stew for the Slow Cooker

123 - Deer Chop Hurry

124 - Slow Cooker Spaghetti Sauce II

125 - Vegetable Cheese Soup II

126 - Moist Poultry Dressing

127 - Old-Fashioned Peach Butter

128 - Corned Beef and Cabbage

129 - Hot Chili Cheese Dip

130 - Grandma B's Bean Soup

131 - Pareve Cholent

132 - Minestrone Stew

133 - Swiss-Style Veal and Mushrooms

134 - Spaghetti Pork Chops

135 - Slow Cooker Cider Pork Roast

136 - Slow Cooker Vegetable Soup

137 - Home-Style Ribs

138 - Slow Cooker Chops

139 - Easy Beer and Ketchup Meatballs

140 - Slow-Cooked Sweet 'n' Sour Pork

141 - Cranberry Apple Cider

142 - Slow Cooker Thai Pork with Peppers

143 - Corn Spoon Bread

144 - Slow-Cooked Flank Steak

145 - Mexican Beef and Bean Stew

146 - Slow Cooker Country-Style Spareribs

147 - Dee's Special Chicken

148 - Slow Cooker Mock-Roast

149 - Wildfire Pulled Pork Sandwiches

150 - Slow Cooker Butter Chicken

151 - Old Virginia Wassail Cider

152 - Slow Cooker Salisbury Steak

153 - Slow Cooker Chicken Dinner

154 - BBQ Meatballs

155 - All-Day Meatballs

156 - Italian Style Beef Sandwiches

157 - Vegetarian Southwest One-Pot Dinner

158 - Slow Cooker Taco Soup

159 - Slow Cooker Apple-Scented Venison Roast

160 - Gone-All-Day Casserole

161 - Cousin David's Slow Cooker Brisket

162 - Savory Slow Cooker Squash and Apple Dish

163 - Slow Cooker Pork Chops

164 - Chicken in Mushroom Sauce

165 - Beef 'N' Bean Starter

166 - Slow Cooker Bean Casserole AKA Sweet Chili

167 - Amazing Hawaiian Chicken Chili

168 - Hot Cranberry Citrus Punch

169 - Cocktail Meatballs

170 - Hearty Split Pea Soup

171 - Slow Cooker Italian Moose Roast Sandwiches

172 - Chicken Tagine

173 - Slow Cooker Ham

174 - Minister's Delight

175 - Southern Pulled Pork

176 - Christmas Morning Oatmeal

177 - Meat Loaf Burgers

178 - Slow-Cooked Pulled Pork Shoulder

179 - Hot Chicken Sandwiches I

180 - Meatballs and Sauce

181 - Asian Style Country Ribs

182 - Spicy Chicken Thai Noodle Soup

183 - Italian Sausage Dip

184 - Slow Cooked Apple Peach Sauce

185 - Slow Cooker Northern White Bean Bacon Chowder

186 - Easy Slow Cooker Carne Guisada

187 - Easiest BBQ Pork Chops

188 - Smoked Beef Brisket

189 - BBQ Cola Meatballs

190 - Meat-Lover's Slow Cooker Spaghetti Sauce

191 - Rachael's Superheated Cajun Boiled Peanuts

192 - Sloppied Flank Steak Sandwiches

193 - Slow Cooker Sweet and Sour Kielbasa

194 - Manhattan Clam Chowder

195 - Party Kielbasa

196 - Kona Chicken

197 - Jennie's Heavenly Slow Cooker Chicken

400 - Hearty Beef Vegetable Stew

401 - Country Cooking Slow Cooker Neck Bones

402 - Campbell's® Slow-Cooker Chicken and Dumplings

403 - Southwestern Style Fifteen Bean Soup

404 - Shredded Beef Sandwiches

405 - Rice Pudding in a Slow Cooker

406 - Slow Cooker Chicken Tortilla Soup

407 - Savory Pork Stew

408 - Slow Cooker Corned Beef and Cabbage

409 - Uncle Bob's Soybean Bread

410 - Slow Cooked Venison

411 - All Day Apple Butter

412 - Sweet-n-Sour Kielbasa

413 - V-Eight Vegetable Beef Soup

414 - Chicken With Orange Sauce

415 - Potato Minestrone

416 - Mom's Easy Roast

417 - Slow-Cooked Tamale Casserole

418 - All-Day Apple Butter

419 - Tangy Slow Cooker Pork Roast

420 - Slow Cooker Beef Stew IV

421 - Spicy Slow Cooker Mac-n-Cheese

422 - Bob's Slow Cooker Braciole

423 - Cabbage Rolls II

424 - Hot Mint Malt

425 - Taco Bean Dip

426 - It's Chili by George!!

427 - Slow Cooker Chicken Creole

428 - Hamburger Salad

429 - Steak Burritos

430 - Wildfire BBQ Beef on Buns

431 - Slow Cooker Ham and Beans

432 - Chicken Paprika

433 - Swanson ® Slow-Cooker Chicken Cacciatore

434 - Charley's Slow Cooker Mexican Style Meat

435 - Savory Cheese Soup

436 - Slim's Bad Attitude Nacho Sauce

437 - Sweet and Sour Meatballs

438 - Slow Cooker Buffalo Brisket

439 - Vegetable Beef Stew

440 - Slow Cooker Pork Cacciatore

441 - Beer Beef Stew II

442 - Cream of Leek Soup

443 - Jeanne's Slow Cooker Spaghetti Sauce

444 - Cheese Dip II

445 - Hungarian Goulash II

446 - Slow Cooker Pepper Steak

447 - Slow-Cooked Pork Barbecue

448 - Chicken and Two Bean Chili

449 - Slow Cooker Carrot Chicken

450 - Warm Fruit Compote

451 - Bavarian Style Meatballs

452 - Easy Slow Cooker Meatballs

453 - Spicy Beef Vegetable Stew

454 - Slow Cooker Balsamic Beef and Onions

455 - Sour Cream Pork Chops

456 - Slow-Cooked, Texas-Style Beef Brisket

457 - Barbecued Country Ribs

458 - Apple Butter IV

459 - Cranberry Pot Roast

460 - The Ultimate Chili

461 - Slow Cooker Venison Chili for the Big Game

462 - Slow Cooker Clam Chowder

463 - Spicy Seafood Stew

464 - Slow-Cooked German Short Ribs

465 - Luscious Lima Bean Soup II

466 - The Sarge's Goetta - German Breakfast Treat

467 - Roast Beef and Gravy

Printed in Great Britain
by Amazon.co.uk, Ltd.,
Marston Gate.